CARMEL IN THE WORLD PAPERBACKS

4

Mary, Mother of Carmel - II

MARY, MOTHER OF CARMEL

OUR LADY AND THE SAINTS
OF CARMEL

II

Redemptus Maria Valabek, O. Carm.

CARMEL IN THE WORLD PAPERBACKS
Rome, 1988

Cover design by Riccardo Palazzi, O. Carm.

ISBN 88-7288-007-6

Institutum Carmelitanum
Via Sforza Pallavicini, 10
00193 Roma

CONTENTS

1

THE SCAPULAR DEVOTION:
MARY'S ROLE IN MAN'S REDEMPTION

*The Scapular Devotion in the writings of
Fr. Raphael of St. Joseph, Carmelite*

Until a few decades ago, devotion to the brown scapular of Our Lady of Mount Carmel was among the most widespread Marian devotions in the church. Today the scapular is referred to much more rarely, even in comparison with the rosary which is flourishing after being updated to meet modern sensitivities and needs. Formerly, the scapular devotion attracted writers and preachers both of the original family of Carmel and of the Teresian reform who seemed to vie with one another in sharing their love and devotion for Our Lady of the Scapular with the church at large. There is a plethora of books on the scapular which makes it embarassingly difficult to choose one which would be representative of the whole vintage. Two experts, Frs. Enrique M. Esteve, O. Carm., and Bartolomé M. Xiberta, O. Carm., both recommend the volume by the Teresian Carmelite, Raphael of St. Joseph, *Signum salutis, Salus in periculis*, Linz, 1718, as a compendium of the best and the crown of literature during the "Golden Age" of writing on the scapular.

The imposing latin title of this volume is a resumé of the contents: "The Sign of Salvation and Safety in Dangers; that is, the benefits and wonders wrought for the holy Order of Brothers of the glorious Mother of God and ever Virgin Mary of Mt. Carmel, as well as for the most ancient and famous Archconfraternity of the sacred, wonder working Scapular ..." The Bohemian author gives the genre of his work: he is not aiming at originality as much as a kind of encyclopaedia on the scapular. He relies on past writers: papal documents, the Annals of the Order, serious authors, recent reports from various parts of the Order. He wishes to provide ample material for preachers for the Marian feasts and Sundays when the sermon should be about Our Lady and her scapular. After 868 large size pages in small print, he adds numerous indices which help trace any aspect about Our Lady and her scapular.

Evident on every page is the love for the Bl. Mother which the author had, as well as the enthusiasm with which he was intent on sharing this treasure with one and all. Even on pages which abound with reports of miracles and wonders, the underlying and basic truth is that Mary is our mother, who is willing to do anything, even extraordinary marvels, for her sons and daughters. What will impress the reader is the humble erudition of the author, who attempts to marshall every element on earth and in the heavens and to show how Our Lady can be found in them. Not only was the author versed in the fathers of the church—he cites the most beautiful passages they penned about Our Lady—but he is also a humanist who knows Greek mythology and the ancient Roman scene.

He also refers to other cultures, nations, peoples, with their different and novel ways of life. A reader asks himself what would the author have produced in our technically advanced age? He would have needed several companion volumes to provide this type of overview of the scapular devotion.

Favors and wonders, normal for a mother

A careful reading of the witness of men like Fr. Raphael will prove that assertions of the decadence of the scapular devotion are vastly exaggerated. An objective reader will admire the way in which that generation of writers aimed to root the scapular devotion in the basic elements of the Catholic faith. They leave no stone unturned in order to show that popular Marian devotion is an authentic manifestation of the religion of Christ Jesus. Nor were these authors naively credulous. They were exacting in discerning the authenticity of the wonders they recorded. They were aware that many "miracles" are not such: "Who dares to offer self as being able to discern—in a sure and infallible way—with so many dangers of hallucination and error, with so many crafty pitfalls—a true miracle worked by divine power from a false and fictitious one? ... Is there any wonder that the rashness of an active mind, together with the ability of a deluded imagination, has devised and given birth to some of them?" (Fr. Raphael, p. 38). Although a goodly part of this volume is given over to miracles—as the mentality of the times demanded—the criteria and the actual type of wondrous happenings described will assure a more critical modern reader that former generations were not quite as gullible as they are often described.

In the Middle Ages and thereafter, even the process of discerning the heroic holiness of a saintly person was based not so much on the heroic way of life as on the wonders worked at his or her intercession. The overriding principle was that a tree is known by its fruits; God performs wonders at the intercession of holy people to approve veneration for them.

Admittedly, the criteria for judging the authenticity of miracles was not as rigid as it is today; still efforts were expended to identify favors from on high as distinct from merely natural, human phenomena. Typographically, Fr. Raphael's book highlights the wonders by printing them in large print. The reported wonders are meant to be proof of the validity of what he has written on a doctrinal level previously. The numerous wonders are collected from previous writers as well as from contemporary witnesses. Many of them have to do with "miracles" in which death is delayed until the scapular wearer could receive the last sacraments. In a thoroughly catholic vision, the scapular never is described in contrast or competition with the sacramental life of the church, but rather as an aid on the Christian's way. The advantage of these accounts of divine favors is that they place grace on a very personal level. Leaving aside abstract discussions by scholars, grace is shown to be God's loving-kindness touching the ups and downs of man's life as it comes from the hands of Mary, particularly through the scapular. As with other popular devotions, so too the scapular and the wonders attributed to its fervent use are a humble extension of Christ's Incarnation, by which he uses the very simple things of our earth to accomplish the great work of our redemption.

Fr. Raphael goes back to Jesus' own example. Jesus called out: "The works that I do give witness to me" (Jn 5: 3). "Mysteries are proposed which practically overwhelm the mind by their difficulty and frighten the will by their challenge. Difficult to approach truths like the Trinity, the Incarnation, the Resurrection and the Eucharist are set forth; the law of the cross is made known to the will, together with the need for penance, the destruction and extermination of venal pleasures. How will the teaching of Christ, so greatly surpassing our human reasoning, merit consent unless it becomes credible by some evidence?" (p. 520). This is the role of miracles: the seal of divine truth. After explaining the church's ordinary teaching of how miracles of various kinds witness to the solidity of Jesus' claims, Fr. Raphael is quick to add that some miracles may not be such in the strict sense. He argues that there are many ways in which God shows that he is the Lord of heaven and earth by working over and beyond the ordinary laws of nature.

The Council of Trent (Session 25) saw that Christ continued his mission of aiding the faith of his followers by means of wonders worked at the intercession of those disciples who ressembled him most: the saints. Marian devotions are an extension of this basic principle: in his loving-kindness God works wonders at the hands and intercession of Mary and through her scapular, as an extension of Christ's own mission on behalf of man's eternal destiny. Names, dates and places of prodigies abound in this volume, all worked through the instrumentality of the Marian devotion of the brown scapular of Carmel. Far from apologizing for dwelling on these wonders, the author sees them as guarantees of what can happen for those who believe in the motherly charity of Mary, as expressed through the Carmelite scapular.

Scapular devotion: Our Lady's overriding role

The spotlight is definitely on Our Lady of Carmel. She is on center stage not just because she mirrors God for us, but because in doing so she reveals the real meaning of the world as it issued from the hands of God. She is "the most beautiful expression of the archetype of the heavenly and terrestrial worlds, the epitome of the whole of the universe" (p. 550). No human being mirrors God's inner life more authentically than Mary: the Father's creative fruitfulness, the express image of the Son's wisdom, the vessel in which the Holy Spirit effected the Incarnation. God's work found no surer complement than in Mary. She who was clothed with the sun, i.e. adorned with God's choicest gifts, could not help that her clothing, her habit, her scapular should reverberate with the brightness of her goodness and kindness and charity. This is the root of the scapular devotion. Mary's person is filled with God's activity, which affects her clothing and makes its symbol, the scapular, "the powerful instrument, in which Mary's power is exercised as the strikingly beautiful compendium of the world of Mary" (p. 551).

There is simply so much of God in Mary that her Godlikeness cannot but overflow into her relations with and her witness to us. Mary who cradled the world's Savior in her arms and offered her own milk as his first nourishment, has not changed in anything except those towards whom she shows her affection, namely, those who belong to her Son as members of his Body, and in a special way those who are devoted to her through practices like the scapular devotion (cf. p. 553-554).

Mary is reflected in nature

So much of what we say about Our Lady is based on this: she mirrors God so faithfully that we find

11

traces of her in nature precisely because God left traces of himself in the handiwork of his power and kindness. If the world about us trumpets forth the glory of its Creator, it will also tell us something about the creature who is brimming over with God and his presence within her.

The magnetic force of Our Lady on Christian hearts is traced to her resemblance to God. If she can break down the resistance of those immersed in sinful living, it is due to "the attractiveness of her motherly kindliness." Citing the Marian author Bernardino de Bustis, O.F.M., Fr. Raphael notes: "'The Virgin herself must attract you who are iron-like, that is, who are obstinate and mired in evil, by the nature of her mercy. Just as God's nature is always to have mercy and to spare, the same holds for his mother.' ... 'Mary's beauty is designated as the magnet of hearts. Heaven's citizens are attracted by it to the deepest of delights. What is even more, the very King of the heavens is attracted' (John of Jesus Mary, *De Amore Reginae coeli* 1, 1). O the power, the unspeakable graciousness by which the Mother of God, the magnet, won over to herself the very Emperor of heaven and earth! Why wonder, then, that Mary is called with all justice the magnet of magnets?" The author goes on to explain how this power of attraction, proper to Our Lady, redounded to her scapular, and has attracted persons of every social standing— from the humblest to the most powerful—to become members of the confraternity of the scapular (p. 624-625). He describes how the devotion is suited to all types of vocations, for instance, for married couples: "The mother of mercy, obtaining delicious wine at the wedding feast of Cana, rendered the yoke of marriage pleasant and the burden light, by incorporating the spouses into our Carmelite association, and adorning them with the wedding garment—the holy and wonderworking scapular" (p. 108).

The author draws up, as well, detailed lists of many important personages, on both the civic and ecclesiastical scenes, who wished to be invested in Our Lady's livery, the scapular. Innumerable kings, queens and royal notables were known for their affiliation to Carmel. The popes too were frequently clients of Our Lady of the Scapular. Fr. Raphael recalls how Cardinal Fabio Chigi, on the way to the conclave that would elect him Pope Alexander VII, stopped at the Carmelite Church of Transpontina and asked the General of the Order to clothe him in the scapular. From that day he began observing the Wednesday abstinence, and asked his cook to observe this practice even on the Wednesday that he was elected pope. "When Pope Leo XI had already been elected Roman Pontiff and was being divested of his Cardinal's clothing in order to dress in papal vesture, the prelate assisting him wished to take off the Carmelite scapular with which Leo had been clothed since he was a child, together with the rest of his clothing. He thought that the papal vesture surpassed every other habit. The pope forbade him with these words: 'Leave me Mary, lest Mary leave me.' He seemed to want to say: 'Do not deprive me of the vesture, the habit of Mary, lest Mary deprive me of her protection and of her support" (p. 81).

The vast majesty of the ocean has often been cited by Christian writers to describe God and his attributes. Spontaneously this usage was also applied to Mary, full of God and of his grace: "The sea is a gathering of waters, Mary is a sea of graces" (p. 758). A medieval writer (Raymund Giordano who styled himself "the Unlettered") explains this comparison: "Just as the sea cannot be exhausted, for all waters flow into it and then flow out and it remains forever full, so the Bl. Virgin receives all the waters of grace and the fullness of good things, so that she might distribute them to us without any diminution of her fullness ... If she shows herself so kind towards individuals and single persons, this gracious mother will offer greater benefits still when there is question of a whole family dedicated to the protection of Mary" (p. 425).

The number of images for Our Lady that Carmelite writers and preachers found in connection with the sea had a decisive impact on the devotion of sailors and seafarers for Our Lady of Mt. Carmel. She has been adopted as patroness of several navies, e.g. Spain's. Fr. Raphael followed the lead of other Carmelites in commenting on St. Bernard's famous sermon in which Mary is presented as the Star of the Sea: "'You who feel yourself far from solid ground and are carried along on the waves of this world and the crest of storms and tempests, do not take your eyes off the light from that star, Mary, if you do not wish to drown.' Think of Mary, call on Mary ... the anchor is lowered in a sea of graces, and in the depths of the sea; when in danger on streams, Our Lady of Carmel is the longed for Cape of Good Hope' (p. 786). Mary is our anchor when all else seems to be overturned by violent waves of unruly nature: "O protectress, O gleaming pole-star, Virgin Mary ... Mother of Carmel you are for us the most solid anchor" (*Ibid.*, cf. p. 778-779). Throughout his work there is reference to Our Lady as the safe port of arrival. Taking his inspiration from a phrase of St. Ephraem, Fr. Raphael comments: he "greets the Mother of God as the all quiet port, the most desired liberator from the violent waves and storms" (p. 764). Our author is never satisfied with theological explanations: he adduces prodigy after prodigy to show in how many ways Mary deserves these titles by the concrete instances in which she aids those in distress by means of devotion through her scapular.

Mary, brim full of God

The clients of Mary followed this reasoning: if God performed wonders in the past by means of externals and symbols—if the scriptures and the history of the church describe for us the innumerable interventions which God condescended to work for mankind through some concrete instrument, why should this same power and mercy be denied to her who is filled with grace and is God's highly favored one? A typical case is the Ark of the Covenant, which Joshua used to divide the waters of the Jordan River so that the people could enter the promised land dryshod. Can the same be denied to the Mother of God's own Son? "St. John Damascene had already reverenced the Mother of God as the living, most venerable ark. She is the Ark of God's Covenant, outwardly gilt with the gold of virtue and inwardly built with the gold of his purest majesty. In her were the Law of God's Covenant, the manna come down from heaven, and Aaron's staff which blossomed. St. Ildephonse, too, defender of her pure integrity and of her unblemished virginity, believed this of the Mother of God. Nor is the right hand of the Almighty less generous. At the entry and presence of the ark the shimmering waves are stilled and become like mountains. Wherever the Virgin of Carmel, the Ark of the Covenant and the Covenant of Peace, provides shelter and care by reason of her gracious assistance, there the uncontrolled voraciousness of the element water comes to a halt" (p. 769).

Our Lady's ability to help those in need and her merciful kindness do not derive from her natural powers or prowess. She is merely a disciple of the Son, who has shared his own saving mission with her. Whatever she has of tenderness and availability and power to save, she derives from Christ Jesus. Fr. Raphael makes this clear when speaking of a panacea, a cure-all. He maintains that more than to any wonderworking drug, we should apply this title to Our Lady. His reasoning is the orthodox faith of Christians: "The expert doctor of the human race distributed the only absolutely universal medicine—he did so with the greatest of ease, extemporaneously, with a single word, gesture, touch, movement or step—and with a stupendous broadness. The evangelist attests of him: 'Power went out of him and cured everyone.'" There was no illness "which could not be healed completely by his extraordinary power. This power he transferred to his disciples with a wonderful fruitfulness. He shared it in the greatest degree with his thrice-blessed mother."

Because of Mary's continued mission to bring Christ Jesus into the world and make his kingdom finally be achieved, she can be called the "pharmacy of our doctor, Christ." The insistence of Carmelite writers on this point might appear naive and unscientific. Yet, their faithfilled conviction was that Christ came to heal the whole man, body and soul. Even in the most enlightened of modern critiques, there is a subtle dualism that would divide man, and at the most allow that Christ has something to do with the spiritual side; modern medicine and allied sciences concern themselves with the bodily side. But man can never be neatly divided into compartments. Christ Jesus came to save man in his wholeness and wholesomeness. He cured both bodies and souls. This is why Mary and the various Marian devotions like the scapular are tied to this truth about Christ's mission. Mary "gave birth to the doctor. From what was hers she produced the medicine for mankind (St. Caesarius). The Queen of Angels graciously supplies the angelic root, the blessed thistle, the blessed fruit of her immaculate womb. The Mother of Life supplies him who is always alive" (p. 800). Without embarassment, and even with pride, Carmelite authors present person after person who, by devotion to Our Lady through the scapular, were healed of every type of malady—from headaches, to mental distress to blindness" (cf., e.g., p. 823-830).

Mary, part of God's eternal plan

The prodigies attributed to Our Lady are not isolated from the whole process of man's salvation by Christ. Mary's extraordinary interventions are the foretaste of things to come. "This rose without thorns is the antidote to illnesses, the remedy of salvation. The eagle of the Apocalypse had seen the new heavens and the new earth. Look at the flourishing earth which authentically blossomed with flourishing life with the splendor of all virtues—look at the virginal earth in which Jesus Christ, the most fragrant flower of all, was produced—look at the earth adorned with wondrous wholesomeness, from whom the Most High created our medicine ... Who will not venerate the Mother of God as the pharmacy of Christ the doctor, in whom the beauty of all flowers flourishes, and whose fragrance spreads" (p. 791). Although even those whose lives were spared by miraculous interventions must eventually die, Mary is the bright beacon reflecting in herself the fact that life in Christ is eternal.

Fr. Raphael traces Mary's intervention in purgatory to her maternal instincts. If Our Lady of Mt. Carmel has, in recent centuries, been identified with

Our Lady of the Scapular and has often been depicted as helping the souls in purgatory, the reason is, according to our author, based on scripture. "'A friend is a friend for all times, it is for adversity that a brother is born' (Prov. 17: 17). Will not this most loving and dear Virgin, a miracle of kindness ... love those especially devoted to her, and prove her love by action, when they are being assailed by the frightful flames of purgatory? ... Then the heart of our Mother ... will melt like wax ... then her heart of exquisite charity will be moved" (p. 333). If parents here on earth are moved to their best efforts and sacrifices to help their children who are afflicted, can less be thought of Mary especially with regard to those who wear her livery, and who are members of her family?

Mary's special role in Carmel

Mary is Mother of all Christians. All religious families and congregations in the church honor her as such. Just as each religious order attempts to incarnate the whole Christian life in its charism, but in fact, stresses certain elements of Christ's mission and life, so the Carmelite Order has perennially fostered a special love and affection for Mary its mother. Without claiming any exclusive monopoly, it humbly confesses that Mary has been extremely gracious to the order as a whole. How has Mary shown herself to be mother to Carmelites? Fr. Raphael lists the ways:

1. The Carmelite Order has never venerated a founder, such as Sts. Francis or Dominic; "the Bl. Virgin is the patroness, Mother and Foundress of the Carmelite family" (p. 397).

2. Mary gave her own name to her religious family, in fact, early Carmelites defended this grace jealously and were not reluctant to cite popes who addressed their order with the title of Brothers of the Bl. Virgin Mary of Mt. Carmel.

3. As a Mother feeds her child with her own milk, so Mary has provided nourishment for her sons and daughters of Carmel.

4. A mother does not merely give birth to her child, but as a symbol of her all-embacing care, she provides clothes for him. The scapular is the concrete symbol of this motherly duty. "The crown of all graces, the summary of perfections and gifts, which divine largesse has heaped upon Mary, is also given to men by reason of her motherly generosity, and especially to the clients bound to her by special affection, by sincere devotion, by a presevering familiarity... A host of authentic events proves that floods of heavenly gifts flow to the Elijan order and to the Fraternity of the Scapular precisely through the scapular" (p. 191).

5. A mother by nature seeks to protect her child from all harm. Throughout the volume the author returns time and again to Ps. 90, verse 4. *scapulis suis obumbrabit tibi*, literally, "He (she) will overshadow you with his (her) shoulders," but the obvious allusion is to the scapular. The latter is "the holy habit proper ro the Carmelite Order, and it is the most important and essential part of our habit" (p. 179).

6. A mother assures a long lineage for her family. The numerous persons affected by Mary and the scapular devotion are to be found on every page.

7. What does belonging to Mary's Carmelite family add to a person's basic Christian commitment? Our critical era is not the first to ask this question; Fr. Raphael faced it squarely. Explaining St Paul's description of the Mystical Body of Christ, Fr. Raphael sees many different members making up the one Body of Christ. "All contribute and cooperate in achieving the good and usefulness of the whole. One shares with his brother; one favors another because of a natural propensity for the one Mystical Body... In the church of God there is a mutual sharing between the saints and their good works. There is an over all communion" in the upbuilding of the Body (p. 480). This is basic to every Christian; Carmelites naturally are not excluded. On another level—"secondary and derivative"—our kindly mother shares

the gifts she has received from God and all the fruits of motherhood with those who belong to her by reason of special bonds with her own Carmelite family (p. 417).

8. Mary is Jesus' final gift to man, willed to us as he was dying on the cross. She is Jesus' representative. In poetic form, Fr. Raphael describes the scene on Calvary: "Why does the world not collapse completely with the absence of God? The reason? Mary was still standing there. Therefore, since last wishes carry a stronger commendation, his last word to men was a recommendation of Mary. He commends John above all, he who knew that no youth was safe except under the protection of Mary" (p. 419). Mary's motherly charity is for everyone who belongs to her Son Jesus; just as Jesus singled out the apostle John by symbolic gesture, the same holds true for Mary's Carmelite family at present.

As is to be expected in a compendium, Fr. Raphael gathers as much information as he can from previous authors, who have explained the various meanings of devotion to Mary under her title of "Mount Carmel." Recurring to scripture and to the fathers of the church as well as medieval writers, the pious friar provides a broad overview of the meaning of *Mount*. He notes that it has traditionally been the place of encounter between God and his people. This basic meaning led to *Mount* being applied to Christ, and not long afterwards to Our Lady as well. After citing numerous church writers who describe Mary as "mount," he cites a fellow Carmelite: "by reason of the eminence of contemplation and of divine knowledge, by reason of the riches of graces which lead to the manifold fruit of good works, Carmel is an elevated and richly endowed mount" (p. 136-138). Page after page the author explains the meaning of "Your head is like Carmel" (Cant. 7: 5) in the sense of beauty and plush fruitfulness.

Man's part in the scapular devotion

The greater part of this voluminous work has to do with Our Lady. She, after all, is Carmel's mother and as such always takes the initiative. However, as is the case with all divine realities, in Marian devotion too man has his contribution to make. Like God of whom she is filled, Mary respects man's free response in love. Although the scapular devotion is mainly from the side of Mary, still man is not inert and passive.

Devotion by its very nature calls for a readiness on man's part to render worship and service to God and to Our Lady. This is done regularly by means of prayer—both liturgical and individual. Interestingly, the author provides references and cross-references to Marian topics for the festivities of Our Lady throughout the liturgical year. He also provides hints as to how to bring out Our Lady in each Sunday's homily. Just to take one example: on the 12th Sunday after Pentecost, the Gospel is from Matthew: "Look at the lilies of the field..." He immediately reminds the preacher of Our Lady's lilylike candor. The Gospel goes on to ask, "Why do you worry about clothing?" Too much worry about worldly values goes against the Gospel. The scapular is an apt antitote in its simplicity, availability and unpretentiousness. "No man can serve two masters," the Gospel concludes. In this context the scapular wearer is called to imitate Mary's purity in her service of God.

July 16, the solemnity for the whole scapular confraternity, is consecrated to the memory of benefits from the hands of the provident Virgin and also to a renewal of the Order's commitment to her service (p. 134). Other feasts in honor of Our Lady are described under her various titles. A special place is reserved for Our Lady of Victories. The Central European author, a son of his land, cannot forget the victory which Catholic forces won on White Mountain near Pilzno in modern Czechoslovakia. The historic battle was fought in 1620 in the war against the invading Swedes: the protagonist on the Catholic side was Fr. Dominic of Jesus Mary, O.C.D., who hung a desecrated image of the Virgin and Child around his neck and dashed among the Catholic forces, rallying them to the defence of their lands and rights. The image is preserved to this day in the Carmelite Church of Our Lady of Victories in Rome.

The scapular devotion had become so much part of the Catholic scene because it embodied various important elements of Christianity. It is not a devotion in competition with and alongside the ordinary schools of Christian spirituality. In other words, besides being close to the simple, easily accessible realities of life on earth, the scapular devotion is also an integral part of the ordinary way of salvation, available not to a certain portion of Catholics, but to everyone. As a sacramental of the church it in no way means to derrogate from the unique efficacy of the seven sacraments left by Christ himself; rather it leads to them and is one way of living the graces of the sacraments after their actual celebration (cf. p. 289).

Even when he takes up the task of explaining the conditions for the Sabbatine Privilege, the author ably shows how they are merely concrete expressions of Christian attitudes and practices. The first condition, chastity according to one's state in life, is a commandment of the Lord for all Christians. The other condition, the Divine Office or the Little Office of the Bl. Virgin Mary, or else abstinence on Wednesdays and Saturdays, is not something proper to the scapular devotion. The Office belongs to the whole church, and fasting and abstinence are part of the church's penitential practices. To give but one example of the edifying instances that fill this volume. Fr. Raphael (p. 382) recalls a widower of many years, Lope Ribera, who would get up at midnight to pray the Little Office of Our Lady. He was used to praying slowly and aloud. When he was struck by the meaning of some verse, he would pause and savor the contents in meditation. At times the Little Office could take three or four hours to celebrate.

The devotion is simple: it requires no specific prayer or pious work. Still, various means are suggested in order to collaborate with the loving-kindness of Mary and show her our gratitude. The first and most solid means is imitation: "The supreme devotion is to imitate the person we venerate" (St Augustine). A second means is a daily intention and a readiness and zeal of soul to serve so great a mother and lady with all our works and activities. But he gives even more concrete suggestions: "First, in the morning on rising (and in the evening when going to bed), kiss the scapular, make the sign of the cross with it over oneself, while saying, 'May the Virgin Mary bless us with her Child,' or at least gaze at it, touch it to one's heart and offer to God the activity of the day under the guidance of so good a protectress. Secondly, in bodily or spiritual dangers and temptations, turn one's mind to the Mother of God and call for her help. Thirdly, to avoid whatever is contrary to straightforwardness ... Fourthly, frequently during the day, at the beginning of some activity, offering it to God and commending it to the Virgin as to one's directress, accepting it and performing it for her honor. Fifthly, to be sollicitous and have the intention (but without scrupulosity) of gaining the indulgences granted to the Confraternity ... To this end it is very useful to say in the morning: 'I intend during my activities to gain the indulgences granted by the Holy See to members of the Confraternity of the Holy Scapular of the Bl. Virgin.'"

* * *

The Teresian friar's final exhortation summarizes the reason for the labor of love he expended in composing this imposing volume (p. 868): "Member and confrère of Mary's Order, wear the scapular constantly, day and night. Do not do so on a material level, as you would a piece of cloth, but as a symbol of the love of Mary. Wear it as a precious gift granted by heaven itself, the seal of motherly kindness and protection. Wear the scapular in a spiritual, authentic way: your spirit should be filled with affection for the Bl. Virgin, you should be intimately committed to her honor and veneration, you should be most devout in celebrating her feasts and her feats. St. Augustine taught, 'The supreme devotion is to imitate the person we venerate.' To reverence the habit of the glorious virgin will also be for you the token and warranty of assisting grace, obtained for you by the Virgin Mother of God and the most gracious Mother of Carmel. Through her intercession you will keep the commandments and will end your life in a holy way."

2

HIDDEN WITH MARY IN CARMEL

*Our Lady in the Life of
St Theresa Margaret Redi*

Among the saints of Carmel, one of the least known is St Theresa Margaret Redi (1747-1770). One of the reasons for this obscurity is because she based her brief earthly pilgrimage very effectively on the imitation of the hidden life of Jesus. Her lustre is often absorbed by more prominent lights. She was no teacher, but rather a noble Tuscan girl who was so overwhelmed by the reality of "God is love" that all else paled in comparison. She was no writer, rather one whose naturally religious outlook led her to lament that not enough attention was paid, not enough affection was lavished on the lover of mankind, particularly symbolized by the newly introduced devotion towards the Sacred Heart (in fact, in Carmel she added "of the Sacred Heart of Jesus" to her religious name). She was no pacemaker; rather she lived her charism in Carmel, glad to accept the structures of cloistered life as graces.

Spirituality for everyone

What makes St Theresa Margaret's witness valuable is the plainness of her spiritual odyssey. Preceeding her sister from Lisieux by two centuries, her life proclaims that the heights of mysticism need not be accompanied by extraordinary phenomena, which were so highly thought of in her own time, but rather by an unswerving faithfulness to Love, with all his crucifying demands. Struggling Christians will not find it hard to identify with this mystic who complained: "It's a torment for me just to think that I must apply myself to the things of God. Just imagine what it's like when I try to keep going ... I fear that in my communions I leave God disgusted with me. I seem to be spiritless, so great is the cold I feel when I ask for his help ... I make constant resolutions, but I'm always the same ... I can't wait for spiritual reading to be over ..." (*Letter*, Summer, 1769, to her spiritual director, Fr. Ildefonsus, OCD, in *Ephemerides Carmeliticae* 10 [1959], p. 362).

While she was tormented in her sensitive nature, God was becoming the ever more dominant figure in her life. His purifying action cleared away the obstacles to his advances. For days after she had been given to understand the meaning of "God is love," she remained in a semidaze, going through her daily duties, particularly that of infirmarian, repeating this one phrase that transfixed her. She came to understand that the greatness of a person lay in the generous acceptance of the love of Jesus' heart, with which a poor creature was now able to love. Man's glory lies in becoming capable of bearing God's way of loving, forgiving, rejoicing and sacrificing—and allowing oneself to be the instrument (Elizabeth of the Trinity would say "be an additional humanity") for God's loving-kindness to appear in our lands once more.

St Theresa Margaret is precious because she shows that the spiritual ascent is not esoteric. Mystic heights are not dependent on exceptional measures, but are available to the Christian who takes seriously the normal approaches of God, to be found everywhere.

The Marian devotion of St Theresa Margaret is a case in point. This contemplative soul shows how down-to-earth her vocation is. It takes in the whole person, body and soul. From the beginning to the end of her life, St Theresa Margaret expressed her Marian devotion outwardly. "As a youngster, that is, at the age of 6 or 7, she took great delight in setting up small altars in honor of the Bl. Virgin" (*Summarium super dubio*, 1836, p. 28). Until she died she continued this Catholic way of showing her veneration for Our Lady. "The Servent of God had found three pictures of the Bl. Virgin. One was on the terrace, the other two in unoccupied locales of our monastery. As soon as she knew of their existence, she began to repair and clean them. With the superior's permission, she placed one of them in her own cell, another she carried with her to bless the sick sisters. The third one, because of her premature death, she could not finish restoring, so she recommended it to me... that I finish repairing what she had undertaken" (*P.O.*, 2167v).

Marian devotion for everyone

During her lifetime if anyone mentioned to Sr Theresa Margaret that she was exceptional in some virtue, her stock reply was "but that's what everyone does." This Carmelite dedicated to "the hidden life" spared no effort to remain unobtrusive. Her devotion to Our Lady followed the pattern. Her message is that using the ordinary means at everyone's disposal, even the heights of holiness can be reached.

The rosary was St Theresa Margaret's companion from her earliest years until she died. Her father, Ignatius Redi, who served as her first spiritual director, made the daily rosary so much part of his daughter's life that the day he accompanied her to the Benedictine boarding school when she was nine, "since the time to go to bed was fast approaching, she reminded the mother mistress that she had not yet recited the rosary" (*P.O.*, 481v). The emotional strain of taking leave of her beloved parents and family, the fatigue of the journey, nervousness in a new environment, none of these could distract young Anna Maria (her baptismal name) from her faithfulness to Marian prayer. Her father later commented; "At the very moment you heard the first sound of the Angelus, you would find her, rosary usually in hand, kneeling... devoutly saying her usual prayers" (*P.O.*, 203). Her eight years spent with the Benedictines introduced Anna Maria to the Little Office of Our Lady. She was proud to be able to pray this age-old praise of Mary when she returned home and was joined by her father in its recitation both at home and while travelling (*P.A. supra famam sanctitatis*, 155).

While in boarding school, Anna Maria had a Marian shrine in her room. Not only did she celebrate her private devotions before the image of Mary, but she also invited fellow students to join her (*P.O.*, 320). She would continue in the same way until she died at 23 years of age. To prepare for Marian feasts she would link the usual triduum or novena with the more assiduous personal practice of some virtue or mortification. Given her way of remaining "hidden in Christ," it is not surprising that her preferred practice was silence. Again, she introduced school friends of hers to the same practice.

At the Beatification Process, those who lived with her testified that the rare occasion when her interior life became somewhat transparent was when she passed by one of the many images of Our Lady in the Benedictine Monastery. She took precautions that no one was about; then she would stop before a statue or painting of Our Lady and, in Italian style, converse animatedly and affectionately with the Bl. Mother (*P.O.*, 983). Our Lady was no abstract ideal for her; she was a living, loving person whom she loved to address as "beloved Mother," or even as "Mom," as her father attests (*P.O.*, 210). This show of affection and tenderness is noteworthy, given the times, when Jansenistic influences frowned on such displays. St Theresa Margaret would never understand a hybrid Christianity which is not rooted firmly in the whole person: filial intimacy and emotions are part of the human condition.

Like many other Christians—St John of the Cross being a prime example—St Theresa Margaret was bound to Our Lady by a concrete episode in which Mary showed herself her concerned mother. All his life St John was convinced that Our Lady had saved him from drowning as a child. St Theresa Margaret had a similar experience as a school girl in St Appolonia's School. While carrying a lit brazier, she stumbled and fell down the stairs. At the bottom of the staircase was an image of Our Lady of Sorrows. Anna Maria appealed to Mary under that title. For all her days she felt obliged to Our Lady for saving her life (*P.O.*, 983v). Mary's concrete intervention elicited from Anna Maria concrete acts of gratitude and praise. "She was especially devoted to the holy name of Mary; . . . she prefixed her name to anything she wrote . . . and daily she venerated her with the recitation of the five psalms whose initial letters form the holy name of Maria" (*P.O.*, 1444v). Anytime Mary's name was mentioned, anytime she passed her image, a grateful Anna Maria would bow her head.

Value of externals

St Theresa Margaret was one Carmelite who showed no scruples about being too attached to externals. Statues, holy pictures, paintings were her normal, lifelong expression of Marian devotion. Before she entered Carmel she had been given a gift of a statue of Our Lady of Perpetual Help. She asked her father to provide a silver crown and gold-embroidered clothing for the statue, which Anna Maria wished to accompany her at her clothing ceremony as a Carmelite. This preoccupation with her favorite statue did not abate as she entered more deeply into the contemplative life; on the contrary, Sr Theresa Margaret, who made few requests, did ask that the statue be placed in a public place where the nuns could venerate their heavenly mother. When the dormitory where the statue had been placed was transformed into a workshop, she asked to move the statue to a more dignified place. Her request was granted: the statue was transported to an oratory near the novitiate wing of the monastery. But her need for concrete symbols did not finish with that. She adorned the statue with flowers and small wax hearts, one each for the sisters of her community and for her parents. This contemplative nun wished to express her concern for the significant persons in her life; she could extend them no deeper affection than to leave them in the hands of her Madonna.

Sr Theresa Margaret did not wish to be seen spending much time in chapel lest people begin to praise her holiness. When she had a free moment, she would take refuge in the oratory before the statue of Our Lady. She confessed that even when she was working in other parts of the monastery, her heart would often be in commuion with Mary, offering her work in Mary's honor (*P.O.*, 144v). True to form, Sr Theresa Margaret on the eve of her profession gave each of the sisters a small piece of Our Lady's veil. She asked the nuns a favor: to trust in Our Lady of Perpetual Help in all their needs, physical and spiritual. This was part of her heritage, one she kept repeating during her five years in Carmel, especially to her peers among the nuns.

Sr Theresa Margaret was a far better doer than preacher. In her difficult moments she ran to the oratory to throw herself at the feet of Our Lady. Many of the nuns in the community were elderly; the young Theresa Margaret was assigned to act as infirmarian and did so until the day she died. She was asked to assist a demented nun who had to be kept locked in her room. Sr Theresa Margaret followed the superior's orders in what she could and could not give to the unfortunate nun. Not so the older infirmarian who, in order to curry the favor of the demented sister, gave in to her hankerings. Sr Theresa Margaret came to be hated by the sick nun to the extent that she turned to physical violence. Sr Theresa Margaret's reaction? Even before she entered the cell, she would have recourse to Our Lady before her statue. And when the sick nun showed her violent streak, Sr Theresa Margaret fled from the cell and ran to Our Lady's shrine, before whom she recouped her composure, and returned to her charge. When the superior, herself sickly, came to know of Sr Theresa Margaret's difficulties, she removed her from the charge of serving the demented nun. But the young mystic volunteered to continue; a grateful superior accepted her offer.

The experience and example of Sr Theresa Margaret are particularly relevant in an age when many "external devotions," e.g., novenas, processions, scapulars, medals, shrines, have been abandoned in favor of a more doctrinal, cerebral devotion. Externals may need revision or even substitution, but an authentic, human devotion cannot do without them.

Certainly there is need for vigilance lest inauthentic elements creep in and suffocate true devotion, as Vatican II pointed out; but this same council strongly recommended additional devotions, besides the Liturgy, as vehicles of Marian devotion.

Prayers to Our Lady

Sr Theresa Margaret used both standard prayers and spontaneous expressions to honor the Bl. Virgin. Her lifelong devotion for the Seven Sorrows of Mary inspired her to address the Bl. Mother with apposite prayers, plus seven Our Fathers, Hail Marys and Glorys. This was her custom every Friday, and other days as time permitted. At times she would substitute the *Stabat Mater*.

Another favorite prayer was one in honor of the twelve gifts of Mary that had led to her glorification. Each day the Carmelite nun recalled these mysteries, praying a Hail Mary or Hail Holy Queen for each of them. Her spiritual director testified that her veneration of Our Lady was such that when she heard of any worthwhile devotion, she attempted to adapt it to her daily schedule. When she was frustrated in this by her increasing duties in the monastery she did the next best thing: she asked to be in communion with those Christians who were most devoted to the Bl. Virgin, as well as with those who now honor Mary in heavenly glory (*P.O.*, 1445).

The Marian prayer which came to be attributed to St Theresa Margaret, because it was printed on holy picture cards in her honor, in reality was taught her by Fr. Ildephonsus, her director, who had in turn learned it from a devotee of the Bl. Virgin. She repeated these acclamations to the Bl. Mother very often and shared her enthusiasm for them with her fellow religious and with her father.

> I venerate you a thousand times, O true Mother of my Lord Jesus Christ: – Hail Mary.
> I venerate you, O sovereign Queen of the Angels, Empress of the Universe: – Hail Mary.

I venerate you, most kindly Virgin Mary, most worthy mother of my one Savior Jesus: – Hail Mary (*P.O.*, 1764v-1765).

The distinctly contemplative tone of these acclamations would have been particularly pleasing to Theresa Margaret: not a word about herself and her unworthiness. What is paramount in the contemplative's experience is the greatness, the searing purity, the terribly demanding love from on high. It is Mary's intimate sharing in the mystery of God which strikes the Carmelite contemplative. Our Lady is an integral part of God's loving plan for mankind, the culminating point of salvation history, providing God's definitive Word for mankind. The breath-taking reality of Mary's motherhood of Jesus and of all who belong to Jesus, and of Mary's perennial concern for all her sons and daughters in Jesus, becomes the eternal reality of which the contemplative is given a finite, but all-pervading experience. The response is a praise-filled acclamtion such as that used by St Theresa Margaret.

This Marian prayer has an authentic ring because it is rooted in Mary's secondary but real role in man's salvation. When compared to the paramount attention paid to Christ Jesus and his Sacred Heart in the writings and witness of this contemplative nun, the place of Mary is refreshingly modest, described within the fuller picture of Jesus and his mission for men. Mary's whole importance depends on her collaboration with Jesus' work. Her incisiveness depends on how faithful a disciple of her Son she is, on how much of God there is in her, and on how faithfully she allows God to use her as the instrument of Jesus, of his reconciliation and of his loving-kindness.

A third characteristic of Theresa Margaret's Marian prayers is her desire to share this treasure with others. This is significant in view of her desire for self-effacement in order to reserve the delights of her interior life for the King. She instinctively understood the dangers of self-deception in becoming an oracle and "showing off" one's spiritual prowess. Yet in the case of Marian prayers, she took it as her mission to share the graces which she knew to be reserved for those who venerate Our Lady. She urged her fellow sisters to have recourse to Our Lady. In fact, the Marian acclamations are recorded for us in that context.

St Theresa Margaret's Marian devotion had a liturgical aspect. In her quaint way, resolutely rooted in the concrete, she would prepare for the great solemnities of the Lord by petitioning Our Lady to obtain for her the graces reserved in the mysteries being celebrated. This was not merely a spiritual exercise: Sr Theresa Margaret wrote notes to Our Lady and placed them at her shrine. One such note has come down to us: "Blessed Virgin, Mother of God, and mine as well, full of faith, I present myself to you with this reminder to beg you insistently for a grace on this dear feastday. I desire a great spiritual fervor and a complete detachment from all those things that prevent me from putting into practice all those aims the Lord had in calling me to a religious order. I feel I am very needy: I know that the honor of God, as well as my sanctification, are your concern. I hope you listen to me. From my beloved cell" (Stanislaus, OCD, *Angelo del Cielo*, 3 ed., 1934, p. 81).

St Theresa Margaret confessed to her spiritual director that the graces she begged of Our Lord in order to grow in the Spirit "she never sought from the Lord except through the powerful mediation (of Mary)" (*P.O.*, 1450). Because she saw in Mary a mother concerned for the welfare of her childen, she spontaneously turned to her when she experienced the indispensable action of God in order to make her over into the image of Christ. Her own surrender to God who is love, her hiddenness in the Sacred Heart of Jesus, these characteristics of her "way" were graces she begged from the mother of mercies.

Among the young religious of her monastery, Sr Theresa Margaret fostered a favorite practice, "a contest of love." Religious life is meant to offer ample and sustained possibilities of growth in the Spirit of Jesus. Creatively taking the initiative, St Theresa Margaret, overwhelmed by the sense of God's infinite love for her and for all, could not stand this becoming a formality. She used every possible means to keep the charism of religious life alive and incisive in the lives of the religious. The "contests of love" were designed to be challenges that the religious offered to one another not to allow the Spirit to be quenched. Much like the charismatic manifestations of today, these practices were meant to bring to an awareness level what tended to become mere routine and formal repetition. By means of these contests, the practice of virtue and prayer was maintained as a priority in everyday living.

Naturally these practices centered on Christ and imitation of him. Sr Theresa Margaret's director testified that she had constant recourse to Our Lady with these devotions (*P.O.*, 1204). At times she made direct reference to the Bl. Mother, as in one "contest" that has come down to us. "In each practice we shall perform these acts, three of adoration, three of contribution, often repeating: 'I adore and love the divine Heart of Jesus, living in the Heart of Mary. I beg you to live and reign in all hearts, especially in mine: consume it in your pure love. Blessed be God'" (*Eph. Carmel*, 10 [1959], p. 387). This "league" which the six enthusuastic nuns formed to help their appreciation of divine love as "the one thing necessary" and at a high pitch, could hardly abstain from calling on the mother of divine love for support. In Mary they had their ideal: through humility, faithfulness, availability, she was filled with divine love more than any other creature.

As mother, the Bl. Virgin was particularly concerned when her children were in distress and trouble. In the terrifying purification of her final year on earth St Theresa Margaret kept seeking the Lord while experiencing only a void. Compared to former experiences, she felt she was lacking even the minimum spark of the Lord's love. As she grew ever more detached from every enjoyment of God, she doggedly and silently remained faithful to her first love. In her misery she had even more frequent recourse to the Bl. Mother. "In that period I used to note that her characteristic good humor and her calm manner did not shine on her face. I saw that more than usual she would have recourse to the image of Mary which she had brought to us" (Testimony of Sr Anna Maria *P.O.*,

737v). This custom was so deeply engrained in her spirit that, as life ebbed out of her during the night of March 6/7, 1770, a nun who was with her noticed that "she remained immobile without the slightest complaint. Only every so often we heard her call on the Bl. Virgin and offer herself to her" (Letter of Sr Theresa Maria Ricasoli). She died the way she lived: invoking Mary and offering herself to her.

Imitation of Our Lady

The ordinariness of Mary's life impressed St Theresa Margaret, as it did centuries later St Therese of Lisieux. Mary's silence, hiddenness, love stronger than death, faith in face of suffering, abandonment as she stood beneath Jesus' cross: St Theresa Margaret spontaneously identified with the Bl. Mother. Although we do not know whether St Theresa Margaret was familiar with it, we do have an outline as to how to imitate Mary's virtues found in the archives of her monastery. It was written at an unspecified date for a novice. The exercise is certainly redolent of the times of the saint. This was the type of devotion that would spark her love of Our Lady (cf. *Eph. Carmel*, 10 [1959], p. 236-237).

"1. *Virtue*: Mary's privilege of being the Mother of God. Humility is why the Virgin Mary pleased the most high God so much.
   External practice: she will have to be sure to find six occasions every day on which to humble herself either in action, in word, or at least in keeping quiet about herself.

2. *Virtue*: Mary's prerogative of being mother by adoption of all the faithful. Filial trust in Mary as a true mother of grace.
   External practice: she will have the mother mistress daily assign her a particular responsibility to seek some special grace from Mary either for herself or for others.

3. *Virtue*: Mary's prerogative of being mother of all of Carmel by a special title, received when St John was given to her as a son.

33

Grateful homage of a daughter towards so great a mother.

External practice: she will ask the mother mistress permission to pay a daily visit to Mary in some image of hers, or else to express some good sentiment towards her which will enflame others in devotion towards her.

4. *Virtue*: Mary's excellence of being mediatrix and universal dispenser of all graces, which we ask of God. Prayer which is the key to all treasures, and without which we obtain nothing.

External practice: she will ask to spend at least a quarter of an hour more in prayer, either vocal or mental, every day."

* * *

Posturing was foreign to St Theresa Margaret. Her spiritual witness is outstanding because it encompasses the core of Christian living, while resolutely refusing histrionics, complacency or display. She surrendered herself to the loving advances of God and when she was passing through the darkness of her final purification, she lived on the memory of God's love until her early death. For this reason, her fervent, filial, and outwardly expressed devotion for Mary is something special. It was an overflow of gratitude and praise for God's goodness in sharing himself with the contemplative nun, but also in sharing other precious gifts, such as Our Lady. She reveals to us God's perennial presence among men in all its variety and beauty and intensity.

Mary, good and faithful mother, leads us to a deeper contemplative knowledge of God. Calling on her in all our needs, temporal and spiritual, we learn how to turn all things, even the most banal and seemingly irrelevant, to our good. The usually reticent Theresa Margaret could never say enough about Mary's indispensable intercession and concern. This sensitive Tuscan nun had recognized Mary's touch in many of the graces she received. She spent her brief life praising and sharing this gift.

TERTIARIES LOOK TO MARY

*Our Lady of Mt. Carmel in the Life
of Liberata Ferrarons, T. O. Carm.
and Carmen de Sojo, T. O. Carm.*

People become Carmelite tertiaries for a variety of reasons. One of the most constant ones is the perennial devotion of Carmel to the Blessed Mother, Carmel's Beauty and Patroness. Two such tertiaries who were drawn to Carmel because of Mary's role were Venerable Liberata Ferrarons (1803-1842) and Venerable Carmen de Sojo (1856-1890).

Several common characteristics link these two daughters of Catholic Catalonia. The quest for holiness—seen as assimilation into Christ Jesus—was the overriding concern of both all through their lives. In what one official of the Roman Congregation for the Causes of Saints recently called "an explosion of holiness in 19th century Catalonia," these two women tertiaries show that the church did not have to wait until Vatican II to recognise that holiness, even of the heroic type, is not reserved to religious, but is a challenge offered to every baptized Christian. The spirit of prayer, understood as the all-pervading presence of God and of God's initiative in their lives, played a paramount role in their earthly existence. Another Christian value which the two of them lived was an appreciation of suffering. Both asked to take on themselves afflictions destined for others.

Liberata, moved by the misery resulting from the civil war of 1841, cried out in favor of the church: "Lord, crush me like salt, grind me like wheat by means of suffering, but do not allow this type of disgrace for poor Spain" (*Process I*, p. 171-172). Carmen, loving wife of a respected doctor and mother of five children, made her byword: "I am very content when I am corrected, I am happy to suffer, I wish to suffer even more, to become the joke, the scoffing of everyone, to be humiliated and trampled upon. However, as I see that I please no one, I am afraid that at times I am not doing my duty—that in my clumsiness I sometimes fail. It seems to me that I work and do what I can. I keep going until very late at night. But because I am so stupid, I do not recognise that I am failing in my obligations or that I should do it in another way" (*Letter* to her spiritual director, Fr. Casañas, in José M. Saenz, *Una heróica víctima del Divino Corazón*, Barcelona, 1947, p. 35). These sentiments were not wishful thinking, but a way of life.

While united in their spiritual vision and pilgrimage, these two tertiaries were as different as is the variety of the Spirit's gifts. While Liberata belonged to one of the poorest families of Olot, her native village, Carmen was the daughter of comfortable, middle-class parents. While Liberata had to take to the steets to beg at the age of 7 in order to feed her decimated family, Carmen's family could afford to send her on trips to Lourdes and Rome. While Liberata never learned to write (and many witnesses at her Beatification Process signed their testimony with a cross or with their fingerprints), Carmen's husband brought in a tutor to teach her French. While Liberata began working in a textile mill at the age of 8 and continued uninterruptedly until she was 29 and confined to bed, Carmen had another problem: she found it extremely difficult when her husband, in a move to be more economical, let her domestic help go. While Liberata remained single and becomes the exemplar of a Spirit-filled single life in the world, Carmen shows that the pinnacle of the mystical experience can be attained by a wife who "adores" her husband and fondles her children. While Liberata never leaves the environs of her small country town, Carmen is absorbed by Catalonia's metropolis, Barcelona. While Liberata is supported and appreciated by her poverty-stricken parents, some of Carmen's deepest sorrow is caused by a misunderstanding and critical mother. While Liberata is known by her whole village and even today is venerated by the people of Olot, Carmen is known only by a restricted circle of friends and relatives (and today her cause of beatification has fallen behind that of Liberata).

But what is deepest in their hearts, their religious convictions and their acceptance of God's will in every instance, unites these differing personalities. Their devotion to Our Lady of Mt. Carmel was one such binding force. Grounded in the Catholic faith of their forefathers, both took for granted the value of traditional forms of devotion. Theirs was no critical look at how the scapular devotion fit into the biblical scheme of things. They were too busy appreciating how God lavished his love and pardon and mercy through this venerable form of piety.

Both tertiaries made Marian shrines and churches the destination of many of their outings and devotional outlets. The *Hail Mary*, the *Angelus*, the *Hail Holy Queen*, the rosary were never highlighted in their writings and in their Christian life. They were simply taken for granted and used as graces. Almost automatically when the name of Jesus is mentioned, so is Mary's. In their prayers, how many times Mary is found immediately following Jesus. Again, this happened in no studied way, but in the spontaneous, natural way of cradle-born Catholics to whom Mary is as much a member of their Catholic family as anyone.

When Liberata on December 26, 1819, at the age of 16, and Carmen on March 24, 1879, at the age of 23, entered the Carmelite Third Order they both understood that their commitment above all was to the spirituality that the Order had to offer them. The Carmelites serviced a church in honor of Our Lady in Olot, which was one of Liberata's favorites. Carmen, a teen-age bride at the age of 15, turned to Carmel's sturdy spirit to buttress her own deeply felt spiritual life. When tertiaries who belonged to several Third Orders were asked by Pope Leo XIII to choose only one, Carmen had no hesitation in choosing Carmel. Carmel paid special devotion to the Blessed Mother, particularly by imitation of Our Lady in her prayerfulness, in her sense of God's presence, in her accep-

37

tance of suffering and of the cross: this form of devotion was a model for Gospel living, which both Liberata and Carmen had absorbed and tried to incarnate in their own lives.

Liberata Ferrarons: Marian devotion of the poor

Liberata's devotion to Carmel was at least partially inherited. Her father, whose sickness confined him to bed for many a year before he died, was the reason for Liberata's begging missions and her assiduity at work. The father, poorest of Olot's poor, had one source of riches for his family, his indomitable faith which included devotion to Our Lady of Mt. Carmel. In fact, he predicted that he would die on the Vigil of July 16 and be buried in the Carmelite Church on the central feast. With the sensitivity of simple believers, he sent for a Carmelite priest on the Vigil. He died soon afterwards. As Carmen took part in her father's funeral on July 16 in the Church of Carmine, at his express wish and prophecy, she could not but have understood the patrimony of Carmelite Marian devotion and of the scapular which her father left behind.

For the rest of her days, she became so well known for her Carmelite devotion that people were reluctant to come to visit her without the scapular. She would inevitably know it. Several witnesses recalled one episode which occurred when Liberata was already confined to bed by her inexorable sickness. "Well known is the case of some young men who had heard of Liberata; on the eve of a feast day they resolved to go and visit her. There were four companions, but one of them was not wearing a scapular, nor did he have a rosary. When he found himself outside the door of her house, he was betwildered by what he had heard and said to the others, 'You go in, I feel some repugnance. I'll wait for you.' These latter ventured up the stairs. As they entered her room, Liberata gazed at them all smiles and said to them, 'Didn't four of you come for a visit? Where is your companion? You can tell him that he can come in with full freedom and without any fear. Don't be hard on him. I know what he is lacking and I have a lot of extras. Look at how many scapulars and rosaries I have. I will certainly give him some.' Then his friends understood the cowardice of their companion and they went to look for him and told him what had happened" (Domingo Balcells, *Liberata Ferrarons, Donzella Exemplar*, Olot, 1923, p. 53-54).

Child labor laws were a long way off when eight year old Liberata began to work in the textile factories in and around Olot. Hard work did not turn her into a rebel or complainer. It strengthened her faith. From the very beginning, the spiritual moorings of Liberata were noted by her neighbors and townsfolk who even while she was alive referred to her as our "little saint." She tried to be this by the example she set for her fellow workers; she prayed the rosary on her way to work (the first factory was an hour's walk away). She invited her companions to do the same. Her homemade devotion was called "the rosary of a happy death." During the recitation of the regular prayers, the girls in one group added: "God grant us a happy death." The other group responded: "God grant us a happy life" (Calvo Morato, *Loose papers* n. 3, in *Process* II, p. 340).

Conscientious in her work habits and serious beyond her years, Liberata was put in charge of others, some even older than she. She could not but show her high moral standards. Her own prayer life deepened to the extent that in the end she asked to work in a room apart, where she would be able, without ostentation, to continue her work in a prayerful and recollected atmosphere. She had led her coworkers in the regular recitation of the *Angelus* and even when she was working alone she would not forget to stir up their remembrance of Mary and the mysteries of the faith in which Mary shared. Antonio Carbó, the owner of the last factory in which Liberata was able to work before her fatal illness, puts it simply in his sworn testimony: "Liberata had a mallet. When the clock struck the hour, she would knock several times, calling on the workers of the other two rooms to pray the *Hail Mary*" (*Testimony of 60 Witnesses* in *Process* II, p. 417). When possible

Liberata initiated the rosary during the long working hours, using this means to sanctify what so often becomes deadening routine, boredom and resentment. In simpler, less evolved days, Liberata was not innovating; she was using a practice common to her time.

Devotion: simple and mystical

This tertiary who was to be graced with extraordinary, possibly mystical graces and equally extraordinary trials and temptations, was traditional in her Marian devotion. From her early years she had the habit of stopping at the Marian shrine of Our Lady of Tura to ask for her protection for her undertakings. Mary, patroness of Olot under that title, became Liberata's model and protectress. The same holds for Liberata's dedication to the Carmelite church. Her Carmelite confessor swore that if the Carmelite friars were able to escape capture during the uprising of 1835, and if the church and monastery were not ravaged, it was because of Liberata's pleadings before the Lord and his Blessed Mother. While she was able she paid daily visits to the Carmelite church, where her devotion to Our Lady led her to her other favorite devotions—to the Blessed Trinity, and to Christ in the Bl. Sacrament, which she received even daily at a period when this was not the rule. She also had special devotion for the cross of Jesus.

Several notebooks of prayers which she used have come down to us. None of the prayers seems to be her personal composition. As with the majority of Christians, so Liberata was content to use the treasury of prayers already composed by other Christians. Those which nurtured her devotion betray her approach to the spiritual life. Spain, ever faithful defender of the Immaculate Conception even before the dogma's proclamation in 1854, clearly appears in Liberata's prayer books.

Antiphon: "You are my one dove, you are my perfect one, you are the chosen one of your mother. Saintly souls gaze at you and proclaim you immaculate. Alleluia.

In your Conception, O Virgin, you were already immaculate.

Pray to the Father, whose Son you bore.

Prayer: O God, by the Immaculate Conception of the Bl. Virgin, you prepared a suitable dwelling place for your Son. We beg you, that as you preserved her from every stain by the merits of his death from which she benefitted in advance, grant us also to reach you with clean hearts. By the merits of that same Jesus Christ. Amen."

Among her ordinary prayers for the grace of repentance, she addressed these verses to the Bl. Mother: "O Mary Immaculate! / O Mother of sinners! / You are the Queen of clemency, / Obtain these favors for me. / Assist me, / guide me / to live well. / And I hope for this grace from you: / that through my tears I may be saved" (*Process, Addenda*).

The final prayer in her collection was also addressed to Our Lady: "O most blessed Virgin, I offer you my eyes, my hands and my whole body. Protect me, please, like a daughter of yours. / Virgin Mary, conveived pure and immaculate, / render my body pure, my soul holy."

A sign of great souls is their appreciation of the ordinary pieties of the faith. While graced with outstanding manifestations of God's presence, Liberata continued to sew scapulars and spread devotion to Our Lady of Mt. Carmel by distributing them as widely as possible. She believed that God granted graces through pieties like the scapular and the rosary; they were not to be squandered. Just as she had given good advice to her fellow workers, so all through her life she shared her convictions about Marian devotion in its concrete forms. "She once mentioned to a poor washerwoman that she was without a scapular. When the latter denied it, she asked to see it. The woman discovered that that morning, inadvertantly, as she was changing her clothes her scapular fell off" (Barcells, *Liberata*, Barcelona, 1925, p. 85). Liberata took this to be part of her apostolate as a Carmelite tertiary. Interestingly, her biographer notes that her concern went beyond the mere material wearing of

41

the scapular, which she so often recommended. She urged Sunday Mass on those who were remiss, she argued with those who had given up on the rosary, and she sought to heal those whose hearts were filled with rancor and hatred (*Ibid.*).

To remain simple and satisfied with her humble status was a top priority with Liberata. She was convinced that her true treasures were all from above. She for whom poverty was a way of life from youth could not but be compassionate with anyone in need. She shared what little she had. Strict with herself even as to what she wore, at the end of the three and a half years she had to spend in bed, always in the same position, she expressed her gratitude to the thoughtful neighbor who had provided her with her burial clothing—the habit of Our Lady of Mt. Carmel. "When my hour arrives, clothe me with the holy habit of the Blessed Mother, Virgin of Carmel, which I have ready. It was a gift to me together with this blouse from the good and charitable lady whom you know" (Nanteli, *Tessatrice*, p. 84).

This down-to-earth tertiary was graced with extraordinary phenomena such as visions and the gift of prophecy. Her lifelong effort to remain faithful led to her being graced with a glimpse of heaven while still here on earth. Despite her contentment with whatever God willed for her, despite her diffidence vis-à-vis the extraordinary, despite her fear that she might be deluded, she was made aware of that life which is eternity and which in most cases becomes apparent only after death. The best guarantee that Liberata's spiritual experiences were authentic and not merely self-projection, is the fact that she did not want them, and that she realized that ultimately it was not these that made her holy. "After all, I do not enjoy them nor are they necessary for justification or for progress or for spiritual profit," she used to say (Nanteli, *Tessatrice*, p. 110).

Our Lady in extraordinary manifestations

It should not come as a surprise that Our Lady has a role in those out-of-the-ordinary phenomena.

It could not be otherwise in the case of someone for whom belonging to Mary's Carmelite family was important. Liberata never considered herself deserving of the graces accorded her. Her confessor, Luis Vila, who succeeded the Carmelite Antonio Bonavia, kept the latter informed about their penitent, who during her years of confinement to bed ate so little that doctors of different persuasions swore that she had to be kept alive by something beyond natural means. Fr. Vila noted what was to become Liberata's rule: Liberata would not cooperate with heavenly visions until she had her confessor's permission. "During these days she received most unique favors which would take too long to describe. The Blessed Mother insisted that she take her Son into her arms. But she considered herself unworthy" (*Letter* Sept. 13, 1836).

She would close her eyes and refuse to look at her heavenly visitors until she was reassured by her confessor that she was not being deluded. Her last spiritual director, Dr. Joachim Masmitjà, records a typical episode: "On another occasion, while she was being assaulted by a violent temptation, the voice of the Bl. Virgin was clearly heard. She was encouraging her, saying. 'Don't weep, little lamb.' — 'My Mother, I can't go on like this, I have no peace. I fear that I have offended God. Please don't increase my distress. Your tears touch me, and make mine worse'" (Nanteli, *Tessatrice*, p. 112).

On another occasion, Liberata perceived the Blessed Mother sheltering her Carmelite family under her mantle. Liberata reflected her times; she noted that some Carmelites were habitless, a result of the exclaustration ordered by the secularist government in 1845. "On this occasion the Virgin Mary appeared; she showed her mantle covering the Carmelites. Some of these appeared without habit. She lamented over this and spoke to the Bl. Mother, that they be allowed to wear their habit without danger. She said jokingly and lovingly, 'Shouldn't you be embarassed with your sons going around without their habit?'" (Fr. Bonavia's account). Liberata's familiarity with Our Lady and her down-to-earth dialogue say something about the authenticity of the experience.

Liberata's struggles with temptations, her battles with the "terrible" demon, who was as real to her as her heavenly visitors, made her wary of her spiritual progress. She was convinced ever more deeply of her personal misery. "Don't worry about me. What I suffer is worth nothing. My sins deserve much more. There is no comparison with what Christ suffered for me" (Balcells, *Liberata*, p. 48). Her physical ills which condemned her to bed for her final 13 years on earth were so varied and acute that visiting doctors wondered how she was surviving. Yet, until her death, Liberata continued with her no-nonsense approach to religion. Clothed as a Carmelite tertiary, she awaited death with those closest to her, her hand clutching a lit candle, blessed and indulgenced at the shrine of Our Lady of the Rosary. She was going to the eternal mansions, not relying on her spiritual prowess, but totally anchored in hope in God's mercy and Mary's motherly charity "at the hour of our death," as she had so often prayed.

Carmen de Sojo: under Mary's protection from birth

Carmen de Sojo had a Carmelite connection from birth. Not only was she born on the feast of St. Teresa of Avila, 1856, but her baptismal patroness became Our Lady of Mt. Carmel. Called *Carmencita* in her family circle, Carmen celebrated July 16 as her name day. As is usual in Latin countries, the nameday takes precedence over the birthday. It was so in Carmen's case during the 33 years she spent on this earth.

When she received her First Holy Communion at the age of ten, Carmen learned by concrete experience that Jesus in communion was a grace to be shared and lived with others. Her straightforward, and sometimes harsh mother took the youngster to the hospital dedicated to Our Lady of Mercy, where Carmen helped to serve the poor during the afternoon hours. This hospital was to play a role in Carmen's future life as well. As became her spiritual way, Carmen did not take her mother's brusque ways amiss. Until the end she expressed her unabashed affection for her mother; if anything, Carmen had misgivings about herself. She did not forget the nameday of her mother, December 8, since she was named Concepción. This Marian feast was not a mere formality for Carmen, but a reminder of Mary's motherly concern. "My very dear mother, in the first place, I rejoice with you for all your days which I hope pass by happily and in the best possible way in the world, with the blessings of the Lord and of the Immaculate Conception. May she lavish her heavenly and also material gifts on you, my mother" (Mario di Franca, *Carmen de Sojo*, p. 25).

Teenage bride

Carmen was only 15 when she and Dr. Jorge Anguera, 15 years her senior, began courting at the suggestion of a mutual priest friend. Carmen's own religious convictions must have been seconded by this daily communicant. Her Marian devotion could not but have been strengthened by this professional who became one of Barcellona's better known doctors and yet died poor because he helped those in need *gratis*. In fact, Jorge had the habit of accompanying the bodies of his patients who had died to the cemetery. On the way he insisted with his colleagues that they pray the rosary. If it were a relative or acquaintance then all fifteen decades were prayed.

The courtship was not long. Carmen did not believe in keeping the love of her life waiting in order to make his affection and concern for her keener. They were married in the chapel of the hospital of Our Lady of Mercy. They spent the afternoon of their wedding day serving the sick poor. In a letter written a month before their wedding, Carmen recalls what Mary meant for both of them: "Love her (Mary) very much, Jorge. I will try to do the same. I'll never forget the day we were together at Mercy (hospital). We placed ourselves under her protection and chose her as our patroness." Carmen never ceased praising God—as her daily letters to her husband when he was away on business attest—for giving her a spouse who shared so many of her religious

45

convictions. What it meant for this teenage bride to be able to consecrate herself to Mary's protection and patronage with her husband at her side, and expressing the same attitude! Over and above the various ways Carmen had of expressing her affection for her husband, she could pay him no higher compliment than to call him "the guardian of my virtue."

Not that all was idyllic. As every marriage, so Carmen and Jorge's had its rocky moments. Jorge was not always satisfied with Carmen's management of the household. He sometimes protested even heatedly that Carmen should be more committed to domestic duties. She wrote in anguish to her spiritual confidant, Bishop Casañas, confessing that she tried to fit in all her duties. She sometimes was still up at 2 A.M. in order to finish everything and still dedicate her two hours to mental prayer and to the Little Office of Our Lady.

A typical episode of how Carmen approached the things of God occurred in December of 1878, when she visited this same Don Casañas, who at the time was afflicted with a case of serious laryngitis. Carmen was so dismayed that she prayed the Lord to cure her spiritual father and transfer his laryngitis to her, but in a way that would appear normal. This is just what happened. When Fr. Casañas heard of her status, he came to pray for and with her. They used a familiar novena prayer, and at the second *Hail Mary* she was healed.

As a professional man, Jorge wished his wife to be recognized as belonging to a certain strata of society. He was quite displeased with the black clothes she habitually wore. After another session of sermonizing, Carmel wrote to her confessor protesting that fashions were not on her list of priorities, yet she wanted to satisfy her husband's desires. Her compromise was to dress in brown, which in Catalan was called *Del Carmine*, or the Carmelite color.

Another crisis occurred when she gave birth to her children. Carmen insisted that she personally nurse them with her milk. Her family wanted to call in a wet-nurse. As happened so often in her lifetime, Carmen had refuge in prayer to Our Lord, to the Bl.

46

Mother and to a personal favorite, Bl. Oriol. Despite her precarious state of health, which led to her death at 33 years of age, she was able to nurse all of her children as she wished.

Carmen's mettle and faith are revealead in her discovery that her baby Jorge was suffering from a notable deformation of his vertebrae. When her husband diagnosed his infant son's condition, he was pessimistic. Carmen's reaction: not recourse to the best medical institutions, but rather to Mary, Health of Christians. She invoked the Catalan favorite, Our Lady of Montserrat, and promised a pilgrimage on foot to her shrine if her son were healed. Without need of any medical device, the youngster grew up healthy. A year later Carmen fulfilled her promise with a pilgrimage to Catalonia's patroness.

The intensity of her spiritual life with its Marian tonality is in evidence throughout her letters. A birthday greeting to a friend, Raymonda, is typical: "My dear sister, how are you spending the birthday of the Queen of Angels and our Mother? Does the Lord grant you the joy and peace that I desire and wish for you? I have prayed so much for this intention to Our Lady in my poor prayers. If you only knew, beloved sister, the hunger and thirst I have for your holiness. My desires increase in proportion to my love for you. My Raymonda, I would have you belong completely, completely to Jesus, hidden in his heart, sated with his love" (di Franca, *Carmen*, p. 168).

Carmen de Sojo is an example of a wife who never ceases thinking up new ways of expressing her love and need for her husband, and on the other hand her ever growing love for the Tremendous Lover of mankind. Her letters abound with signs of affection: "You can't imagine, my husband, how much I miss you this time. It seems that Our Lady of Mt. Carmel's feast (her name day) will never arrive. The days that remain seem to be centuries to me. I am sure that the same is happening to you, and that you are thinking a lot of your wife and little son. Am I not right? We have not been separated for so long a period in a long time. I feel it so much the more. I am impatiently looking forward to tomorrow so that I can be with you. I miss you. All intent on seeing you is your wife whom you know lives only for you" (*Letter* in *Post. Arch.* IV, 11, p. 25). Her letters are filled with details about the children. Nothing seems to have escaped her notice. She was particularly intent on sharing her religious convictions and practices with her children. Time and again she stated that the worst thing that could happen to them would be to fall into sin.

Love for the person of Jesus

Positively, her love for the person of Jesus overwhelmed her as she made spiritual progress. The place of Mary in her spiritual vision is aptly summed up in the act of consecration to Jesus which she and her husband both made. Their marriage became a true sacrament and outward sign of the burning furnace of love that Jesus has for his own. "Most beloved and dear Jesus of my soul! By your great goodness and grace I consecrate to you completely and uniquely for always my soul, my body, my senses and my faculties to be like your angels and ardent seraphim. My beloved Jesus, accept this consecration of mine which I present to you through my dear Blessed Mother Mary, through beloved Bl. Joseph Oriol and through my guardian angel. I ask you to let me die a thousand times rather than sin against this consecration even slightly, which the most miserable of your creatures makes to you. September 7, 1881" (di Franca, *Carmen*, p. 182).

Like Liberata before her, Carmen received ever higher forms of divine favors, accompanied by immense sufferings, both physical and moral. This purification process made Carmen rely only on the Lord. She understood by the weakness of her flesh and of her inner life that whatever was worthy in her was from the Lord. He constantly convinced her of the immense floods of love he had for her. She was given to understand by Mary, whom she constantly invoked, that the crosses she had to bear were gifts from on high. While she was introduced by Mary,

Joseph and a band of angels to the grotto at Bethlehem in one of her meditations, "afterwards it seemed that the Bl. Virgin nodded to me and put a very precious small cross into my hands. I don't know the material of which it was made because I cannot form an idea of it from the things of this world. As I accepted it, I felt that it was heavy in an incredible way. I could not begin to think of how to support it. My dear patron, [Bl. Oriol] came to my aid. He held it on one side; and the cross lost much of its weight" (*Ibid.*, p. 240-241). The meaning was clear: the purification process to follow was from the Lord. Mary was the messenger of the ray of hope that would be needed as Carmen was oppressed day and night in ways that could become a textbook of the trials of souls close to the Lord. In the years that followed, she had frequent recourse to Mary in her moments of keenest suffering.

The perfect and limitless love of Jesus was alone able to satisfy the longings of Carmen to repay in her own inadequate way the goodness which was lavished on her. To allow this love of Jesus to have his way with her in sufferings and in good times, as he willed, was supreme happiness. "This is truly heaven: to suffer for Jesus, to live dying for my Jesus." This contemporary of St. Therese of Lisieux shared her fellow Carmelite's experience. The love of Jesus' heart overwhelmed one in the cloister, the other with her family at home. Both Carmelites understood that their hearts needed more than human means to be able to support such a show of affection on Christ's part. Both cried out, in their anguish, for a share in Mary's heart which had embodied so well what a human being was capable of. Carmen expressed it so: "Virgin Mary, my most sweet mother, give me your heart, ardent with love, with which to love my Jesus" (Saenz, *Una Heroica Victima*, p. 211-212).

In this description of the status of her prayer life, she is acting under obedience to her spiritual mentor, Bishop Casañas. As a true mystic, she had little confidence in her own abilities to express herself, or to reciprocate the immensity of God's love for her. Her native confidence in Our Lady, our mother and model, must come to her aid if she is to be able to shoul-

4

der the burden of God's love for her. Because Mary was so filled with God's grace/love, she was much more able to cope with the resonances of this love than any other creature. "My Father knows how to do it better, he himself is better.... But I, such a small child, I wish to stay with my Father and unite my poor heart with his in order to love you, Jesus, the more. Yes, mother of ours, yes, let us love Jesus with a single heart. Present us to Jesus and chant our love to him in our name. We are your children, my mother, and we wish to die consumed by love. Tell Jesus, tell our love that we wish to be his completely and exclusively. Tell Jesus that we love him, that we die of love. Recount it to him, O loving mother, recount it to him, O loving mother, recount it to him for us. Our life, our sweetness, our heaven and love of our heart, Jesus of our soul, being of our being, our one love, we love you with the angels and with millions of seraphim and with the heart of your saints and with our dear patron [Bl. Oriol] and our most beloved mother, your mother Mary."

Mary's natural role in mysticism

While she was engaged to Jorge, a month before their wedding, she wrote to her fiancé about what she understood Mary's role to be in their life together. In context the 15-year old was commenting on how happy she was that he had the pleasure of taking part in a public manifestation of the Catholic society to which he belonged: "What is more beautiful and greater than to sing well to Mary, to our mother, to our hope, to our model, to the greatest and most beautiful of all women? In this way, my friend, I think that if you believe that I have some good qualities (I assure you, you are wrong, because they are far from existing in me, and yet you love me so much); then how much you must love the Virgin Mary, who you positively know possesses all grace, all virtues and all attraction, and that she is superior to every creature" (*Letter*, Dec. 11, 1871).

Carmen uses the experience of human love, of the obvious affection her fiancé has for her, to point beyond and higher. Her point is that if he can be so taken in by Carmen's goodness, which is something precarious and not as real as might appear at first glance, how will he have to react to Our Blessed Mother in whom goodness is rooted, who is "full of grace" by the Lord's own admission.

Although she had once been miraculously cured of tuberculosis, Carmen was mortally afflicted by this illness at the age of 33. This time she was convinced that she would not recover. She obeyed her confessor and prayed for healing, but inwardly she thought the opposite. She was sorry for her children whom she was to leave at such a tender age, but she felt eternity itself was calling her. Her husband was with her when she died. The telltale sign of her true state was confirmed when she spat up blood.

Typically, this deeply spiritual, even mystic soul went to her beloved Lord Jesus not with some elevated insight which she shared with those around her. Her doctor husband, seeing the end was near, and speaking out of his own deep faith in Mary's protection and motherly charity, simply asked his wife. "Are you wearing the scapular?" Her last words were a simple. "Yes, I am." On that Marian note she died.

* * *

Liberata Ferrarons and Carmen de Sojo understood, as tertiaries who stood close to the sources, that belonging to the Order of Brothers of the Bl. Virgin Mary of Mt. Carmel meant above all living the spirituality of Carmel. For them prayer was not so much a set of programmed formularies as delighting in the overwhelming and loving presence of God, as a milieu in which the primacy of God was not something to be argued about, but rather something to be enjoyed and appreciated. This "having time for God" followed the path trod by Christ Jesus when he was on this earth with us. That path inexorably led to the cross on Calvary. Carmen expressed it so: "I do not want, I am not able to live without suffering. On my own I can do nothing; but with Jesus I can do all things. My ambition is to live dying for him. I ask to suffer, to suffer ever more. To live long to suffer more, to be more sensitive and so be able to suffer more" (di Franca, *Carmen*, p. 207-208). Only the experience of Jesus' love could rouse such profound convictions.

In the Carmelite family, this Gospel spirit is lived in the unobtrusive but all-pervading warmth of Mary's motherly concern. In fact, both Liberata and Carmen took Mary's presence and protection for granted. When they mention Mary it is never in polemical tones. She is simply there because Carmel was her idea to begin with; it is her family. This is why these two tertiaries experienced Mary's presence both on the heights of their contemplative experiences and sufferings, and also in the simple but effective scapular devotion. Typically, both of them—worn out with suffering and out of love for the Lord Jesus—had one final wish: to be buried wearing the habit of Mary's Carmelite family.

4

CARMEL: AT HOME WITH MARY

*Our Lady in the lives of
Bl. Raphael Kalinowski and
Bl. Mary of Jesus Crucified, Carmelites*

Teresian Carmel continues to provide the church with models of Christian holiness. The inspiration given to the reform of Carmel by Sts Teresa of Avila and John of the Cross has been so strong as to produce saints in every generation. Recently, two followers of Carmel's reform have been added to the album of Blesseds: Raphael of St. Joseph (Kalinowski) and Mary of Jesus Crucified (Miriam Baouardy). The surprising variety of the Spirit's gifts is only too evident in these two fervent Carmelites, whose living out of Jesus' Gospel was so authentic and heroic that the Church willingly and gratefully indicates them as models.

A study in contrasts

If a study in contrasts were being etched among the saints, these two figures could serve as excellent examples of how the work of forging saints by the Holy Spirit takes the most disparate types, and transforms them into the living Gospel of Jesus Christ. Bl. Raphael was born into a noble Lithuanian-Polish family; Bl. Miriam's (we shall use her native Arabian name throughout this article) parents were among the poorest inhabitants in the poverty-stricken village of Abellin, not far from Nazareth. The friar's schooling included the School for Nobles in Vilno, capital of Lithuania, and several specialized colleges in Russia; the Carmelite nun's schooling was nonexistent. Although they were not wealthy, the Kalinowski family was able to provide a decent education and positions in life for all nine children whom the father, Andrew, had by three successive wives; Miriam Baouardy's parents both died when she was two, and for the better part of her life she worked with various families as a housemaid.

While the allurements of a comfortable life in various Russian cities led to a period of ten years in which Bl. Raphael gave up on the sacraments of the church, the "little Arab" Miriam was left for dead when attacked by a Muslim who wanted to convert her to his religion. The Slav, elevated to the rank of captain in the Russian military, resigned to take active part in the Polish-Lithuanian revolt of 1863 against Russia, and was named minister of war in the provisional government; the cloistered Sr. Miriam wished to remain a lay-sister rather than a choir nun all her life—she could not read sufficiently well to be able to celebrate the Divine Office, despite efforts to teach her. While the future Carmelite friar was condemned to death by a military court because of his share in the insurrection, a sentence commuted to ten years hard labor in the Siberian salt mines, the future Carmelite nun's life was determined by the peregrinations and wishes of the families for whom she worked, travels which took her to Egypt, Jerusalem, Beirut, France.

The quiet, recollected, generally serious personality of Fr. Raphael contrasts sharply with the voluble, expansive, almost irrepressible portrait left us of Sr. Miriam. The saintly friar was known for his dedication to regular observance—he was constantly calling for an exact observance of the Order's Constitutions; Sr. Miriam was more charismatic and spontaneous in her spirituality. Even a cursory study of the prayers left by the two blesseds is striking. Bl. Raphael prefers the tried and true; Bl. Miriam is full of ingenious intuitions and sparkling images of her life in the Spirit. While Fr. Raphael was esteemed during his lifetime universally as a saintly figure. Bl. Miriam had a more difficult time of it: in Mangalore, India, where she was sent to help establish Carmel, she found the whole community together with the bishop turned against her. While it was Fr. Raphael who had to keep reminding people that he was a sinner, grateful for the gift of repentence, Bl. Miriam was told that she was possessed by the devil, and in fact was exorcized several times. While Fr. Raphael spent a good deal of his time as a Carmelite priest hidden in the confessional, counselling, guiding, abolving, Sr. Miriam gave the best of her efforts to the building of the Carmelite monastery in Bethlehem.

Naturally, even more elements could be found which *united* these two saintly spirits in the Carmelite family. The essentials of their commitment to Gospel living in Carmel were shared by both. One of those ingredients was their love for the Blessed Mother, whose Carmelite family became their home. The blesseds are sterling examples of the ways of the Spirit: while gracing them with a new religious family explicitly dedicated to Our Lady, still the Spirit had already given both Carmelites their own native love and devotion for Mary. Bl. Raphael would for all his days reflect the Polish-Lithuanian mystique of Mary, mother and potent defender of her people by her prevenient mother's love. Bl. Miriam would, all her days, reflect the intimate way in which Mary is encountered as another member of one's family in Eastern Christendom. Both blesseds were born into religiously oriented families (after having lost their first 12 children, Bl. Miriam's parents had made a long pilgrimage to Bethlehem on foot, to beg God's mercy and the survival of at least one child). For neither of them was Mary ever a problem or a theory, or a mere idealization of the spirit of motherhood. In a genuinely Catholic sense, in both families Our Lady's place was taken for granted and took on the national and cultural characteristics of each.

As so often happens in a person's relationship with Mary our mother, so in the case of the two blesseds. Aspects of their personalities which were not always evident surfaced and were evoked by the presence of Mary in their lives. In the case of Bl. Raphael, devotion to the Bl. Mother helped this well educated and well-bred member of the intelligentsia to remain simple and direct. Although he had to work through religious crises in his own life—and subsequently helped many others do so, addressing himself even to deeply religious and theological questions— still in his piety and preaching and pastoral practice he remained the down-to-earth son of the humble handmaid of the Lord. Bl. Miriam, on the other hand, had no intellectual pretensions whatsoever— she found the touch of her beloved triune God in nature about her and in her ordinary life as a religious. Yet in describing Our Lady and in composing spontaneous prayers to her, she expresses insights that have solid theology behind them. For Bl. Miriam, Our Lady becomes a concrete example of the marvels of God's grace, which cannot be left unadmired nor unattended. It is a moving religious experience to meditate on the description of Our Lady left by this unsophisticated, uneducated lay-sister, and discover the down-to-earth, accessible way she has of expressing the deep and often abstruse descriptions of theologians.

Bl. Raphael Kalinowski:
Devotion etched deep in the Slav soul

Bl. Raphael, whose mother died shortly after his birth, found dedicated motherly concern in his successive stepmothers, but as a true son of Lithuania he learned as well to rely on the motherly charity of the Madonna of his people. The deeply religious Kalinowski family often went to pray before the icon of Our Lady of Ostra Brama, second in importance in these lands only to Częstochowa. The delicate, tender features of the image of Our Lady are part of Vilno's defensive walls (and so the name *ostra brama*); faithful Lithuanian and Polish people to this day believe that more than any army, more than any leader, more than any human expedient, the one responsible for the survival of their national culture and identity is the Mother of God. Although we have no record of his sentiments, the youngster Joseph Kalinowski could not but be touched by the beautifully compassionate, concerned visage of the Madonna of Ostra Brama. In fact, each time he returned "home," an obligatory visit was to this mother of faithful love.

Childhood impressions are often lasting; rapport with mother and father have lasting impact on the future of the child's personality. We know from the testimony of an eyewitness that all his life Joseph was impressed by this heavenly mother who had been his refuge so often as a youngster. Even as a Carmelite friar he lived on the memory of so much goodness experienced from the heart of his mother in heaven. In fact, he asked to have an image of Vilno's Madonna sent to him. John Czech, a shoemaker who tried his vocation with the Teresian Carmelites and spent much of his life working in their communities, gave an eyewitness report: "He had a special devotion for the Madonna of Ostrobrama; once I met the Servant of God in front of a copy of the image of the Virgin of Ostrabrama, which he had sent to him. I remained amazed at the great veneration and at the great recollection that you could read on his face. The Servant of God was very glad to possess this picture" (*Summarium*, Roma, 1963, p. 333).

Only a Slavic soul, such as that of Pope John Paul II, can appreciate how deeply rooted in the Slavic people is their lovetie with their heavenly mother and protectress. Some of their fondest religious hymns, often sung from memory verse after verse, are expressions of their grateful memory of someone who never forgets them and bends down to them particularly in their greatest needs—as a nation, as families, as individuals. Bl. Raphael had this experience. In his youth, after he had finished his studies and was successfully positioned in Russia as a military engineer, a certain sadness and melancholy—typical of the Slavic character—overwhelmed him. His future was clouded. He tried the usual expedients of young people his age: immersion in the entertainments, friendships and amusements of young people climbing the ladder of success in the world. This is the period in which he was alienated not so much from the faith as from the practice of his religion. For ten years he kept away from the sacraments. How could he ever forget the simple way in which he found his way "home." It made a deep impression on him, as he describes his homecoming in his *Memoirs*.

He was in Kursk, working on the construction of the first railroad track between Kiev and Odessa, alone and confused. A friend and a simple book were his salvation. "Of that time spent there, I didn't profit because of my work, for which I was not that suited, but because of a religious book which fell into my hands. I had this book with me, given to me by an assistant, an engineer, a Pole. He had received it from his mother before he left home. The reading of this book edified my soul considerably. It particularly roused in me the sentiments of certainty in the help of the Blessed Virgin. The point it made on the usefulness of reciting the 'Hail Mary' in times of need was etched deeply in my memory when one day I found myself in great danger of losing my life. I recited the Hail Mary with fervor and my life was spared. What a mighty weapon is prayer! How all-powerful is the intercession of the Blessed Virgin. How many means of salvation the church gives us by means of books of devotion, by which the truth of God has access to us" (p. 96-97, in *Responsio ad animadversiones Promotoris*, Roma, 1976, p. 13). The simple objects of piety often are the choice instruments of God in his plan for talented and well educated persons such as Joseph Kalinowski. In other situations more sophisticated means might be needed: what made sense to him at this point was the simple, personal touch of a mother's love, available not just to the elite, but to all her children.

Condemned to the Siberian salt mines

But even this intervention did not reconcile Joseph completely to his religious duties. He still remained alienated from the sacraments though his interior life was being strengthened. Only before his forced march to exile in Siberia did he get to confession and comunion. All his life he blamed himself for being away from the Lord for such a long time. His strong attachment to the Bl. Virgin evidently was operative during his years of wandering, because when he was arrested shortly after his first sacramental reconciliation one of the ways in which he filled up his days in prison was by singing aloud the

Litany of the Bl. Mother (Poles are not beyond singing the rosary in its entirety!) In the meditation book he kept in prison, the first page had a design of the Cross and of Our Lady of Częstochowa (small wonder that the first Polish Pope chose these two realities to be emblazoned on his coat of arms). When he was dragged in for his grueling interrogations, his prayer was: "Under your protection. O holy Mother of God . . ." as he placed himself in the hands of his heavenly protectress. He remained calm even though he knew that most of his compatriots had been condemned to death; he escaped with a sentence to the Siberian salt mines—a trek which was two thirds on foot and which lasted more than half a year!

Ten years of forced labor in Siberia has broken the spirit of many a man. In Joseph Kalinowski's case it made him into a saint. Already on the long trek across the vast Asian continent, in freezing weather often 40 degrees below zero, this Lithuanian patriot was sculpted into one of the beautiful people of God, to the degree that his fellow prisoners used to pray, "By the prayers of Joseph Kalinowski, deliver us, O God." Not only was his interior life buttressed by the hours of prayer and recollection in those vast tundra regions, but his character, always sensitive and attached to people, turned to those who were most in need—to the poor, the abandoned, the children. He became a "savior" for many, even sharing the monies his family sent him to sustain him in his exile. His talents at teaching youngsters were particularly appreciated by this family oriented populace. Till the end he included the native Russian people in his charity. (Later on, among Poles again, during the Russo-Japanese War of 1901, some Polish confreres wished that every Japanese bullet would reach ten Russians. Fr. Raphael's corrective, despite all his sufferings in Siberian exile, was: "Brother, we should not talk like that—to wish that on our enemies is wrong. Rather, we should ask God that they be converted. After all, they are our brothers" (Fr. Charles of the Heart of Jesus, O.C.D. in *Summarium*, p. 44). The deep feelings of the Poles vis-à-vis the Russians make this approach all the more Christian.

In Siberia, again by means of a book, he came to know about the Carmelite Order with its roots in the Orient and its great devotion to the Bl. Mother. "I found a mention of the Order of the Bl. Virgin Mary of Mt. Carmel, of its existence first in the East and then its transfer to the West. It struck me: here is an Order which should bring those who fell into schism back to the holy church. I could not conquer that inner desire to see Russia converted. Guided in a miraculous way by Providence, I entered that order ten years later" (p. 208, in *Responsio*, p. 17).

Carmel, Mary's home

To enter Carmel was not an impulse which followed his likes and dislikes (for years he had spoken of a life as a Capuchin). Fr. Raphael believed it was part of God's providence and the initiative of the Bl. Mother that led him to her own family. The cloistered nuns to whom he dedicated many of his priestly ministrations had prayed and prayed that he enter Carmel precisely to restore the Polish Teresian family. The superior of the Breslau Carmel remembered Fr. Raphael's teaching: "He loved Our Blessed Mother as a son loves his mother. He often repeated to us that we should be particularly thankful to the Blessed Mother for having welcomed us into her order" (Sr. Mary Joseph Nowosielska, O.C.D., in *Summarium*, p. 280). Among the nuns the general opinion was that he wished to enter Carmel because of his special love for the Mother of God (cf. Sr. Margaret of the Bl. Sacrament, O.C.D., in *Summarium*, p. 98).

A precious witness has been left by Fr. Bronislaus of the Bl. Trinity (Jarosinski), O.C.D., who gave a resumé of Fr. Raphael's Marian devotion: "The Servant of God fostered a special devotion to the Bl. Mother. I know that he had copies made of the image of the Madonna of Berdyczów, of Ostrobrama, of Godohaj and of Our Lady of Consolation in Lublin. He begged Fr. Wenceslaus Nowakowski, O.F.M.Cap., to publish a booklet on the miraculous image of Our Lady of Mt. Carmel in Berdyczów. In Wadowice I saw in the Servant of God's cell a prayer to the Bl.

Virgin Mary, composed by him and which he kept on the desk of his cell. After the death of the Servant of God, I took the manuscript of this prayer as a souvenir. It remained in Berdyczów where it probably has been lost. The Servant of God, Fr. Raphael, taught his confreres what kind of devotion we should have for Our Lady most Pure. Before the feast of Our Lady of Mt. Carmel, the friars were called together for a spiritual conference on the Bl. Virgin. In his position as prior, the Servant of God presided over this meeting and appealed to the monks that each say something about Our Lady. One of our confreres said among other things, that the Carmelite Order gloried in having the title 'Brothers of the Bl. Virgin.' At the end of the spiritual conference the Servant of God himself spoke and insisted on this title in a special way. He said that to glory in the title of Brothers of the Bl. Virgin would serve no purpose if the life of a Carmelite were not worthy of such a mother. He showed his displeasure that the church had not been adorned with garlands of flowers for the feast of Our Lady of Mt. Carmel, since he himself had given the order the decorate the church... The prayer composed by him proves his great reverence, love and dedication to Our Blessed Mother. In the prayer he affirms that he has bound himself by a vow to the Bl. Virgin. 'Blessed Virgin, Immaculate Mother, kindly look on the misery of my soul, which is bound to you forever by a vow'" (*Summarium*, p. 187-188). Another confrere had been impressed by the fervor with which Fr. Raphael used to intone the *Salve Regina* on the vigils of feasts of Our Lady and on Saturdays (Fr. Bogumil, O.C.D., in *Summarium*, p. 234).

To the members of the Carmelite scapular confraternity and of the Third Order, Fr. Raphael often centered his sermons on the role of Our Lady in Carmel's spiritual life. In the restoration of Carmel in Poland he knew the importance of lay Carmelites; his instructions to them covered the core values of Carmel's spirituality: prayer and devotion to the Bl. Mother. "During the meetings of the Third Order the Servant of God most often and most willingly gave us conferences on Our Blessed Mother. From these teachings of his you could understand how much the Servant of God himself loved Our Lady. He sought to transfer this love to the souls of each of the tertiaries. He zealously exorted us to imitate the virtues of Mary and above all, her innocence. He often repeated to us what was obviously the motto of his own life: 'Mary, always and in everything.' His sermons in church also made a deep impression on me" (Anna Michalik, T.O.C.D., in *Summarium*, p. 323). The Third Order chapters in Kraków, Wadowice and Przemysl all benefitted from his fervent exhortations to live the spirit of Our Lady in the world. Great soul that he was, Bl. Raphael recognized the need for externals: he was a firm believer in the scapular devotion. He enrolled numberless persons in the scapular: what he urged constantly was a warm, simple, loving approach to Our Lady, who had begun the love process by showing so much favor to the Carmelite family.

Fr. Raphael was able to reach Romania with his fervent scapular devotion. A noble Roumanian lady claimed that Fr. Raphael had cured her of a psychosomatic disease, and she, together with her husband, showed her gratitude by helping spread the scapular devotion in their native land. The clergy of the area became so enthusiasic that a new wave of fervor was tangible, to the extent that there was talk of spiritual transformation.

Although he was not known as a writer, his Marian devotion and the need of his people led Bl. Raphael to compile two books on Our Lady: *Mary, Always and in Everything*, Kraków, 1901, and *The Veneration of the Mother of God in Polish Carmel*, Lwow-Warsaw, 1905.

The confessional, to which he was studiously faithful, was another venue in which he explained how Mary was our guide on the path to holiness. One of the novices whom Fr. Raphael had confessed testified: "He must have had a very lively devotion to Our Lady in his heart because when he heard our confessions, he always urged us to love Our Lady, and he wrote a nice book on Our Lady entitled, *Mary, always and in everything*, which was of great use to me throughout my life to rouse this devotion in me"

(Fr. Thomas of the Heart of Mary, O.C.D., in *Summarium*, p. 216). Although he was not a great preacher—people were edified by his sincerity and authenticity of life—still his deep-seated love for Mary could not but characterize his sermons: "His sermons were easy to understand and were noted for their simplicity. In them he urged us especially to the veneration of the Bl. Virgin Mary and to prayer" (Frances Zabudzinska, in *Summarium*, p. 17). Interestingly, this much loved yet austere friar was known for the seriousness with which be undertook his duties. Yet one ray of joy and sunshine irradiated from the Bl. Mother: his dramatically adventurous life had taught him how all earthly joys pass. Our Bl. Mother is part of God's lasting kingdom: "He used to preach about the Bl. Virgin Mary and often repeated with exaltation: Mary is the cause of our joy. You could see that he himself was affected by a great joy at this" (Maria Podolecka, in *Summarium*, p. 51).

He was convinced: "Every good mother loves her sons and wishes their happiness. There has never been and never will be a mother as good as the Blessed Virgin" (Preface to *Mary, always and in everything*, cited by Sr. Theresa Mary, O.C.D., in *Summarium*, p. 257). A diocesan priest who had been guided in his vocation by Fr. Raphael, recalled another detail: "At every step he showed himself to be devoted to the Bl. Virgin. He began with Mary and with Mary he finished. He used to leave me with the words, 'May the Virgin Mary bless us with her holy Infant...' He encouraged in attractive ways, especially young people, to have devotion to Our Lady, and to receive the sacraments on her feasts" (Rev. Rudolf De Formicini, in *Summarium*, p. 260).

In his writings

A few of Bl. Raphael's extant writings will betray the reasons for his warm, tender Lithuanian-Polish devotion towards Mary. He does not see her apart from her Son Jesus: "One of the motives for devotion and love for the Virgin Mary is that, in the plans of divine providence, the Incarnation of God was neces-

63

sary for our redemption. Without her virtues, Mary would not have been a choice vase. God would not have had the means by which to come; there would have been no redemption. O Maria, what would happen to us without your virtues? Why is it we understand and love you so little? We should deplore this lukewarmness of ours" (Notes from Siberia, Smolensko, 1874).

Although looked on as a saint while still alive, Fr. Raphael would have none of it—he repeated that he had too many sins on his conscience and his trust was uniquely in the mercy of God and in the goodness of our heavenly mother. This is how he expressed himself in a prayer he often said: "O most blessed Virgin, Immaculate Mother, look kindly on the anguish of my soul, which is bound to you forever. For me you are my shield of protection against the arrows of the evil one. Calm the tempests of my agitated spirit, chisel in my heart the passion of your divine Son, fill it with repentance solely for love of him. Show me the path of sincere penance for my repeated betrayals. Prepare me for a death out of love of God. Keep me as the very least of those in the kingdom of saints and of the just, do not delay. Free me of the constant anguish for my salvation, amid so many traps of this earthly life. Lead me, although I am full of unworthiness, by your mercy to the eternal enjoyment of God. March 15, 1900 — Your prodigal son, Raphael of St. Joseph" (Honorat Gil, *Rafael Kalinowski*, Madrid, 1981, p. 126-127).

We have the text of a conference Fr. Raphael prepared for his confreres at Wadowice on November 20, 1906. It shows how solidly his Marian devotion was rooted in the faith. Firstly, he surveys Christendom, sees so much lukewarmness and indifference; the one area that seems to be better in his day than in the earlier years is "Marian fervor." This factor could well be labelled a "seed given as a gift by the merciful providence of God to mankind, in order to achieve salvation." Secondly, Bl. Raphael points out that only God himself knows how many graces he bestowed on this magnificent creature from whom his Son was to receive a type of existence he never had before. Forever Our Lady provides for

Jesus all that a human mother provides for a son. Thirdly, "because of her motherhood Mary is like a book in which the eternal Word, Jesus the Lord, presents himself to the world to be read." Fourthly, Mary by her motherhood of Jesus becomes the mother of all men. Fifthly, all this accrued to Our Lady insofar as she obeyed and pronounced her world shattering words, "Let it be done to me according to your word." The will of God is vital for each of us. Finally, Mary stays with us "until the hour of our death;" "no one better than ourselves, doubly sons of Mary, should imitate her so that as faithful sons we might be enriched with the fruits of her motherhood; and seeking 'the one thing necessary,' the only thing necessary for salvation, she might guide without danger the ship of this life, during our austere pilgrimage through this world, safe from the convulsions of our times. And then to obtain with our prayers for all of mankind the grace that so many calamities cease and that light dawn on the horizon of the world" (*Ibid.*, p. 105-108).

Bl. Miriam Baouardy:
A Palestinian's love for the Daughter of Sion

Miriam Baouardy, baptized in the Greek Melchite rite, in the poverty-stricken village of Abellin, halfway between Nazareth and Haifa and in view of Mt. Carmel, even as a child showed a remarkable piety. She could not but have imbibed the warm, constant and close contact of the Bl. Virgin with her people.

The Eastern Liturgy is more a way of life than mere ritual: among the people it is not a thing; it is the living presence of the divine persons who touch our daily lives. The Bl. Mother is part of this divine presence from the time of the Incarnation, thus becoming a living and loving member of Christian communities. In this type of atmosphere it is understandable that this future mystic even as a child would have begun to fast on Saturdays in honor of the Bl. Mother. "As a small child she loved to set up small altars in honor of the Bl. Virgin and to decorate

5

them with flowers" (Marguerite Leclaire, in *Summarium*, Roma, 1933, p. 172).

Miriam's closeness to Our Lady also can be traced to the death of her mother when the child was just over two. Adopted by her paternal uncle, the filial affection she felt was at least partially directed towards her who was fully alive and presented to her by the church's liturgy. From her earliest yers, the prayer life of the church attracted Miriam; people who knew her as a child testified that she was outstanding, someone alive to religion and spiritual realities. A priest testified: "A certain Hanna Michail told me that he had gone to the house of [Miriam's] uncle, and he found Miriam there, at the time about 10 years old, kneeling in front of an image of Our Lady. She was all wrapped up in prayer with a devotion that was transparent on her face. Hanna Michail began to talk to the uncle and two hours passed by. By then, Miriam finished her prayer and came to greet Hanna, whom she knew. Hanna told her: 'Don't you get tired of praying so much?' But she answered him: 'A daughter is never bored to stay near her mother. Our Lady is my mother and I enjoy staying near her'" (Mons. Boutros Said, in *Summarium*, p. 79-80).

The significant moments of Miriam's early years are marked by the presence of the Bl. Mother in a spontaneous way, without any artificiality. Such was Miriam's reaction to her uncle's arrangement for her marriage at the age of 13. By this time the family was living in Alexandria, Egypt; the uncle was following cultural traditions in providing a husband for his orphaned niece. But from her deep-seated religious convictions, Miriam would have none of it: she explained that she would remain a virgin in honor of the Bl. Mother who had stood by her so faithfully. When the uncle persisted, Miriam prayed to Our Lady for guidance—and cut off her beautiful hair. Although she had to bear the daily wrath of the family, she never changed her resolve.

A Muslim acquaintance, irritated and then enraged when Miriam energetically resisted his efforts to convert her to Islam, impetuously grabbed a scimitar, the traditional Arab curved sabre and struck her on the neck. Till the day she died, Miriam affirmed that she thought she was dead and had been brought back to the land of the living by the ministrations of the Bl. Virgin Mary. A sister who had lived with Sr. Miriam for six years recalled the episode as related by the "little Arab:" "He struck her with the scimitar on her throat and left her practically dead, bathed in her own blood. With nightfall he wrapped her in a sheet and went out to discard her on a deserted street ... She came to her senses in a cave where she was cared for for several weeks and healed by a religious sister whom she believed was the Bl. Mother. I myself, after the death of the Servant of God, saw the scar which she had on her neck: it extended from ear to ear. The scar was one centimeter wide and was whiter than the rest of her skin. I heard that during her lifetime a doctor of Marseilles and another doctor from Paris had examined the wound and ascertained that her neck lacked some of the bones necessary for life and that she was alive by a miracle" (Sr. Marie Therese Carrère, O.C.D., in *Summarium Additionale*, p. 17). This latter observation was confirmed by three doctors in 1929; they examined her mortal remains and found two rings of the trachea to be missing.

Housemaid – handmaid

She worked as a servant in Beirut; she was remembered years later as a hard worker whose piety was outstanding. During May she would take time out to pray her rosary before a particular image of the Bl. Virgin, inviting acquaintances to join her (cf. Mons. Boutros Said, in *Summarium*, p. 62). In two episodes, which the first biography of Miriam recorded, the Bl. Mother again had a decisive role. At a certain point of her service with the Atalla family, Miriam went blind for six months. Naturally she was discouraged; "she began to weep and to pray to the Bl. Virgin that she be good enough to cure her. 'Look, mother, at all the trouble I cause in this house; I have never been better cared for by my own parents. If it be pleasing to your Son and to you, grant me my sight'" (*Vie meraveilleuse* I, p. 18). Regardless of the medical diagnosis of the case, Miriam never doubted that Our Lady had once more intervened as her mother when she regained her sight.

A like episode strengthened her trust in Mary: while hanging clothes on the terrace roof, she fell off and was so battered and bruised that the doctors gave her little chance of recovery. The Atalla family themselves attested later to the veracity of the facts: that Miriam prayed to the Bl. Mother to take her to heaven. Instead she received, as she perceived it, a visit from the Mother of God. She told her that Miriam's book of life was not complete yet and recommended three things: blind obedience, perfect charity and an immense trust in God. The village—including Christians, Moslems and Jews—was in such an uproar at the "miracle" that Miriam, in her humility, decided to move on. No amount of begging by the Atalla family, to whom she was deeply indebted, could dissuade her.

In preparing the Cause of Beatification of this "little Arab" (called such in France because of her halting, almost infantile French, and also because of her naive, spontaneous mannerisms), the promotors of her cause had to show how the extraordinary gifts evident on almost every page of Miriam's life were authentic. It was no easy task to show how the gift of prophecy, of the reading of hearts, of vision, of ecstasies, of the stigmata, were manifestations, albeit of secondary rank, of the work of the Spirit. It was no easy task to show how the devil was constantly badgering this simple unlettered nun to the extent that she had to be exorcized several times. One thread running through her life which puts things in place is her undying commitment to the Bl. Virgin. During the manifestations of her extraordinary gifts, the Bl. Mother's role is ancillary, but still much in evidence. The unobtrusiveness of Mary's presence in Miriam'a mystical life merely shows how deeply engrained Mary's presence in her life was. In reading the account of her extraordinary prayer life, commanded to be recorded by the local bishop, it would take much time to point out every reference to Mary, particularly since Mary's presence is taken for granted in so many instances.

A nun who lived with Sr. Miriam for six years testified: "She had a remarkable devotion towards the Bl. Virgin. You could hear her cry out at times: 'Ah, my dear mother!' She used to improvise songs for her. She often spoke to the sisters about the Bl. Virgin. She shared with them the graces she had received from her. You just had to look at her and listen to her to be inflamed with love for the Bl. Virgin" (Sr. Marie Therese in *Summarium Additionale*, p. 22). Her favorite prayer corner was the shrine of Our Lady of Mt. Carmel in the Pau monastery garden: there she was granted some of her most sublime mystical graces.

Sensitive and lively, Sr. Miriam, in the way of holy people, had to suffer physically, but even more interiorly. The physical pains, which she endured on Fridays in particular and which accompanied her stigmata, were slight when compared to the spiritual torments caused by the devil. He made her say things and do things contrary to all she stood for. She often confessed how ashamed she was for her behavior. Our Lady was her one sustaining force— not only did she warn Miriam about her impending share in Jesus' cross, but Miriam experienced her powerful protection when assailed by devilish tricks and obscenities. Once while praying to Our Lady with her mistress of novices, she began to dialogue with her heavenly visitor. When asked what Our Lady had said, she naively replied: "But you can see and hear as well as I. The Bl. Virgin said: Happy, very happy is the soul who suffers!... Time is short, very short... After having suffered a bit on earth, she will be with my divine Son in the house of the heavenly Father." Her Mistress asked her: "But didn't she say anything to you in particular?" "Oh yes, she always tells me: humility, humility! What, then, is this humility?" (*Summarium Additionale*, p. 120).

In her meditations Miriam often returned to this aspect of Our Lady which makes her so suited to be our model. She is humility and faith in the flesh. "You, Mary, were a virgin in the world. Who would have thought you would ever be the Mother of God? Yet that is what you actually became, and because of your humility. The angel of the Lord appears to Mary to announce her divine motherhood. Powerfully enlightened by God, she understands that the Creator ef heaven and earth is going to become her Son and she is filled with a sense of lowliness. The more the angel revealed to her, the more she humbled herself before God. O Mary, how humble you are, and how loveable in your humility!

"Mary is the model of faith as well. How pleasing that faith was to the heavenly Father! It was her faith that made Jesus grow more and more each day in her. If we have such faith it will make Jesus grow in our hearts. Because of her faith and humility, Mary feels unworthy to become the Mother of God. On earth, children cannot be born without a mother: it is a woman who brings them into the world. And it is also a woman who brings us into heaven. Ever since the fall men have been waiting for the Fruit of Mary, the Fruit of the gentle, humble, holy virgin. O thank you, Mary!" (*Thoughts of Sr. Mary of Jesus Crucified*, ed. Buzy, Jerusalem, 1974, p. 40-41).

Our Lady's beauty was habitually contrasted to the ugliness of the devil and what he suggested to Sr. Miriam. Throughout her spiritual odyssey, Sr. Miriam was supported by the kind virgin to whom she often called: "Glory to Mary! Get ready for her the softest velvet, and all that is most beautiful for my dearly loved mother. Oh, what beauty is Mary's! Her crown sparkles with diamonds that are brighter than the sun. But the light is most of all radiant in her breasts and arms—the places where Jesus nestled" (*Thoughts*, p. 40).

Bl. Miriam was a woman close to earth and nature, without sophistication, with a directness that, when it took the form of correction of faults in religious life, could even appear rude. How many times she apologized for her hurtful mannerisms. Her encounters with the spiritual world were also graphic, concrete, person centered. Typical was a vision she had about Our Lady and her role for us: "I seemed to see many children in procession, with Mary leading them. And a multitude of stars, like waving torches, went before her. I saw her enter a very arid garden, where nearly all the trees were dead. She came upon a fallen tree that was still green. She lifted it up and carried it away and heavenly music was heard. And the grass touched by her shadow became green again. The mountains seemed to greet her as she passed, the water rose in the channels, the springs gushed out more plentifully. The enemy fell before her, as he fled before God. And Mary returned to her starting point, and the procession followed, the stars staying with them all the time. The stars, which always go before Mary, signify the love of God. This love Mary shares with us, for we belong to Mary and Mary belongs to God and God to Mary. Everything trembles before her because she is so powerful and so much loved by God" (*Thoughts*, p. 41-42).

In what could best be described as a *credo* of Mary's place in our spiritual life, Bl. Miriam expressed her eternal gratitude to the life given her by Our Lady, who brought true and eternal life to earth in the person of her beloved Son Jesus:

> At the feet of Mary, my dearest Mother, I have found life again.
> All you who suffer come to Mary: I have found life again.
> At the feet of Mary, salvation and life will come to you.
> You who work in this convent, Mary counts your steps and labors.
> Say to yourselves: at the feet of Mary, I have found life again.
> You who live in this convent, detach yourselves from all that is of earth.
> At the feet of Mary, salvation and life will come to you.
> To you who live in this convent Mary says:

My child, I have chosen you out of millions, to
place you in my temple.
At the feet of Mary, you will find life.
Mary says to you: I have placed you in my temple,
Where you will not hunger or thirst and where
I shall feed you with the flesh and blood
of the Innocent One.
You who say I am an orphan, look, I have a
mother in the heights of heaven:
Fortunate the child of such a mother!
I dwell in the heart of my mother, and there I
find my Well-beloved.
How then can I be an orphan?
The serpent and the dragon tried to snap at me
and take my life;
But in this calling, and in this convent I shall
evermore remain.
At the feet of Mary, I have found my life
again

(Thoughts, p. 42-43)

Her impulsive, dynamic, expansive nature caused
Sr. Miriam to be irrepressible and at times to miss the
mark of perfection. Again it was Our Lady who
helped her set things aright and climb the steep path
of the Spirit. In her favorite nook in the hermitage
of Our Lady she often went to meet her "good mother of love." She was heard chanting:

I greet you, dear mother; do not be sad dear
mother;
I will love you a bit more than I did before.
Everything will end. I can no longer live in
this life.
Good mother, keep me near you. I can't go
on; take me near you, dear mother!
My repast, the food which I eat, is to see you,
dear mother!
The water I drink to refresh my soul is to love
you, dear mother.
In loving you, I come back to life; in loving I
am refreshed.
The rest I take is to seek you night and day!

(Supp. Additionale, p. 371)

* * *

The ardent love of Blesseds Raphael Kalinowski and Miriam Baouardy for Our Lady drew its initial impulse from the Catholic milieu in which they were born and nurtured in the faith. Neither of them could ever finish thanking the mother of love and mercy for deepening this love in Carmel. Neither felt worthy of such a favor from on high. Bl. Raphael, still in Siberia (1873), noted a lifelong attitude: "O Mary, vase of honor, pray for us who are so weak." Bl. Miriam (*Summ. Additionale*, p. 130) insisted: "My mother, how beautiful you are! I am not worthy to be called your daughter. You, you can give me this name, but as for me, I call myself your little servant, the servant at your feet."

MORE MOTHER THAN QUEEN

*Our Lady of Mt. Carmel
and St Therese of Lisieux*

At times St Therese's "Carmelite" spirit has been suspect. She hardly fits the schemata for spiritual progress traced by the "greats" of Carmel like Sts Teresa of Avila and John of the Cross. In recent times, however, there is increasing evidence that Therese of Lisieux captured the essential traits of the Carmelite rationale like few other members of this religious family. One of the telltale signs of her Carmelite roots is her tender, confident, intense devotion to God's Mother and ours. In her famous statement, "Mary is more mother than queen," Therese shows how anchored she is in Carmel's original approach to Mary. Whereas at the time of the discalced reform, due to cultural and political factors, Mary was often venerated as "Queen of Carmel," the more primitive appreciation of Mary was as mother. The fact that Therese did not make this statement for philosophical or theoretical reasons, but because this was her lived out experience in Carmel, actually reinforces the conviction that Therese was a "natural" Carmelite.

Thoroughly Catholic that she was, Therese had no restrictive concept of her Carmelite moorings: they were as broad as the view of the Mediterranean from the slopes of Mt. Carmel. In her devotional life she embraced all that she found worthwhile in the life of the Catholic Church. She chose all as a child; she never changed. With regard to Our Lady this included devotions to Our Lady of Victories, Our Lady of Perpetual Help, Our Lady of the Smile. Therese dedicated poems to the first two devotions; the latter is represented by a statue of Our Lady, transferred to Carmel from the Martin household. Therese always believed that Our Lady had smiled on her, curing her of a strange illness as a young teenager. When she is giving advice to her cousin Marie Guerin on the question of worthiness to receive communion, she has no doubt that Mary will hear her prayers on that day, the last of her month of May (May 30, 1889). She recommends that her cousin "pray a lot and, if you can, place a candle before Our Lady of Victories . . . I have such confidence in her!" (Letter 92).

Therese's charism was to grasp the inner dynamism of the very commonplace ways in which God lavished her with his love. She would have been untrue to form had she not apprehended the central role of Our Lady in the Order of Carmel dedicated specifically to her. The order has no "founder" in the ordinary sense; through the centuries Carmelites have looked to Our Lady as the original inspiration of their way of life. Therese takes this for granted in a number of ways. In a poem she penned for her cousin Marie's entrance into Carmel she wrote:

> It is in the blessed Order of the Virgin Mary
> That I can find genuine wealth (Poem 21,
> August 15, 1895)

From their very first chapel on Mt. Carmel dedicated to Our Lady, Carmelites have been convinced that their family has the Virgin Mary as its mother. Therese expresses this traditional view: "The Blessed Virgin is truly our mother because our monasteries are dedicated to her in a special way" (Letter 154 to Leonie, Dec. 27, 1893).

Therese is of the opinion that Mary attracted her to Carmel in the first place. "I love to think that it is for this reason that she [Mary] was so kind as to make me her child ever more perfectly in granting me the great grace of leading me to Carmel" (Letter 70 to Mother St. Placid, Dec. 1888). Therese, who had become Mary's child previously on her First Communion Day when she had become a member of the sodality of the Children of Mary (*Ibid*), knows Mary as the sure guide who even in the dark night keeps pointing out the summit of Carmel which is

Christ himself. In the depths of frightful sufferings, Therese bravely writes:

> O queen of the heavens, my beloved
>   shepherdess,
> Your invisible hand knows how to save me.
> Even while I was playing on the rim of
>   precipices,
> You were showing me the very summit of
>   Carmel.
> I then understood the austere delights
> That I must love if I am to fly off to heaven.
>   (Poem 53, May 1987).

Poem to Our Lady of Mt. Carmel

We possess a poem that Therese addressed to and entitled in honor of Our Lady of Mt. Carmel. Previously unedited, the poem is not one of Therese's most inspired pieces. It was occasioned by July 16 being the birthday of her novitiate mate, Sr. Martha, so that most directly the poem is for her fellow sister; but Therese's devotion for her "Star, who gives her Jesus and unites her to him" (Poem 5, June 1, 1984), cannot but make its mark. In fact, several characteristics of devotion to Our Lady of Mt. Carmel make the poem important in assessing Therese's Marian vision. The initiative of Mary is the first striking "constant" which Therese stresses: mother that she is, Mary is protecting her children even when they are too young to be aware of it:

> At the very first moments of my life
> You have taken me into your arms,
> From that day, O beloved mother,
> You protect me here below.
> To preserve my innocence
> You placed me in a pleasant nest;
> You protected my childhood
> In the shadow of a blest cloister.

As every mother, so Mary wishes her child to be well set up in life. It is again her initiative that stirs an attraction for religious life in Carmel. Hers it is to show that Jesus is the sure summit of the spiritual ascent of Carmel.

> Later, in the years of my youth,
> I heard the call of Jesus!
> In your unspeakable tenderness
> You showed me Carmel
> And kindly you said to me,
> 'Come, my child, be generous;
> Near me, you will be happy,
> Come and immolate yourself for your Savior.'

Once a mother, always one. Mary as Mother of Carmel sustains those who have heard her invitation and have followed. Particularly in difficult moments she is there, even if no one else is. Mary will never be lacking with the support she provides for those who acknowledge her as Mother of Carmel:

> Near you, O my tender mother,
> I have found rest for my heart;
> I want nothing else on earth:
> Jesus alone is my whole happiness.
> If sometimes I feel sadness
> Or fear assails me,
> Always, O mother, you uphold
> My weakness and are so good as to bless me.

Our Lady of Mt. Carmel has traditionally been linked with man's final journey on his earthly pilgrimage. Not only does her Sabbatine Privilege promise Mary's aid to those committed to her on the first Saturday after death, but she is also committed to those who wear her livery, the scapular, especially at the hour of death. This eschatological dimension of Carmelite devotion to Mary is not lost on Therese:

> Grant that I be faithful
> To Jesus, my divine Spouse.
> And one day, may your gentle voice call me
> To soar among the elect.
> Then, no more exile, no more suffering;
> In heaven I will repeat for you
> The song of my thanksgiving,
> O lovable Queen of Carmel.

Because of her penchant for the ordinary ways, it would be strange had Therese not appreciated the meaning of the Carmelite scapular. From her correspondence we know that she understood the basic values of the scapular devotion: a sign of predestination insofar as it is a symbol of dedication to Our Lady, and also a sign of aggregation to the family of Carmel. Lisieux Carmel at this time was able to earn some income by the making of scapulars (cf. *Correspondance Générale*, p. 864, note f). Therese, however, intuited the spiritual side of the devotion. She is writing to a childhood friend, Céline Maudelonde, when she shares her convictions about the scapular. It is July 16: "Oh, how beautiful our religion is! Rather than shrink hearts—as the world believes—it raises them up and makes them capable of *loving,* of *loving* with an *almost infinite* love, since it is to continue after this mortal life. We have been given this latter only in order to reach our true country in heaven where we will again find the cherished persons whom we loved here on earth! My dear Céline, I begged from Our Lady of Mt. Carmel the grace that you obtained in Lourdes. How happy I am that you are clothed with the holy scapular! It is a sure sign of predestination. And then by it aren't you united more closely still with your little sisters in Carmel?" (Letter 166).

The scapular as Mary's vesture symbolized the constant care that Mary had for those devoted to her. An ordinary part of a mother's care is to provide clothing for her children. In the spiritual life there are various ways in which this motherly charity of Mary is symbolized. Beyond the scapular, Therese habitually referred to the veil of Mary, under which her children were sheltered (Poem 13) or hidden (Poem 1, 13). Overwhelmed by the goodness Mary showed her so splendidly, Therese saw her supreme good as resting beneath the veil of this loving mother (Poem 5), sleeping peacefully and safely (Poem 54).

For Therese, holiness came not from below—from her own efforts—but essentially from above—from God and his mother as well. Her main preoc-

79

cupation became not to lose a single manifestation of this heavenly goodness. Childhood means complete dependence; an infant forgotten by his parents would shortly die. Therese saw that Jesus would be most comfortable with her the more she expressed her dependence on him and let him have his way with her however and whenever he wanted. Mary and her role fell into the same category. Abandonment to Mary's intervention is symbolized by the wholesome security afforded by remaining under her veil. In one of her poems Therese makes this connection explicitly, as she puts these words on Mary's lips:

> I will hide you under the veil
> Where the King of the heavens is sheltered,
> My Son will be the only star
> That from now on sparkles in your eyes.
> But so that I might always shelter you
> Under my veil, close to Jesus,
> There is need for you to remain small,
> Adorned with childlike virtues (Poem 13).

Far from being an escape, being hid under the veil of Mary was important for Therese because it was there that Jesus was to be found. "Jesus sleeps in peace under the folds of your veil" (Poem 54: 12). And for Therese Jesus is everything (Poem 45: 5). In this sense, for Therese Carmelite life is nothing else than remaining under the mantle of Our Lady. The white cloak of the Carmelite habit was a constant reminder of the mantle of Our Lady, which in medieval images covered the whole spectrum of various members of the church. In Carmel this cloak of white symbolized the purity of heart by which members of this religious family were to be characterized in the Mystical Body of Christ. Therese appreciated these truths even before she entered Carmel. She describes her experience at the Parisian shrine of Our Lady of Victories, as she and her loved ones were about to embark on their trip to Italy. "I understood she was watching over me, that I was *her* child. I could no longer give her any other name but *mamma*, as this appeared ever so much more tender than mother. How fervently I begged her to protect me always, to bring to fruition as quickly as possible, my dream of hiding *beneath the shadow of her virginal mantle!* This was one of my first desires as a child. When growing up, I understood it was at Carmel I would truly find the Blessed Virgin's mantle and towards this fertile Mount I directed my steps. I prayed Our Lady of Victories to keep me far from everything that could tarnish my purity" (*Autobiography*, trans. Clarke, p. 123; *Ms. A*, 57r; italics are Therese's, as in other citations as well).

For Therese, life in Carmel hardly had a more basic purpose than to remain under Mary's protective mantle in order to present a pure heart reserved to the Lord. Mirroring the ancient Carmelite *Institution of the First Monks*, Therese intuited that Carmelites have as their charism "the offering to God of a holy heart, purified of every actual stain of sin in a way that not only after death, but also in this mortal life, they could to a certain extent taste in their hearts and experience in their minds the power of the divine presence and the pleasantness of heavenly glory" (*AOC* 3 [1914-1915] 348). Therese merely added the Marian dimension: "And the Blessed Virgin? Ha! Céline, hide yourself in the shadow of her virginal mantle, that she may *virginize* you!... Purity is so lovely, so white! 'Blessed are the pure of heart, for they shall see God.' Yes, they shall see him—even upon earth, where nothing is pure, but where all creatures grow limpid when we can look at them with the face of the loveliest and whitest of lilacs between!...." (Letter 105, May 10, 1890, *GG*, p. 529-530). As she recruits Céline to pray for the renegade Carmelite friar, Hyacinth Loyson, she feels responsible for this brother in Carmel, who for that reason is a son of Mary. "In any event, it is not our merits but those of our Spouse, which are *ours*, that we offer to our Father who is in heaven, in order that our brother, a son of the Blessed Virgin, shall come back vanquished to throw himself beneath the cloak of the most merciful of mothers" (Letter 129, July 8, 1891 in *GG*, p. 641).

Interestingly, Therese describes the only mystical experience she recognized as taking place under the veil of Our Lady. It was the summer of 1889 when Therese, a novice, found herself in the far corner of the monastery garden. "... It was as though a veil had been cast over all the things of this earth for me... I was entirely hidden under the Blessed Virgin's veil. At this time, I was placed in charge of the refectory and I recall doing things as though not doing them: it was as if someone had lent me a body. I remained that way for a whole week" (*CJ* 11.7.2).

This abstracted state was the epitome of life committed to give pleasure to the good God, to pay him attention and reserve one's heart for him. "'Virginity is a profound silence of all this world's cares,' not only useless cares, but *all cares*... To be a virgin one must have no thought left save for the Spouse, who will have nothing near him that is not virginal, 'since he chose to be born of a Virgin Mother'... Again it has been said that 'every one has a natural love for the place of his birth, and as the place of Jesus' birth is the Virgin of virgins and Jesus was born by his choice of a lily, he loves to be in virgin hearts'" (Letter 122, Oct. 14, 1890 in *GG*, p. 621). Traditional Carmelite spirituality hardly finds a more able spokesman than Therese, who sees the hidden life of Carmel as a Marian desert experience (cf. *Poésies* II, Cerf, 1979, p. 90).

Mary a living person

Devotion to Our Lady, in Therese's spirituality, is not a principle, nor even an ideal: it is an awareness of the presence of a living, loving and caring person. In fact, because of her glorified status, Mary is part of the "real" world that does not change or pass away, whereas everything else here on earth does. Basically this is why Therese was convinced that we can never love Mary too much. "Do not be afraid of loving the Blessed Virgin *too much*, you will *never* love her enough, and Jesus will be glad of your love for her because the Blessed Virgin is his mother" (Letter 92, May 30, 1889, in *GG*, p. 487). Rarely, however, does Therese dwell on the heavenly glories of Mary; rather she is enthralled by the fact that Our Lady lived our type of life here on earth—an ordinary, common life, extraordinary only by the inner intensity with which it was lived. "What does me a lot of good when I think of the Holy Family is to imagine a life that was very ordinary. Not all those things they have told us, all those things they imagine. For example, that the Child Jesus, after having formed some birds out of clay, breathed on them and gave them life. But no! Little Jesus would not perform useless miracles like that, not even to give pleasure to his mother. But no, everything in their life happened as it does in our own" (*CJ* 20.8.14).

One of the reasons why Therese would have whished to be a priest was so that she could preach about Our Lady as she deserved. Supreme realist, Therese was put off by much of what was said and written about Our Lady. She felt that she could sum up her thoughts in a single sermon. She would begin by pointing out how little we really knew about Mary's life. "We shouldn't say unlikely things or things we know nothing about! For example, that when she was very little, at the age of three, the Blessed Virgin went up to the temple to offer herself to God, burning with wholly extraordinary sentiments of love. Perhaps she went there very simply out of obedience to her parents" (*CJ* 21.8.3).

Therese could not imagine Our Lady under the constant spell of Simeon's prophecy that a sword would pierce her heart. In fact, Therese intuited that joys come from God as well as sorrows. Mary would not have been so ungrateful as not to have rejoiced in the good things that God sent her. In her ode to Our Lady (*Why I Love You, Mary*), Therese, buffeted by her dark night, courageously wrote:

> Your motherly glance banishes all my fears,
> It teaches me to weep, it teaches me to rejoice
> Instead of despising pure and holy joys,
> You wish to share them and are so good as to
>   bless them

(v. 18).

Even Therese's sisters did not intuit that this was Therese's profound conviction—in fact Agnes changed the words "pure and holy joys" to "the days of sacred feasts" (in all editions until the last, critical 1979 original version). This is precisely the kind of thing that Therese wanted to eliminate!

The Gospels were Therese's reference point: they describe Mary's real life as quite simple and accessible "For a sermon on the Blessed Virgin to please me and do me any good I must see her real life, not her imagined life. And I'm sure that her real life had to be very simple. They show her to be unapproachable; they need to show her as imitable and bringing out her virtues, telling us that she lived by faith like we do, and giving proofs of this from the Gospel. There we read: 'They did not understand what he said to them.' And that no less mysterious saying: 'His parents marvelled at what was said of him.' This marvel supposes a certain amazement, doesn't it?" When she pronounced these words, Therese was herself passing through the crucible of her trial of faith. She could identify perfectly with Mary.

Certain expressions especially irked Therese. She could not understand how Mary's glory could be made out to eclipse the greatness of her children the saints. It is in this context that Therese states categorically in purest Carmelite tradition: more mother than queen. "We know very well that the Blessed Virgin is the queen of heaven and earth, but she is more mother than queen. We shouldn't say that by reason of her prerogatives she eclipses the glory of all the saints, just as the sun at its rising makes the stars disappear. My God! How odd that is! A mother who makes the glory of her children vanish! As for me, I think just the opposite. I believe that she'll greatly increase the splendor of the elect."

Exaggerated superlatives meant to exalt Mary to the stars did not impress Therese. Quite the contrary. "It's all well and good to speak of her prerogatives, but we should not stop at this. If, during a sermon, we were forced from beginning to end to exclaim with *oohs* and *ahs*, we would soon have had enough. Who knows whether there wouldn't be some soul who would reach the point of feeling a certain estrangement from so superior a creature and would say, 'If that's how it is, it's better to go into one's own corner and shine there as well as possible.'"

Therese acknowledges Mary's advantage over us in not being under the influence of original sin. But she is far from overawed. In fact, positive as ever, she intuits one way in which we have an advantage over Our Lady, ingenuous but true: "What the Blessed Virgin has over and above us is that she could not sin, since she was exempt from original sin. But on the other hand, she was less fortunate than we, because she had no Blessed Virgin to love. That's one pleasure more for us, one less for her."

Therese's Ode to Our Lady

Not content to tell what she did not like about contemporary preaching about Our Lady, Therese, in what could be considered her swan song, called on the full reserve of her poetic talent to record all she wished to say about Our Lady. When already seriously ill, she confided to Céline, "I still have one thing to do before I die. I have always dreamt of expressing in a hymn to the Blessed Virgin all that I think of her" (*Apostolic Process*, Rome, 268). Mary's month of May was the apropos setting for one of Therese's great poems, *Why I Love You, Mary*, especially when her other sister, Marie, urged her to formulate in verse all that she thought of Mary (*DE*, p. 649). Her two sources were her typical inspiration: the Gospels and her own experience ("my heart reveals to me," v. 15). On the one hand Therese, in using the present tense, felt herself to be a protagonist in the events of Mary's life. On the other hand she was not merely contemplating historical events; she strove above all to capture Our Lady's interior sentiments as she lived out her humble, ordinary life. Three things in particular struck Therese and became the leitmotifs of her poem: Mary knew suffering by personal experience; Mary loves us as Jesus loves us; Mary, challenged by the the night of faith, was content to live in silence. Therese's own experience at this time made her identify with these basic attitudes of Our Lady.

85

The title of Therese's poem already betrays her intention. She had proposed to write about what she *thought* about Mary; now she changes her mind. She wishes to tell why she *loves* Mary so much. Therese's experience of motherly love has been so deep that not even her trial of faith can cancel its memory: "No, the Blessed Virgin will never be hidden from me, because I love her too much" (*CJ* 8.7.11).

O Mary, I should like to sing why I love you,
Why your sweet name makes my heart thrill,
And why the thought of your supreme
   grandeur
Will not be able to inspire fright in my soul.

Therese wrote these optimistic lines as she was assailed by doubts of an afterlife, tempted to despair. Her heroic greatness lies in that she continued *wanting* to believe and love. Spiritual realities might be a closed book for her. She still had Mary. So delicate to let God have his way with her, Therese would not pray to him either to live or to die. This is why she asked Mary to present her prayers to God—her mother would know how to present her requests in a way that would put no pressure on the Lord, and he would be free to do what pleased him. "The Blessed Virgin has performed my commissions well. I'll give her more! I often repeat to her: 'Tell him never to go to any trouble over me.' He understood and that's what he has done" (*CJ* 10.6). The reason why Therese has so much confidence in Mary goes to the heart of her experience: she is Mary's *child* in the sense of having a communion of life with her. Therese is not looking at Mary's life as an outside observer. She is reliving the same reality, just as a child has received its life from its mother and continues to live on by that life.

If I should contemplate you in your sublime
   glory
Surpassing the brilliance of all the blessed
I could not believe that I am your child;
O Mary, before you, I would lower my eyes.

Therese knows that Mary is glorious in the heavens, but she prescinds from this. She takes up her favorite book, the Gospels, and finds there the Mary whose life she is sharing—a life of suffering, of exile, of tears. How this similarity touched Therese, who had controlled herself and her outward show of suffering so admirably, but now could not help herself and often found herself in tears. Her physical pain forced gasps and cries from her; her embarassment was mollified by the figure of Our Lady, who also had walked the way of suffering. This is how Therese felt herself to be Mary's child:

> For a child to cherish his mother
> She must weep with him, share his sorrows.
> O my dear mother, on this foreign shore
> How many tears you shed in order to attract
> me to you!
> In meditating on your life in the holy Gospel
> I dare to gaze on you and approach you.
> It is not difficult to consider myself your child
> Since I see that you are mortal and suffering
> just like me.

To share suffering is the sign of deepest communion of life between two persons. The "little way" of St Therese is anything but a way that seeks to eliminate suffering on an easy way to heaven; rather, it enters into the world of Jesus and Mary and seeks to continue their way of life. As she meditates on the life of Mary soberly depicted in the Gospels, Therese finds the motives for her childlike love of the Mother of God.

Therese's virginal love finds justification in the Annunciation scene. Like Therese Mary offers God her heart and never goes back on her generous gift. In fact, Therese sees that this pure, fresh, faithful heart is the only suitable abode for the Son of God made the Son of man. The "humble, pleasant valley" of Mary's soul is the only proper dwelling for the ocean of love who is Jesus:

> When an angel from heaven bids you to
> become the mother

Of God who should reign for all eternity,
O Mary, I see that you prefer—what a
    mystery!—
The unspeakable treasure of your virginity.
I understand, O Immaculate Virgin, that your
    soul
Is dearer to the Lord than his divine abode.
I understand that your soul, humble and
    pleasant valley,
Can contain Jesus, the ocean of love.

Only a soul whose love is reserved exclusively for the Lord and his will is capable of containing the vast ocean of love. Therese never ceased marvelling at Christ Jesus' predilection for being among the sons of men. She often applied this to her love for the presence of Christ in the Eucharist and, in this context, to his choice of Mary.

Humble Mary

The other trait that impresses Therese is Mary's humility. If Mary has power over the Trinity it is because she won over the heart of God, so to speak, by her hidden life of goodness. A heart such as Mary's has a power of attraction over the Father, Son and Holy Spirit to such a degree that "O Trinity! You are the prisoner of my love" (Poem 17: 2). Mary is the living proof of the validity of Therese's little way of hidden humility:

O, how I love you, Mary, calling yourself the
    handmaid
Of God, whom you ravish by your humility.
This hidden virtue makes you all-powerful.
It attracts the Blessed Trinity to your heart.
And so the Spirit of Love covers you with his
    shadow,
And the Son, equal to the Father, takes on flesh
    in you . . .
Truly great will be the number of his sinner-
    brothers
Since we must call him: Jesus, your Firstborn!

Earlier on her spiritual pilgrimage, Therese had seen sinners in a category apart from herself. Now, assailed by temptations and doubts that made her feel like a blasphemer, Therese experiences a solidarity with sinners. She understands that Jesus is for them above all—and Mary provided him with his humanity which makes him the new head of a redeemed mankind.

Theological principles hardly affect Therese. She knows God is always the same. He treats his beloved the same today as previously. As Mary's child, Therese understands that in her littleness she has the same treasure as Mary. A mother gives her whole self to her child; whatever she has she willingly and lovingly shares with her infant. For this reason, Therese can exult. She is weakness itself (Letter 247, June 21, 1897, in *CG*, p. 1021). But Mary has taken the initiative in being her mother. Necessarily, if she granted the greater gift, motherhood, could she now deny her child all else—her virtues, her love? Sorely tried, racked with pain, Therese could keep smiling even at fellow nuns who thought aloud that she was being babied by her sisters, because she realized that she was not alone. Her mother Mary's life of virtue was hers.

> Well-beloved Mother, in spite of my smallness,
> Like yourself, I possess the All-powerful in
>   me.
> But I do not tremble in realizing my
>   weakness:
> The treasure of a mother belongs to the child.
> And I am your child, O my cherished mother,
> Your virtues, your love, are they not mine?
> Just as when Jesus, your gentle lamb.
> Descends into my heart, he thinks he is resting
>   in you.

This last conviction of Therese is not pretty wishful thinking; it is just what she wants to affirm as the reality which she lives. She had prayed to live constantly in an act of perfect love (*Act of Oblation*) and has discovered her vocation to be love in the heart of the church. Mary had been her predecessor in this vocation. Carmel's Marian spirit could hardly be better expressed: a continuation of Mary's interior life, to the extent that Christ Jesus finds himself at home in a Carmelite heart as he did in Mary's heart. Already in her first poem (1893), Therese had had this conviction:

> The ever so pure arms of your dear mother
> Had provided a cradle for you—your royal throne.
> Your pleasant sunshine is the bosom of Mary
> And your dew is her virginal milk!...
> Still, soon for my sake you will leave your mother;
> Love already is pressing you on to suffer.

All her life Therese thrilled to the fact that Christ Jesus thought so much of her that for her sake he left the congenial company of Mary. Her human dignity could hardly be affirmed more cogently.

Common life of Mary

However Therese, in the sixth stanza of her poem, finds in Mary a confirmation of her own spiritual "way." In Mary she finds that the simple, unspectacular, humdrum, everyday virtues are given flesh and blood. Therese is convinced that she must remain small, never wishing to grow to the stature of extraordinary saints. Mary is so precious to her because the greatest of women confirmed the veracity of Therese's "little way."

> You make me feel it is not impossible
> To walk in your footsteps, O Queen of the elect,
> You have made visible the narrow way to heaven
> While always practising the most humble of the virtues.
> Close by you, O Mary, I love to remain small,
> I see the vanity of grandeur here below.
> In the home of St Elizabeth, receiving your visit,
> I learn to practise ardent charity.

Therese had confessed (*Autobiography*, trans. Clarke, p. 219; *Ms C*, 11r) that only during the last months of her life on earth had she learnt the perfection of total charity—always looking for the good in others; like Jesus excusing others, realizing that in the eyes of God a fall out of human weakness might not be as culpable as lukewarmness or "virtue" in someone who had no great effort to put out.

When she reflects on Our Lady's canticle of praise and thanks, the *Magnificat*, Therese finds her own convictions perfectly reflected. Whatever is good in her, as in Our Lady, does not come from her own efforts or expertise, but from the generous hands of a heavenly Father. He it is who does great things in his lowly servants. And so man's glory is the handiwork of the Lord's loving-kindness towards him. Man's true greatness lies in letting God's action in him be realized.

> There, ravished, I listen, O gentle Queen of
>   angels,
> To the holy canticle that springs from your
>   heart.
> You teach me to chant the divine praises,
> To be glorified in Jesus my Savior.
> Your words of love are mystical roses
> Which will offer their scent to the ages to
>   come:
> The Almighty has done great things in you—
> I wish to meditate on them, so as to bless him
>   for them!

Passivity is not worthy of someone who has received so much. There must be acknowledgement, praise, thanks. This was Therese's "apostolate:" praising God for his great glory resplendent especially in his children.

Mary's silence

In the episode of Joseph's discovery of Mary's being with child, what strikes Therese more than anything else is Mary's silence. With a single word she would have calmed Joseph's fears. She remained silent. Why? Out of humility, but even more deeply, because she had to put *all* her trust in God. He would provide, even in this episode obviously full of anguish:

> When good St Joseph was unaware of the
> miracle
> Which in your humility you wished to hide,
> You let him weep close to the Tabernacle,
> Which veils the divine beauty of the
> Redeemer!...
> O Mary, how I love your eloquent silence,
> For me it is a pleasant, melodious concert
> Which tells me of the grandeur and all-
> powerfulness
> Of a soul who waits for help only from
> heaven.

Bethlehem leaves Therese breathless as she contrasts the pride of mankind to the humility of God. And Mary is part of the latter. Seldom is Mary more loveable and great than in the narrow confines of a stable after she has been repulsed by all the inhabitants of David's city. Therese cannot comprehend man's small-mindedness.

> Later, in Bethlehem, O Joseph and Mary!
> I see you repulsed by all the inhabitants.
> No one wants to accept poor strangers
> In his inn, there is room only for the
> important.
> There is room for the important; it is in a
> stable
> That the queen of heaven must give birth to
> God!
> O my cherished mother, how loveable, how
> great
> I find you in this so poor a place.

Woman that she was, Therese could not but feel pity for Mary, forced to give birth in such miserable circumstances. Her greatness and true humility shine in her conduct.

The depths of God in the flesh are not lost on Therese. She recognizes that she is not merely contemplating a mystery; she is actually living by its effects. She has no need to envy the angels, because she has become not their sister, but a sister of "my dear brother," Jesus. Therese's "little way" springs from her share in the same life that Christ lived, and like Jesus she too must look to Mary as her mother:

> When I see the Eternal One wrapped in swaddling,
> When I hear the feeble cry of the divine Word,
> O my beloved mother, I have no envy of the angels
> Because their mighty Lord is my beloved brother!
>
> How I love you, Mary, you who made this divine flower
> Bloom on our shores.
>
> How I love you as you listen to the shepherds and the magi
> And as you carefully keep all these things in your heart.

Typically Therese valued Mary's ability to perceive the inner meaning of things in her heart. Once, when on her sick bed she had been misunderstood, Therese referred to this trait. "The Blessed Virgin did well to keep all these things in her 'little' heart ... They can't be angry with me for doing as she did" (*CJ* 8.7.10).

Queen of Martyrs

Mary's humility at the presentation of Christ in the temple is rewarded in a simple way by allowing her to share in the passion of the Lord. From this point on, Therese sees Mary as queen of martyrs.

> I love you as you mingle with the other women
> Who had directed their steps towards the temple.
> I love you as you present the Redeemer of our souls
> To that fortunate old man who hugs him in his arms.

> At first, with a smile, I listen to his canticle
> But soon his words make my tears flow:
> As he casts his prophetic gaze into the future
> Simeon presents you with a sword of sorrow.

The flight into Egypt is but the first concrete instance of Mary's Way of the Cross.

> O queen of martyrs, up to the twilight of your
> life
> This painful sword will pierce your heart.
> Already you must leave the soil of your own
> country
> In order to avoid the jealous fury of a king.
>
> Jesus peacefully slumbers under the folds of
> your veil,
> Joseph comes to beg you to depart at once,
> And immediately your obedience reveals itself:
> You depart without delay, without any
> questions.

Reflecting on her own experience, Therese studies not external details but Mary's inner spirit. And she finds her joy in no way altered; after all, she possesses Jesus and he is one's native land *par excellence*. Heaven is one's true country and heaven is where Jesus is. So Mary's real exile was when she lost her twelve year old son in Jerusalem.

> It seems to me, Mary, that in Egypt land
> Your heart remains joyful, even in poverty
> Because is not Jesus the most beautiful native
> land,
> What does exile matter, you possess the
> heavens? . . .
> But in Jerusalem, a bitter sadness
> Will flood your heart like a vast ocean.
> For three days, Jesus is hidden to your
> tenderness;
> Then you have real exile in all its harshness!

Because she herself was passing this way—of Jesus' disappearance from her sight—Therese allows herself to delve into the inner depths of Mary's experience. The Gospel episode affords Therese a glimmering of light in the thick darkness that blots out her longed for native land completely.

Finally you find him and joy carries you away.
You say to the beautiful Child who charms the
  doctors:
'O my Son, why have you acted in this way?
Look, your father and I have been searching
  for you in tears!'

And the Child-God replies—what a deep
  mystery!—
To his beloved mother who holds her arms out
  towards him:
'Why were you looking for me ... Don't you
  know
That I must be about my Father's business?'

Therese, blocked off from heaven by a wall, continues to look for Jesus mainly by the smiling charity
she extends to the sisters who irk her most, who
make light of her atrocious sufferings. She goes further: she seats herself at the "table of sinners" (*Ms C*,
6r). The night of faith for Therese, as for Our Lady,
does not deter her for one instant from seeking Jesus.

The Gospel teaches me that growing in
  wisdom
Jesus remained subject to Joseph, to Mary,
And my heart reveals to me with what
  tenderness
He always obeys his beloved parents.
Now I understand the mystery of the temple,
The enigmatic words of my beloved King:
Mother, your gentle Child wants you to be the
  example
Of the soul who seeks him even in the night of
  faith.

Happiness even in suffering

Therese's heroic soul never reveals itself more
clearly than in the following stanza. She leaves the
Gospel account and gives her own experience. Suffering on earth can actually be happiness. Therese
will not regret that Jesus takes back all his gifts to
her so long as she can go on loving him, even in darkness, in temptation, in suffering. Mary provides The-

rese with the example of how to suffer faithfully, even desiring to do so if such be God's will. Christ actually willed that his mother suffer through the three days and nights without him; Therese is called to follow for even a longer time.

> Since the King of heaven willed that his mother
> Be plunged in the night, in anguish of heart,
> Mary, is it then something good to suffer here on earth?
> Yes—to suffer while loving is purest happiness!
> Everything that Jesus gave me he can take back.
> Tell him never to take pains with me ...
> He can hide himself, I agree to wait for him
> Until that sleepless day, when my faith will fade away.

At Nazareth Mary is still a model, not only for Therese but for so many little people who are not in high places, who do no outstanding works, whose voices are not heard at the world's councils. Mary shows this multitude how to become truly great without miracles, but content to tread the "common way."

> I know that at Nazareth, O mother full of graces,
> You live very poorly, wanting nothing more.
> No delights, no miracles, no ecstacies
> Embellished your life, O queen of the elect!
> The number of little ones is surely great here on earth;
> They are able to raise their eyes to you without trembling.
> O incomparable mother, it is by the common way
> That it pleases you to walk, to guide them to heaven.

What is important is to love, whether one's task be great or small matters little. In fact Therese is convinced that Mary teaches her not only to bear her sufferings, but also to enjoy herself if such be God's will. Far from masochistic tendencies, Therese is as content with joys as with sorrows, so long as she gives pleasure to the good God.

> O my beloved mother, as I await heaven
> I wish to live with you, follow you day by day.
> While contemplating you, mother, I am
>   overjoyed and immersed
> In discovering the abysses of love in your
>   heart.
> Your motherly glance banishes all my fears,
> It teaches me to weep, it teaches me to rejoice
> Rather than look down on pure and holy joys.
> You wish to share them, you are so good as to
>   bless them.

Mary's extended family

After her encounter with Mary at Cana and with the crowd that listens to Jesus' preaching, Therese gives a precious exegesis of Jesus' reply, calling his mother, brother and sister all those who do the will of the Father. Far from being saddened, Mary rejoices because she sees God's family extend to all those who become disciples of her Son. Jesus gives not teachings, ideals, ideas, but himself, his life, a share in his divinity. How not love a mother who shows so much love and humility in these circumstances?

> O Immaculate Virgin, tenderest of mothers,
> As you listen to Jesus, you are not saddened;
> Rather, you rejoice that He makes us
>   understand
> That our souls become his family here below.
> Yes—you are overjoyed that he gives us his
>   life,
> The infinite treasures of his divinity! . . .
> How not love you, O my beloved mother,
> When I see so much love and so much
>   humility?

Therese intuits that Mary's love for us is the same as Jesus' love for men. It is totalitarian, holding back nothing; a true lover seeks no pleasure for self but only the true good of the beloved. Mary loves us so much that she agrees to be bereft of her Son, while taking care of us. Therese seldom felt closer to the refuge of sinners:

> You love us, Mary, like Jesus loves us
> And you agree, for our sakes, to withdraw from him.
> To love is to give all and to give oneself.
> You wish to prove this, while remaining our support.
> The Redeemer knew your immense tenderness
> He knew the secrets of your motherly heart.
> Refuge of sinners, it is to you that he leaves us
> When he leaves the cross to await us in
> heaven.

Under the cross, Therese sees Mary as becoming our mother in consenting to Jesus' atrocious death. Our Lady is like a priest in offering her Firstborn for those children who would follow. Therese cannot compare any sorrow to Mary's as the queen of the martyrs suffers the deepest stab of the sword predicted by Simeon, but accepts it and gives her blood "for us."

> Mary, you appear to me at the summit of Calvary
> Standing beneath the cross, like a priest at the altar,
> Offering your well beloved Jesus, the gentle Emmanuel,
> In order to appease the justice of the Father...
> A prophet has said it, O desolate mother,
> 'There is no sorrow like your sorrow!'
> O queen of martyrs, by remaining in exile
> You lavish all the blood of your heart for us.

Therese merely hints at the sorrow Mary suffered when John was assigned to take Jesus' place. But then she contents herself with the few details about Our Lady that the Gospel provides. Therese thinks that no small portion of heaven's joys will be Jesus' account of the hidden grandeur of Mary's life.

> The house of St John becomes your sole
> shelter

The son of Zebedee must replace Jesus...
This is the last detail that the Gospel provides
About the queen of heaven; it says no more.
But, O my beloved mother, does not its deep
    silence
Reveal that the eternal Word
Himself wishes to chant the secrets of your
    life
To entertain your children, all the elect of
    heaven?

Forever Mary's child

In her final agony Therese never ceased calling
on Mary: "I can't stand it any more! Please pray for
me!... Jesus! Mary!... Yes I agree to it, I really
do agree..." (*CJ* 29.9.5). "O my good Blessed Virgin,
come to my aid!" (*CJ* 30.9). The mother prioress, a
few hours before her death, placed a picture of Our
Lady of Mt. Carmel on her knees and assured Therese that she would soon be caressing the Blessed
Mother as Jesus was doing in the picture. Therese's
reaction: "O my mother, quickly present me to the
Blessed Mother, I am really a baby and can't stand it
any more!... Prepare me to die well." As life was
being snuffed out of her emaciated frame, Therese
kept her faith and hope and love directed in one
direction. As Mary taught her, she would let nothing
allow her heart to stray from him who had lavished
so much loving-kindness on her. Therese had a good
memory. There were no consolations, no awareness
of Jesus' presence now, but she remembered who he
was. He never changed. This is why she is such a
Marian, such a Carmelite soul. Purification, exile,
sufferings: these were part of the "all" that love
demanded. Mary had lovingly accepted all. So
would Therese. She penned her last stanza:

Soon I will hear this pleasant harmony,
Soon, in beautiful heaven, I will go to see you,
You who came to smile at me in the morning
    of my life.
Come to smile at me once more,
O Mother ... evening has fallen!...

99

I no longer fear the splendor of your supreme
   glory,
With you I have suffered and now I wish
On your knees to chant, O Mary, why I love
   you
And forever repeat to you that I am your
   child.

6

OUR LADY OF MT. CARMEL
PATRONESS OF CONTEMPLATIVES

*Our Lady in the life and writings
of Bl. Elizabeth of the Trinity, Carmelite*

Does contemplative prayer have any room for Our Lady? Contemplation is the invasion of a person by the Blessed Trinity. The overwhelming initiative of the three-Personed God is so pervading as to be almost exclusive. The contemplative person is delighted to remain passive as he exclaims, "Lord, it is good for us to be here!" God is so predominant in an authentically contemplative experience, that any role assigned to Our Lady seems redundant.

Carmel, whose mainstays over the centuries have been devotion to Our Lady and prayer, has given to the church sons and daughters who in their spiritual approach have shown that the two go together, even on the heights of contemplative prayer. One of the most convincing witnesses is Sr. Elizabeth of the Trinity. This nun of Dijon's Carmel, who died in 1906, has become the modern apostle and witness to the fact that the Blessed Trinity truly inhabits a grace filled Christian. In silent adoration she strove to provide a worthy temple for God in her own person.

The Christian faith is a living and loving encounter with the Father, Son and Holy Spirit. This means heaven on earth. "We live with God as with a friend. We make our faith living so that we can communicate with him by means of everything: that's what the saints do. We carry our heaven within ourselves, because he who ravishes the saints glorified in the light of vision, gives himself to us in faith and mystery. It's the same person! It seems to me that I've

101

found my heaven on earth because heaven is God, and God, that's my soul" (Letter to Mme. Sourdon, c. June 15, 1902).

Thoroughly Catholic soul that she was, Sr. Elizabeth never finished telling of the Blessed Mother's role in her one ambition in life: to become "as it were an incarnation of the Word, that I may be to him another humanity wherein he renews all his mystery (Prayer to the Trinity, Nov. 21, 1904, Feast of the Presentation of Our Lady). Elizabeth had no hesitation: just as Mary provided Christ Jesus with all that was human in him when he took his flesh from her exclusively, so when Christians recognize their prime vocation to be that of letting the image of Christ dominate in their persons and lives, they must have recourse to Mary. "No one has penetrated the mystery of Christ in all its depths as did Mary... She—and this is beyond description—'treasured up and reflected on the secret in her heart' (cf. Lk 2: 19); no tongue can express it, no pen translate it! This mother of grace will so form my soul that her little child may be a living, 'striking' image of her Firstborn, the Son of the Eternal One who himself was the perfect praise of his Father's glory" (*Last retreat*, Day 1).

A simple and contemplative piety

What surprises is that this contemplative nun had such a simple devotion towards Our Lady. As so many great souls, she showed no embarassment in making use of statues, images, novena prayers in honor of Our Lady. And this not only when she was young, but right up to her last days at the age of 26. As a youngster she often made Marian shrines and sanctuaries the destination of her excursions. Her *Diary* is full of allusions to Our Lady under her various titles; Mary was a familiar person in her maturing process. Lourdes in particular, which she visited four times, made a deep impact on her, to the extent that it seems that she entertained the thought of entering the Carmel built just on the other side of the river from the Grotto. Even before she entered Carmel she recognized Mary's mission as providing a prelude to the eternal dwelling-place . . .

> O lily of Carmel, kind virgin,
> Our Lady of Lourdes, beloved mother,
> You alone can obtain for me the favor
> Of belonging to Jesus forever,
> The consummate joy of being his bride:
> This is my one, ardent aspiration!
> But what I ask of you above all and always
> Is that his will be mine.
>
> (*Poem*, May 1898)

Her appreciation of Lourdes as the venue of God's visitation of his people in the person of Mary— and the diverse wonders subsequently worked there—increased rather than decreased as the years went on. On her deathbed in the monastery infirmary, she asked her mother to lend her the family statue of Our Lady of Lourdes, because as a youngster she had received so many favors in praying before it. She and the statue became inseparable, even when she struggled to the chapel balcony from which she could participate in the liturgy. The favorite title of Our Lady during these last days on earth became Gate of Heaven (*Janua caeli*); thus the praise of God's glory, Elizabeth herself, would be introduced to heaven by Mary the gateway to the Trinity. "When I shall have pronounced my 'It is consummated,' it will again be the 'Gate of Heaven' who will conduct me into the heavenly courts, softly saying to me those mysterious words: 'I rejoiced when I heard them say, we will go up to the Lord's house'" (*Last retreat*, Day 15).

Expressions of Elizabeth's girlhood devotion to Our Lady help to trace the spiritual growth of this youngster, whose character was by nature quite stubborn and self-assured. An artistic type who could find the Lord's footprints in all of creation, she excelled at piano playing and even in the cloister continued to write verses. This artistic talent included a propensity to attach herself to whomever would show her affection and accept hers. It was not without a lifetime struggle that she detached herself from human consolations. The fourteen year old adolescent was praying:

> Sad, seductive world,
> Fatal deceiver of the spirit.
> I prefer to be loved
> By Jesus and by Mary
> And to say to you forever: Goodbye,
> Let me be alone with my Lord.
>
> *(Poem,* August 20, 1894)

The priest who prepared her for her First Holy Communion was frightened by her unbridled, emotional approach and observed that she would be either a saint or a demon. She confessed that any unjust correction made "my blood boil in my veins, all my being rebels!" *(Diary,* Jan. 30, 1899). With the very next breath she mentions that she has consecrated herself to Mary, a consecration she renews on every Marian feast, and that she has thrown herself into Mary's arms with total confidence *(Ibid.,* Feb. 2).

She begged for humility as a gift from Our Lady: "O Mary, daily I beg you to obtain humility for me; come to my aid, break my pride, send me many humiliations, my good mother" *(Diary,* March 24, 1899). In her adolescent years she took refuge in the all-pure Virgin in her own efforts to remain chaste and pure:

> Always keep me chaste and pure,
> Preserve me from all stain,
> Keep careful watch over my feeble heart
> That it be pleasing to my well-beloved Savior.
>
> *(Poem,* December 8, 1897)

Mary is the gift Christ gave to us as his last heritage. Mother of all men, she receives us in sorrow under the cross and will not be done until we—if we so wish—arrive home in heaven. God "thinks that there is nothing better than a mother who inspires the greatest tenderness, a mother capable of touching and moving even the most hardened hearts. And God gives us a mother, the tenderest, the most compassionate that we could imagine. There she is, upright at the foot the cross. Before her dying Son, she adopts all of us as her sons. If we extend our hand to her, she leads us to the port, happy and safe" (*Diary*, May 22, 1899).

The scapular devotion

Her devotion to Our Lady took the way of the traditional forms of piety. The scapular devotion, widely spread among the faithful of her time, found easy acceptance in her approach to Our Lady. During the 1899 parish mission she noted the three main devotions to Our Lady: the scapular, images, the rosary. "The scapular is the emblem of Mary. A soul who wears it and who, of course, expends all its efforts to be saved, cannot go to hell; it's impossible. Let us never leave our scapular aside!" (*Diary*, March 23, 1899).

Life in Carmel helped her to deepen her appreciation of the scapular. In the last year of her life, she prepared a scapular for one of the other nuns on the anniversary of the latter's profession day. She has Our Lady explain the meaning of the symbolism of the scapular. Seldom has the meaning of the scapular been expressed more convincingly and deeply. "Behold your Mother. 'It was in my arms that Jesus entered the world and first offered himself to the Father and he is sending me to receive you [in profession]!... I am bringing you a scapular, as a guarantee of my protection and of my love and also as a '*sign*' of the mystery which will be worked in you. My daughter, I have come to finish 'clothing you with Christ Jesus' (Gal 3: 27) so that you 'walk in him' (Col 2: 6) the royal way, the light filled path, so that you are '*rooted in Him*' in the depths of the abyss with the Father and the Spirit of love; so that you are '*built on him*' your rock, your fortress, so that you are '*confirmed in your faith,*' in this faith in the immense love which showers down into the depths of your soul from your home above. My daughter, this all-powerful love *will do great things in you* (Lk 1: 49). Believe my words. They are a mother's, and this mother is ravished with joy, seeing with what *special tenderness* you are loved. Do remain in your interior self. *Look at Him* who is coming laden

105

with all his gifts. The abyss of his love surrounds
him like a vestment. It is the Spouse. Silence! Silence! Silence!" (Letter to Mother Germaine of Jesus, Sept. 24, 1906). Obviously, Elizabeth valued the
scapular devotion as the epitome of what Carmelite
life entails.

Especially when her mother opposed Elizabeth's
entry into Carmel, the young girl had recourse to
Mary. "With the fullest confidence I recommend my
future, my vocation to her" (*Diary*, Feb. 2, 1899).
When her mother, in tears, finally relented and gave
her permission to enter Carmel when she reached her
twenty-first birthday, the heart of the future contemplative nun could not be contained. She spoke of a
miracle, of Mary's special intervention, as the real
reason why she felt attracted to Carmel (cf. *Poem*,
March 26, 1899).

> My mother, kind hope of mine,
> To you goes my first cry of gratitude,
> To you goes my first prayer.
> How good you show yourself to me!
>
> It's so beautiful that I think I'm dreaming,
> Reflecting on my littleness.
> O mother mine, how great
> How good is he whom I love!

It is Mary who explains the real meaning of Elizabeth's call to Carmel:

> Some day, answering my call,
> You will leave everything—sister, mother,
> Tears and prayers notwithstanding,
> Because I wish you in Carmel.
> To love, to expiate, to suffer,
> In deep solitude,
> Yes, my daughter, there are souls,
> There are such privileged souls!
>
> What joy to taste his sorrows,
> To be the confidant of his heart,
> His humble spouse, his beloved!
> You have received the more beautiful portion.
>
> I do not wish you any other joy
> Than that of carrying my cross,

Of drinking the whole bitter chalice
Of my sorrows, until Calvary itself.

Mary and the life of prayer

Our Lady, mother and patroness of Carmel, is
intimately linked to the life of prayer and recollection, the center of the Carmelite charism. "Love
silence and prayer, because they are the essence of
life in Carmel. Ask the queen of Carmel, *our mother*,
to teach you how to adore Jesus in deep recollection.
She is our prime patroness" (Letter to Germaine de
Gemeaux, Sept. 14, 1902). The liveliness of Elizabeth's faith reveals itself in her attitude towards
Mary. She does not know theological abstractions
and niceties, nor does she dwell on Our Lady's outstanding privileges. When she kneels before her statue, she engages in a personal, intimate conversation
with a mother who has the good of her children at
heart. She had no hesitation to bring the needs, the
"business" of her friends and acquaintances, to so
good a mother (cf. Letter to Mme. de Sourdon, July
15, 1906). She joins her community in the novena for
the feast of Our Lady of Mt. Carmel, and she has the
intentions of very specific persons to present to the
attention of the Blessed Virgin, "and you know that
no one has ever invoked her in vain" (*Ibid.*) She is
convinced that her loved ones would be united to her
in no surer way than under the mantle of their common mother, the Immaculate Mary (cf. Letter to Abbé
Chevignard, Nov. 29, 1904).

Sr. Elizabeth intuits that in Mary we have the
perfect point of encounter between heaven and earth,
between God and man. There is no surer way to
reach the Blessed Trinity than, united with her loved
ones, in the heart of Mary. "During the month of
May I will be wholly united to you in the soul of the
virgin; it is there that we will adore the Blessed Trinity." In fact, in surprisingly contemporary terms, she
need go no further to describe her ecclesial, Carmelite vocation: "I envisage my life as a Carmelite in the
light of this double vocation: virgin-mother. Virgin:
espoused by Christ in faith. Mother: saving souls,

107

increasing those adopted by the Father, coheirs of Christ Jesus" (Letter to Abbé Chevignard, April 27, 1904).

Carmel's Marian charism

Elizabeth had no identity crisis in her religious life: she realized that she could not be nor do everything in order to be virgin and mother with Mary. In Carmel she could "carry the cross together with Mary" (*Poem to Immaculate Conception*, Dec. 8, 1898), especially by her hidden life of solitude and adoration of Christ Jesus, of the Father and of the Holy Spirit living within her. Our Lady's way of life provided an insuperable example for Elizabeth. Imitation of Mary was the surest way she could live up to her vocation as the praise of God's glory:

> To love is to imitate Mary,
> Exalting the greatness of God
> Just like her when enthralled
> She raised up her canticle to the Lord.
> Your main thrust, O faithful virgin,
> Was self effacement.
> It is always by humility
> That your soul magnifies him.
> (*Poem*, July, 1905)

What joy and gratitude surged in Elizabeth's heart when she recognized that the "praise of God's glory" was not merely a beautiful idea, but one that found its epitome in the person of Our Lady. After Jesus no one on this earth embodied this trait better than Mary. Since she signed herself as "the praise of glory" especially in her latter years, it is not surprising that Our Lady meant something even more to her as she approached the eternal mansions.

"After Jesus Christ, doubtlessly with the distance there is between the Infinite and the finite, there is a creature who also was the great praise of the glory of the Blessed Trinity. She fully corresponded to the divine choice of which the Apostle speaks; she was always 'pure, spotless and unreproved' (Col 1: 22) in the eyes of the thrice holy God. Her soul is so simple. Its movements are so deep that a person cannot absorb them. She seems to reproduce on earth the life of the divine being, the simple being. She is so transparent, so luminous that someone might mistake her for the light itself. Nevertheless, she is only the 'mirror' of the sun of justice: the *Speculum justitiae*. 'The Virgin treasured up all these things in her heart' (Lk 2: 19). Her whole history can be summed up in these few words. It is in her heart that she lived—and at such depth as to be lost to our gaze" (*Last Retreat*, Day 15).

Sr. Elizabeth intuits what many Christian writers have stated: there is so much of God in Mary that, left to our own devices, we could easily identify her with the Godhead itself. This is why she is such a sure guide: her whole being mirrors the justice and the love of God in such rich simplicity that in becoming the praise of her love, a Christian reaches his eternal destiny. In a poem dedicated to Our Lady of Mt. Carmel (July 16, 1906), Elizabeth expresses her certainty that those who have become the praises of Our Lady's love on earth will be led to heaven by the queen of heaven and earth. She associates herself with another sister who is sick in the infirmary with her:

> Your two children, good mother, would like
> To celebrate the queen of Carmel with you.
> Committing our whole life to her,
> We shall be the praises of the love
> Of our spotless queen.
> O well beloved mother of ours,
> Keep us ever faithful.
> Soon, O mother welcome us to our homeland,
> Place us near yourself in life everlasting.

Cultivation of the interior life

Although firmly rooted in the very concrete realities around her—and precisely through them—Sr. Elizabeth engaged in an ever growing interiority. What really mattered, what deserved priority always and everywhere, was the life of the Trinity which Christians had dwelling in their hearts. She exulted in the teaching of St John of the Cross, her spiritual father in Carmel: "At the moment I am reading some very beautiful pages of our blessed father St John of the Cross on the transformation of the soul into the three divine persons. To what an abyss of glory we are called! How I understand the silence, the recollection of the saints who could no longer leave their contemplation. Thus God was able to lead them to the divine heights where the 'one' is consumed within him and the soul becomes a spouse in the mystical sense of the word. Our blessed father says that the Spirit then raises the soul to such a wondrous height that he makes it capable of producing in God the same breathing forth of love that the Father produces with the Son and the Son with the Father, a breathing forth which is none else than the Holy Spirit himself! To be able to claim that the good God calls us by our vocation to live in this holy brightness! What a wondrous mystery of love!"

Elizabeth, on her part, could best identify with the Blessed Virgin when she came to describe her own reaction to God's overwhelming gift of himself in the contemplative experience. "I would like to reply to him by spending my time on earth as did Mary, 'treasuring up all these things in her heart,' burying myself, to put it so, in the depths of my soul in order to be lost in the Trinity, which dwells there in order to transform me into itself. Then my motto, 'my splendid ideal,' as you call it, will be realized. I shall truly be Elizabeth of the Trinity" (Letter to Abbé Chevignard, Nov. 28, 1903).

The mother of one of her best friends, Mme. de Sourdon, had sent her a print of the Annunciation scene. As was her custom, Elizabeth made much of it and when she moved to the infirmary she would not be without it. She explains why it meant so much to her: her life, in imitation of Mary, had to center itself on the Incarnation of the Word of God within her. "In the solitude of our cell, which I call my 'little paradise,' because it is full of him by whom we live in heaven, I shall often gaze at the precious picture and I shall unite myself to the soul of the Blessed Virgin at the moment when the Father overshadowed her, while the Word took our flesh within her and the Holy Spirit came upon her to work the great mystery. The whole Trinity in action, God yielding, God giving himself. And shouldn't the life of the Carmelite be lived in submission to this divine action?" (Letter, Nov. 12, 1905).

The strong action words should be noted. Sr. Elizabeth experienced the activity of the three divine persons as supreme. The best thing that ever happened to this sad and yet potentially great world of ours was the clothing in human flesh of the Son of God. This was the summit and sum of God's marvellous love for men. A whole lifetime on earth could not exhaust the marvels of God's loving-kindness incarnated in the person of Christ Jesus. Sr. Elizabeth, an ardently loving soul, could not do anything better than follow the lead of her who was chosen by God himself to effect this marvel of his love. Mary showed her how best to gather in and to appreciate this gift: by humble acknowledgement, by silent appreciation, by adoring obedience.

"'If you but knew the gift of God' (Jn 4, 10) said Christ one evening to the Samaritain woman. Yet what is this gift of God, but himself? The beloved disciple tells us: 'He came to his own and his own did not receive him' (Jn 1: 11). St John the Baptist could address this word of reproach to many souls: "There stood in your midst, *within you*, one whom you did not know' (Jn 1: 26).

"'If you only knew the gift of God . . .' There is a creature who knew this gift of God, a creature who lost not a single particle of it . . . The faithful virgin: she is the faithful virgin, 'she who stored up all things in her heart' (Lk 2: 19). She was so lowly, so recollected before God's gaze in the seclusion of the temple, that she attracted the good pleasure of the Blessed Trinity: 'Because he has looked on the lowliness of his handmaid; henceforth all generations will call me blessed!' (Lk 1: 48). The Father bending down over this lowly creature, so unaware of her own beauty, wished that she be the mother in time of him whose Father he is in eternity. Then the Spirit of love, who presides over all the activities of God came upon her. The virgin uttered her Fiat. 'Behold the handmaid of the Lord, be it done to me according to your word' (Lk 1: 38), and the greatest of mysteries was accomplished. And by the descent of the Word into her, Mary became forever the prey of God.

"It seems to me that the attitude of the virgin during the months which transpired between the annunciation and the nativity is the model of interior souls, of beings whom God has chosen to live interiorly, in the depths of the bottomless abyss. In what peace, in what recollection, did Mary dispose herself and prepare herself for all these things! How the most trivial actions were divinized by her! Because through everything, the virgin remained an adorer of the gift of God! Yet, that did not prevent her from spending herself outwardly when it was a question of charity. The Gospel tells us that Mary diligently hastened through the Judaean hills in order to be available to her cousin Elizabeth. The indescribable vision which she contemplated within herself never took away from her external charity. For, as a pious author says, if contemplation 'is directed to the praise and towards the eternity of the Lord, it never has and never will lose its unity'" (*Heaven on Earth*, Day 10).

Centered on the Incarnation

There is so much to the gift of God *par excellence*, his perfect image, the Word made flesh, that only a reverent adoration will begin to appreciate its meaning for mankind. Elizabeth did not write about any subject more frequently nor more enthusiastically than about the Incarnation of Christ. It was through this event that God showed how close he wanted to be with men, so close that he became one of them. If the second person of the Blessed Trinity did not hesitate to take on human flesh in the virgin's womb and dwell among men as one of them, then it is not difficult to accept the further reality of the three persons dwelling within the Christian soul.

For Elizabeth these religious facts are not the object of theological reflection; the Incarnate Word, the Trinity, Our Lady—these are living and loving persons who are so good as to bend down and take up their abode in our interior lives. Theirs is the eternal initiative towards us; man's sole duty is to remove the obstacles and to show his willingness because the immensity of God's love will never invade a heart that is unwilling to have him. God is so delicate as to respect the freedom of men even as regards the greatest gift, namely, himself, and not just something outside of himself.

Our Lady was the first and the best at penetrating the meaning of this unspeakable gift, not in any ostentatious way, but with the gentleness and hiddenness of God's own coming among men.

> Mother of the Word, do tell me your mystery.
> From the instant of the Incarnation
> Tell me how, on earth, buried
> In adoration, you spent your time.

> In a totally unspeakable peace
> A mysterious silence,
> You break through to the fathomless being,
> Bearing 'the gift of God' within you.

> Keep us always
> In the divine embrace;
> So that I bear the imprint
> Of this God who is all love:
> "I love Christ."
>   (*Poem*, Christmas, 1903)

Mary leads to the Trinity

Mary had the delicacy and the nobility to imitate, in her aceptance of God's gift, the very manner in which God gave it. Faithful and passive and all-accepting, she could never pretend to put something of her own or of herself in the way of God's coming. Lost in contemplation of the wonders God worked in her, she became the mother and exemplar of contemplative souls, whose sole ambition in life is to disappear and let God take over completely in their lives, letting Christ himself become their holiness and justice and goodness. The Marian and contemplative

113

8

dimensions of Carmelite life could hardly be better combined:

> In a deep silence, an unspeakable peace,
> A godly prayer which has no end,
> Mary, the faithful virgin, remained day and
>   night,
> Her soul completely overwhelmed hy the
>   eternal splendor.
>
> Like a crystal, her heart mirrored the divine,
> The guest who dwelt in her, beauty without
>   decline,
> She attracts heaven; the Father actually
> Is about to hand his Word over to her to be his
>   Mother!
>
> Then the Spirit of love covers her with his
>   shadow,
> The Three come to her, all of heaven opens,
> Stoops and bends down to her, adoring the
>   mystery
> Of this God who becomes flesh in this Virgin
>   Mary.
>
>   (*Poem* for May 25, 1902)

Mary, then, is constantly pointing the faithful to Christ Incarnate, but through him also to the Blessed Trinity. What is particularly moving in Elizabeth's case is that she wrote some of her most luminous words—those of her *Last Retreat* for instance—as she was plunged into the darkest of nights of faith. Like her sister, St Therese of Lisieux, she was ravaged by Addison's discase; because of this she could admit of no food or drink. At the same time she found herself strangely deprived of the awareness of God's presence (something she only confided to her superiors), and she was even tempted to commit suicide. However this experience allowed her to identify the more authentically with Our Lady as she had watched life ebb out of life itself, her Son Jesus hanging and dying on the cross. During her lifetime she could not pass before the statue of the sorrowful mother without recalling the tears of her own dear mother who finally gave her permission to enter Carmel. In her generosity, Sr. Elizabeth had prayed that her mother's grief become her own and that her mother be spared the pain of separation. This trait marked Sr. Elizabeth all her days: she would suffer in silence (cf. *Poem*, Dec. 8, 1899).

> O Virgin, hear this prayer,
> It is a cry from my heart:
> I commend my mother to you,
> Do not let her know about my sorrow!
>
> Allow me to be the only one to suffer,
> Always the only one to be alarmed;
> You, the queen of martyrs,
> You will sanctify my tears.

She was so committed to the "Three" within her that inevitable sorrows which accompany every human existence, and which naturally afflicted her as well, were not allowed to obtrude into her concentration on "the more important thing."

With Mary under the cross

In one of her long poems to Our Lady, she notes that it is Jesus' call to Carmel that necessarily is a call "to love, pray, expiate and suffer."

> Ah, this vocation is sublime
> In its sorrows, its trials.
> What joy, what supreme good fortune
> To suffer with him whom one loves.

She appeals to Mary who knew the suffering of being separated from her loved ones:

> O Mary, O mother of sorrows,
> Do place this balm in their hearts;
> Show them how great, how beautiful is
> The way on which the well beloved calls me.
> (*Poem*, March 26, 1899)

Rather than diminishing, the purifying action of the Holy Spirit increased in Sr. Elizabeth. She accepted all suffering with as much grace as the most pleasant consolation:

> Beneath the gaze of our kind queen ...
> We are plunged into the burning furnace

Which transforms everything to a Godlike
   existence . . .
Our blessed Master leads us to Calvary;
It is there he wishes to consummate our
   union . . .
We shall rest in the cross of the Savior
Waiting for him to take his victims . . .
                    (*Poem*, July 7, 1906)

On the following Feast of Our Lady of Mt. Carmel, she explained quite plainly what Our Lady
meant in her life. She was writing to her only sister
Marguerite; when describing her vocation as love,
she exclaimed: "Today I surely gave you to the
Blessed Virgin together with your angels [her two
daughters]. Really, I've never loved her more. I cry
with joy when I think that this all-serene, all-shining
creature is my mother, and I enjoy her beauty like a
child who loves her mother. I have a very strong
attraction towards her. I have appointed her the
queen and guardian of my heaven and yours, because
all I do, I do for both of us" (July 16, 1906).

This same month she wrote to her spiritual mentor, Canon Angles, about her condition, wondering if
she would last the year, fretting over how her sickness was affecting her mother. Yet she saw it all in a
spiritual light: "Ask that my resemblance to the
adored image [Christ] be every day more perfect.
'Moulded into his death' (Phil 3: 10). This is what
keeps me going, what gives my soul strength in suffering. If you only knew the destructive action I feel
in my whole being: the road to Calvary is open and I
am totally happy to walk on it like a bride at the side
of the divine Crucified One." She reminisces about
her life, six years of which had been spent in Carmel.
She asks the canon to consecrate her in the chalice of
the Blood of Jesus so that she might live by his and
not by her own strength, and in this way she would
be able to go on suffering for what is lacking to
Christ's passion in favor of the church which is his
Body. In this context, she includes Our Lady, on
whose motherly charity she relies at the end of her
days as she has done throughout her life. "Please
also consecrate me to the Blessed Virgin. It is she,
the Immaculate One, who gave me the habit of Car-

mel. I ask her to clothe me in this 'robe of fine linen,' with which the bride adorns herself in order to take part in the banquet of the marriage of the Lamb" (Apoc 19: 8-9). If all her life she sought to clothe herself with the virtues which typified Our Lady, she was not about to change now. She only wished to be adorned with those characteristics of Mary who stood by her Son in his death and shared in his work of redemption, bringing all men back to the bosom of the Trinity. There their overriding experience is that of being loved "with too great a love," one that can never, not even in eternity, be adequately fathomed.

Elizabeth knew she was dying. In her torments, she could find no finer exemplar than the strong and heroic virgin, standing beneath the cross. Elizabeth took Christ's words on the cross as addressed to her personally: "Behold your mother." Mary was, then, sharing the life which she provided for her Firstborn, now with Elizabeth as well. It was in the shadow of the cross that Elizabeth understood that she would be providing another humanity to Christ in order that through her he would bring his Body the church to completion.

"This queen of virgins is also queen of martyrs. But again it was within her heart that a sword pierced her (Lk 2: 35), for in her case everything happened within her!... How beautiful she is to contemplate during her long martyrdom, so serene, enveloped in a kind of majesty that is both strength and gentleness at the same time ... It's what she learned from the Word himself; how those whom the Father had chosen as victims should suffer—those whom he resolved to associate in the great work of redemption, those whom he 'knew and predestined to be conformed to his Christ' (Rom 8: 29), crucified for love.

"She is there at the foot of the cross, *standing* with strength and courage. And my Master says to me: 'Behold your mother' (Jn 19: 27). He gives her to me as mother ... And now that he has returned to the Father, that he has put me in his place on the cross so that 'I suffer in my own body what is lacking to his passion, in favor of his Body which is the church' (Col 1: 24), the virgin is still there to teach me how to suffer like him, to tell me, to help me understand the last chants of his soul which only she, his mother, could catch.

"When I shall have pronounced my 'it is consummated,' it will again be she, the 'gate of heaven,' who will conduct me to the heavenly courts, softly whispering the mysterious words: 'I rejoiced for what was said to me: let us go to the Lord's house.'"

Last Retreat, Day 15

7

MARY AND OURSELVES: GOD BEARERS

*Our Lady of Mt. Carmel in the Life
of Blessed Titus Brandsma, O. Carm.*

Great people have a knack of appreciating the small, simple, beautiful things taken for granted by others. Holy pictures are used as book markers by even ardent students of the spiritual life. Truly holy people see them as occasions of grace. St. Therese, as she lay on her deathbed abandoned by all other consolations and even doubting of heaven's existence, had her favorite holy card pinned to the curtain around her cot. Fr. Bartholomew Xiberta, even during the celebration of the Divine Office which meant so much to him, would sneak in a kiss of his favorite image of Mary, which he jealously guarded in his breviary. Fr. Titus Brandsma, Carmelite martyr in the Nazi concentration camp of Dachau, had no greater joy in prison than that of being able to gaze at an image of Our Lady. His Breviary had not been taken from him when he was interred in Scheveningen prison. "I had no stray holy picture of Our Lady in my breviary—and surely her image ought to be in a Carmelite's cell. I managed this too. In the part of the breviary we are now using, and which fortunately was left me, is the beautiful picture of Our Lady of Mt. Carmel. So now my breviary is standing open on the topmost of the two corner shelves, to the left of the bed . . . At my table I only have to look a little to my right and I have her image before me. When I am in bed, my eye catches at once the star bearing Madonna, Hope of all Carmelites" (*My Cell*).

This was no awkward or desperate gesture by the renowned university professor of philosophy and of the history of mysticism. It was his normal, spontaneous reaction. Titus Brandsma's Marian devotion was as unsophisticated as the rest of his life. One of the best known clerics in his native Holland, involved in a prodigious amount of religious initiatives, he never lost the simplicity of approach of his Frisian forebearers. Although he formulated a mysticism of Marian devotion, as we shall see, far from despising the simple, Catholic forms of Marian devotion, he revelled in them. A telltale episode: when taken prisoner, he could not explain to himself how he could have forgotten to transfer his rosary from his religious habit to the black suit he wore to jail. He considered it a singular grace when a protestant minister was able to provide him with a rosary, which witnesses report he always prayed slowly and devoutly.

Until the end, when a deadly injection was administered to him, Titus kept being friendly with his captors. Other prisoners told him to give up. He never ceased speaking kindly to the Nazi guards. On his deathbed, when his body was being used for humiliating experiments by the physicians, Titus noted that the attending nurse was from Holland and a Catholic. "How did you end up here? I shall pray for you a great deal." And he gave her his cherished rosary. She protested that she could no longer pray. Titus' reply: "Well, if you can't say the first part of the Hail Mary, surely you can still say 'Pray for us sinners.'" The nurse tried to be evasive with the comment that there were so many bad priests. Titus, not be beaten, asked her to look at the sufferings of the imprisoned priests in Dachau. He confessed that he himself was glad to suffer for God's sake. (The nurse, subsequently, returned to the faith.)

Mary in Titus' young years

His trust in the motherly charity of Mary, Titus inherited from his own pious mother. Once when he and his brother Henry both fell ill, the doctor was seriously concerned. The mother invoked Our Lady with rosary after rosary. A distant Carmelite cousin, Fr. Casimir De Boer, was visiting home at the time. The pious and concerned mother with a heart full of confidence in the mother of us all asked the friar to invest the boys in the scapular. Henry, who later became a Franciscan, notes that it is impossible to be dogmatic, but in fact the next day Titus was cured and was able to get out of bed. Regardless of what others thought, he personally felt indebted to the Mother of God. He induced his younger brother to recite the Little Office of Our Lady for a whole month as a token of gratitude.

When it was time for Titus to decide what type of religious life he would join, there was again a Marian connection. He had been educated by the Franciscans, but healthwise he could not keep up. When his cousin, Fr. Casimir the Carmelite, described how Carmel lived its charism, the two elements which caught Titus' attention were a life of deep prayer and a pronounced Marian devotion. As he was later to formulate, the two were not separate elements, but interpenetrating. The taking of the Carmelite habit on September 1, 1898, was the beginning of a lifelong attachment to Mary's family. For Titus, the habit was not primarily something he put on but something that Mary in her goodness clothed him with. "We consider the scapular no longer as a badge which we have put on on our own, but as a royal sign of honor from the queen of heaven, as a uniform, a livery with which her chosen servants are clothed" (Leaflet, *Maria*).

The distinctive white cloak of Carmel, which Titus unfailingly wore on the more solemn occasions, made an impression. It was all the more noticed during the year he served as Rector Magnificus of the Catholic University of Nijmegen (1932). Someone noted to Titus that he had believed Carmelites to be humble religious, yet their white cloaks made them stand out at any gathering. Titus had no apology, but only an explanation: "My friend, don't be amazed that I am so happy to wear this cloak. It is a sign of Mary's protection. I have so much trust, actually certainty, in her help!"

For this esteemed professor and organizer, Carmel cannot be imagined without Mary. "Both superiors and members should help to promote the double spirit of the order with the cooperation and help of the order's patroness Mary, under whose patronage they should place every work and in whose honor they should sanctify all their labors. The order is totally Marian not only in name but also in its works: for if it were not Marian it would not be Carmelite." Philosopher that he was, Titus intuited that what a person does follows on what a person is. So an order like Carmel, which from its beginning committed itself to the Marian ideal, must also show this inner involvement in its apostolate. "The contemplation and meditation of the apostolic life of the Redeemer and that of the co-redemptrix, Our Blessed Virgin Mary, should inflame each one's heart to divine works in the divine task of saving souls."

Although not given to exuberance of rhetoric, Titus could hardly be clearer as to his conviction: the Carmelite vocation is intrinsically bound up with imitation of Mary. In his mature years, while lecturing on the Carmelite charism in the U.S.A., Fr. Brandsma revealed the kernel of his thought. He refers to a "constant" in the medieval Carmelite credo: the foreshadowing of the Virgin Mary in the cloud which the prophet Elijah spied over the Mediterranean from his Carmel retreat. "It was on Carmel's summit that the prophet after sevenfold prayer saw the little cloud—bearer of the rain which would deliver the parched earth. It is not necessary to give an authentic explanation of this vision. Still I may say that many commentators of the Holy Scriptures have seen in this cloud a prototype of the Holy Virgin, who bore in her womb the Redeemer of the world." The professor then notes that in the Old Testament a cloud was often a symbol of God's descent among men. "In the order this vision of Elijah has always been seen as a prototype of the mystery of the Incarnation and a distant veneration of the Mother of God. And it was because of this belief, according to the tradition of Carmel, that the old sanctuary dedicated to the Holy

Maid was built on the mountain and in the midst of the hermits' caves" (*The Beauty of Carmel*, p. 32-33).

Fr. Brandsma then gives a spiritual meaning to this episode: "In our barrenness and dryness, Mary is the providential cloud which draws redemption to us. Let us greet her. Let us trust in her. With her intercession we are sure of the grace of God. The cloud that she is, she overflows on us with copious rain. Immeasurably great is the grace of God, much greater than we deserve. We are like the people of Israel. Mary is the mother of mercy. 'Hail, holy queen,' and after this our exile, 'Show us Jesus.' Banishment, exile are our life without God, or in any case, without intimate union with God ... May she always make our eyes be fixed on Jesus" (*Ejercicios bíblicos con María para llegar a Jesús*, ed. Cesca, 1978, p. 26). Professor of the history of mysticism, Fr. Titus could not be faulted for taking an historical stance towards Carmel's Marian roots. In fact, he makes much of the title Carmelites have had since their origins: "Brothers of the Virgin Mary of Carmel." "Devotion to Mary was intimately allied to their institution, and the name which the neighboring population called them after this sanctuary, stamped the former crusaders, who laid down their swords on the altar of Mary, as knights of Our Lady" (*Beauty of Carmel*, p. 59).

Called to be other Marys

But history is only an aid to better understanding Carmel's perennial commitment to Mary. Titus Brandsma categorizes this commitment under three headings: imitation, union, similarity. "We should not think of imitation without thinking of the union, nor of the union without the thought of the imitation. Both flow into each other, but in one period the former is more prominent, in another more attention is paid to the latter. We should rather see both trends blended together into one harmonious whole" (*Beauty of Carmel*, p. 63). In teaching which forshadows that of Vatican II, Fr. Titus sees Mary to be all that the church aspires and desires to be. "The *imitation* of Mary, the most elevated of all creatures, set as an example before us by God himself, shows Mary the pattern of all virtues. She is the mirror in which we should ever watch ourselves, the mother whom her children ought to resemble ever more " (*Ibid.*) This imitation of Mary can be found at the origins of the order, as attested by the first commentary on the Carmelite Rule, which John Baconthorpe compares to the life of Our Lady.

But there is more. Imitation leads to similarity and even to *union*. " If we wish to conform ourselves to Mary in order to enjoy fully the intercourse with God by following her example, we should obviously be other Marys. We ought to let Mary live in us. Mary should not stand outside the Carmelite, but he should live a life so similar to Mary's that he should live with, in, through and for Mary" (*Beauty of Carmel*, p. 64-65). The historical precedents for this Marian vision Professor Brandsma finds in Ven. Michael of St Augustine of the Carmelite school and in St Grignon de Montfort.

The Dutch Carmelite sees his order's mission without any identity crisis: it is to produce other Marys. He says this in no sentimental, vague or pietistic sense, but bases himself on the solid theology of the Incarnation itself. Anyone who takes the enfleshing of God in Christ Jesus seriously, sees human dignity reach an unsurpassed apogee in that gesture of God. Mary provided everything human to Christ; if Christ is to be conceived in and for our society there is need for constant "Marys" to give flesh to Christ Jesus. This is the Carmelite vocation. "We should attain *similarity* to Mary, especially in that we recognize her as the highest perfection which human power by the grace of God has attained. This perfection can also be developed in us to a considerable extent, if we reflect ourselves in Mary and unite ourselves to her. This ought to be the aim of our devotion to Mary, that we be another mother of God, that God should be conceived in us also, and brought forth by us. The mystery of the Incarnation has revealed to us how valuable man is to God, how intimately God wants to be united to man. This mystery draws the attention of our minds to the eternal birth of the Son from the Father as the deepest reason for this mystery of love" (*Beauty of Carmel*, p. 66).

The liturgy spoke of these profound truths to Fr. Brandsma. Occasionally he left important university meetings in order to be with his community for the praying of the Divine Office (and rosary), to the point that some colleagues criticized him. There this son of Mary opened his heart to the riches which the liturgy not only represented symbolically, but also perpetuated in a real, mystical manner. "In the celebration of the three Holy Masses on Christmas, the birth from the Father is first celebrated, secondly from the Holy Virgin Mary, thirdly God's birth in ourselves. This is not done without significance and this threefold birth must be understood to be a revelation of one eternal love. It should ever be Christmas to us and we should remember that threefold birth as phases of one great process of love. Mary is the daughter of God the Father, mother of God the Son and spouse of God the Holy Ghost. In her that threefold birth has been realized. We should learn from her how to realize it in ourselves. We also have been chosen by the Holy Trinity for a dwelling, to share the privileges which we admire in Mary, but which God is willing to bestow on us also" (*Beauty of Carmel*, p. 66-67).

Marian and mystical dimensions

Carmelites, then, are to prolong in the church what God had so admirably worked in Our Lady. As members of her family, as bearers of her distinctive garb, they have no higher calling than to provide a fresh possibility for Christ Jesus to enter the world again. This is the reason why Titus Brandsma envisioned the Marian dimension of Carmel so intimately bound up with the spiritual and even mystical dimension. All Christian spiritual striving aims to put on Christ; it first happened in Mary's case. Following her lead, Carmel is meant to stress in season and out of season the fact that spiritual values, while they do not crush out material values, still have priority over them. For Titus no factor was more important in

125

Mary's case than the fact that she was God's mother (*Theotokos*—bearer of God). As God-bearer she remains inseparably united to God as only a mother can remain united with her son. "However, it is the characteristic of the Carmelite vocation—and in a broad sense of the vocation of all Christians—to be other God-bearers."

In a famous conference delivered at the first Congress on Mysticism, held in Nijmegen in 1920, Titus made this one of the three major dimensions of Carmelite mysticism. For him this was the summit of Carmel's rationale. Someone who wishes to follow the prophet and live in closest union possible with God can find no richer nor more convincing likeness than that of Mary. In his openness to the contemplative life, the Carmelite seeks to live with Mary so that like her he too may, by a free and unmerited gift of God, give birth to God and live on in him. Grounded in this union, the Carmelite brings God to the world through his apostolic works, just as Mary gave her divine Son to the world (cf. Brocard Meijer, O. Carm., *Titus Brandsma*, Italian trans., p. 281).

This is not an ideal attainable only by an elite few. In Titus' mind it is the characteristic element of the Carmelite mystique. It would be difficult to find an article he wrote, a sermon he delivered, advice he offered, conference he held, in which Mary was not mentioned. A typical example is the widely discussed conference he delivered in 1932, the year he was Rector Magnificus of the Catholic University, which dealt with modern man's notion of God. He discussed the approaches of many contemporaries. When, in the epilogue, he wished to present an ideal illustration to his listeners, he asked them to fix their gaze on the living image of the Mother of Jesus. A surprised murmur rippled through the crowd, yet Fr. Brandsma was undeterred. "We live and willingly speak in images and similitudes, willingly we make use of examples. For the development of our representation of God, we are not lacking images.

"There was once a virgin who became the mother of God-made-man; she presented us with God as

Emmanuel. The latter died on the cross to allow us to live in union with God and to fill us with his grace. Thus he was also born in us in the order of grace. It was in order to rectify union with God even in the order of nature and to make that union even more intimate and overflowing. Thus the Mother of God made us a gift of this intimate union with God, while she presented herself as a model for the most intimate communion. May this example be ever before our eyes. But here we have more than an example. She is called to direct our gaze towards God, just as led by revelation we recognize God in the Child in her arms, so may she lead us through our intellect to the vision of God in all that he has created in order that, just as he lived in her, he may live in us and out of our activity he may be revealed to the world" (*Notion of God*).

There were critical voices raised to this ending; a well-known Dominican concluded that what had begun as a serious dissertation ended up as a Marian sermonette. Few understood that Fr. Titus meant every word of what he said, no more no less. Far from apologizing or excusing himself, in his humility Fr. Brandsma lay the blame on his inability to express himself better. "This ending about Mary has not been well received! I had a feeling that it would be misunderstood. Perhaps, in order to open the minds of all, I should have given a more elaborate explanation of how Mary, in relation to our notion of God, really does have something to say. Oh well, next time I'll know better." This was his conclusion to what was one of the most significant contributions he made to scientific theological thought: not that Mary is a pious afterthought that could be left out, but that he must explain himself better in order to share this precious insight with his audience.

In a Marian retreat that he preached he explained himself further: "The true concept of the Incarnation entails the notion of the divine maternity. There are various ideas of this maternity. For some it is only apparent, merely exterior respect. They will not be convinced of the 'born of the Virgin Mary.' They interpret it in an eminently spiritual, symbolic manner without penetrating reality...

127

Mary is the mother of God in a real, true and complete sense. We must admire this wonderful mystery with respectful love. It represents the extraordinary sanctification of human nature. No falling before the grandeur of this mystery—rather admiring the divine omnipotence which here seems to exhaust itself. Let us consider that the same God lowers himself towards us to unite himself to us. Let us never cease gazing on Mary to see and admire how God transformed her, to what glory he raised her." Practical as usual, Fr. Titus wished that this dogmatic truth be lived incarnationally. "Desire to belong to the number of those who consider the glorification of Mary as the principal task of their lives. Enjoy the beautiful representations of the Blessed Virgin, enjoy hearing chants in her honor, in praise of her. Participate in activities dedicated to her. Tell her all these things" (*Ejercicios*, p. 83-85).

Mary, living and caring

For Fr. Titus, Mary was not simply a woman filled with grace who lived on planet Earth 2,000 years ago, not only she who was assumed body and soul into the glory of heaven; more importantly she was a living, dynamic, concerned person who stands as the model human being, accessible to all men. Just as God made her necessary for his coming among men, so she is necessary for our vital intimacy with God. Titus Brandsma was one who would subscribe to St. Bernard's famous dictum, "You can never say enough about the Blessed Virgin." In fact, the Dutch Carmelite used every occasion—from the Sunday sermon to the learned conference—to implement his conviction: Mary's role can and should be understood by her Son's people.

Typical was his intervention during the Marian Days held in Zenderen in August, 1931. "Sublime creature that she is, Mary is after all what she is—like us she is in debt to grace and to divine goodness. It is true that his grace was reserved for her by an extra special divine disposition, to which, however, she corresponded without the slightest reservation.

On her part, she allowed herself to be totally dominated by it. Mary opened her heart to God. He admired her in her total commitment and gave himself completely to her.

"We want to be one with Christ. We want to receive Christ in our hearts, which too often, however, open themselves to his visit very badly. Instead, Mary was dedicated completely to God from her very first years. From her going up to the temple, her whole life was nothing other than continued service, a constant offering to him, and so her heart always remained open to him. From Mary we must learn how to banish from our hearts everything that does not belong to God and how to open our hearts to him in such a way that we are filled with divine grace. Then will Jesus descend into our womb, he will grow in us, he will be born again from us, he will become visible in our deeds and live in our life. Much too little are we filled with God; much too much we live our own lives. With Mary we must, filled with God's grace as she was, lead the life of God and seek our glory and our salvation in our union with God."

The place of Mary in men's lives was Titus' favorite Marian theme. He naturally appreciated Mary's privileges and graces, but his personal preference in his prayer life and in his priestly work, in his capacities as preacher and teacher, fell on Mary's role in men's lives and how she shows us in the flesh what it means to be united with God. A catholic spirit, Fr. Titus would enjoy a vacation in some European country if it were made possible for him. So he got to visit many parts of the world. Invariably when he visited famous museums he would search out the Christian art section, and give first priority to paintings of Our Lady and Child. Those who frequented him remember a constant bit of advice he gave: "Particularly, think of Mary. That is our vocation. Like her we are to became *theotokoi*, God-bearers and God's heralds."

St John of the Cross, Marian mystic

In an unpublished article on the devotion that St John the Cross had for Our Lady, Fr. Brandsma delights to point out that the Spanish mystic revealed himself as an authentic Carmelite through his esteem for the Mother of God. "Clearly St John acknowledges the necessity and usefulness of devotion to the saints and in the first place to the Blessed Virgin Mary. But he wishes this devotion to be healthy . . . The mystic doctor certainly does not condemn the honor and prayers due Mary and the saints, but he wants to see them used as a means of reaching God. Here again it is not union with the saints that should be the goal, but a lifting up of the heart to God, a new step towards union with him."

Dr. Brandsma reiterated this view on his lecture tour in the USA (1935), which was published as *The Beauty of Carmel*. "For St John of the Cross, Our Lady is the ideal of the soul that strains upwards towards God, and is drawn by God towards himself." To summarize his thought he appeals to the conclusion of a contemporary scholar, Fr. Gabriel of St Mary Magdalen, O.C.D.: "Indeed, she is for him, as is truly reasonable, the ideal of a soul aspiring to the summit of Mount Carmel. He has not dedicated many words to her, but the few which he has written about her show that he regarded her as the archetype of a soul aspiring to the enjoyment of that unity, to the teaching of which he seems to have dedicated his life as an author. Other souls approach this ideal only in a lesser degree" (*The Beauty of Carmel*, p. 92).

In St John of the Cross, Titus Brandsma finds the pinnacle of Marian devotion in Carmel. The images used by the Mystic Doctor provide insight into his obvious love for Mary. She is like a *window through which the sunlight passes.* "If the pane of glass be clean and spotless, the sunbeam will lighten it up and change it in such a way that it seems to be the light itself and gives out light itself. That is the reason why Our Lady deserved to become the mother of God—because she offered not the slightest hindrance to the divine indwelling. Like Our Lady we must absorb the divine light."

Another image used by the saint is that of *overshadowing*. "To overshadow means to cover with a shadow, to protect, favor, pour full of grace ... The shadow thrown by the lamp of God's beauty will be another beauty according to the kind and quality of God's beauty; ... We may say the soul equals Our Lady upon whom the Holy Ghost descended in all his fullness and whom the strength of the All-high overshadowed in the most perfect way."

After expounding other images of the mystical life, Titus recommends that St John's poetry be studied: there one will find "confirmation of the Marian character of the mysticism of St John of the Cross ... Let us, especially the Carmelites, not underrate this. Mary, our mother, our glory, is our example, our prototype, when God selects us also for his divine favors ... Illumined by him she shines for us as the mystical rose, whose sweet odors waft through the garden of the church, so that we can repeat what we so often chant in our Office—that we draw near her by the odor of her sweetness. Like bees, we fly towards this mystical flower to behold in it the fairness of the mystical life in its highest bloom, namely God become man in her, so that he can also be born in us who belong to her" (*Beauty of Carmel*, p. 98).

With perspicacity, Fr. Brandsma forestalls objections that Our Lady in the thought of St John of the Cross is just too far removed from us and our real condition; the theme of Mary on her pilgrimage of faith and suffering hardly appears. "I think it extraordinarily remarkable that St John of the Cross who evidently always saw Our Lady on the loftiest heights never reveals her on the way to mystical union, but only in the glory of her love." From incidents in Mary's life that recur in St John's writings— the visitation, Cana, Mary under the cross, Mary with the apostles awaiting the descent of the Holy Spirit— the underlying theme is "a revelation of love, a radiation of love, a radiation of her union with him (God)." This is how Titus summarizes Mary's role on the heights of Carmelite mysticism: "She is for us, even in the most close union with God, an example and a mediatrix who can procure for us the grace of having God become man in our souls also, one with us, the eternal Son of the Father, through the wonderful indwelling of the Holy Trinity, a source of vision and love" (*Beauty of Carmel*, p. 101).

Mary present at the heights

Fr. Titus was convinced that Carmel's contribution in the history of mysticism was in the specific role of Mary through whom Jesus could be reached. He could understand the nuptial imagery of St Bernard better in the light of Mary's complete commitment to the Lord. He could appreciate better the centrality of the Trinity in the mystic vision of Eckhart and Ruysbroeck because Mary was the visible masterpiece produced by the three persons of the Trinity. In the person of Mary we can avoid an overly abstract and nebulous notion of the heights of the spiritual life. She shows us how this sublime state makes a person human *par excellence*.

During a conference that Fr. Titus held at the Marian Congress in Tongerloo (August, 1936), he tried to make this insight accessible to the diversified audience before him. Though he seemed to have lost them in the body of his talk, his ending caught their attention once again: "In the Communion of Saints, which is an article of faith, Mary is seated on the most sublime and unique throne. It is impossible to reach those heights, but this does not mean that we have no part in her glory, that we are not one with her ... From all eternity God has also chosen us, and in creation from all eternity he loved us and predestined us to live in intimate union with him, who wishes to inhabit us by his grace. And if this union is not as sublime as that of the divine maternity of Our Lady, still we too with full rights can be called God-bearers and to us too the Lord sends his angel to ask us every so often to open our hearts to the light of the world in order to carry it about like a lantern, as Ruysbroeck says. We also must receive God in our hearts, carry him under our hearts, feed him, and make him grow in us in order that he might be born of us and live with us as God-with-us."

Evidently there were few themes dearer to Fr. Titus than this one: like Our Lady we must conceive the Word, allow him to grow within us, and then give him birth in favor of the world around us. Bl. Elizabeth of the Trinity had a similar intuition with her well-known *humanité en surcroît*—an additional humanity. With his resolutely optimistic view of reality, Fr. Brandsma saw God's touch in all of creation. If he saw all the earth shot through with God's goodness and glory—he even considered being in jail a great grace, because then finally he could have the recollection of a cell, so much part of the Carmelite way of life—it was a spontaneous reaction to find God revealed most surely and clearly in the finest creature issued from his hands: the Blessed Virgin Mary, Mother of his Son.

In fact, he found that nature leaves traces of Mary: much as does the church's liturgy, he too wished "to see frequently in the clouds, in the dawn, in the morning star, in so many other symbols or images of Mary, in order to be more aware and appreciate our supernatural election" (*Ejercicios,* p. 30). It was the natural thing for him to do, then, when in prison: his very first prayer after the Sign of the Cross was a greeting to Our Lady of Mt. Carmel, followed by three Hail Marys. Though he lived in a predominantly protestant country, and he had to lament the fact that many of his countrymen looked on devotion to Mary as an aberration from the purity of the faith of the scriptures, Titus could never say enough about Mary's mediating role in uniting men with God. He regretted not being able to convince the world of this fact because in his life it had turned into an ongoing experience. His love for God's mother and ours could not be contained in his heart. He witnessed to it humbly, constantly, warmly.

Devotion through preaching

One method he employed was preaching retreats in a Marian perspective. Fortunately we have the text of one such retreat recently made available in a Spanish translation, edited by Fr. Melus (*Ejercicios bíblicos con María para llegar a Jesús*, CESCA, 1978). "In my status as a Brother of the Blessed Virgin of Mt. Carmel, I wish to lead into the land of Carmel those who with me love and venerate Mary as their cherished mother, so that at the hands of the mother and splendor of Carmel, they can achieve the most intimate union with God, given that this union is the scope of contemplative life in Carmel. 'I have led you to the land of Carmel that you might eat its fruits, and its very best' (Jer 2: 7). Just as Mary meditated on all she heard her Son do and say, just as she gave an example of a retreat in waiting for the coming of the Holy Spirit with the apostles, so she is the surest guide for men.

"Because we are sons of Mary, we know that she—called the mirror of justice—is the most perfect model of union and intimacy with God. No one was more like God than she whom he chose as his mother. Our union with her, the imitation of her life, are the surest guarantee of our union with Jesus, of our imitation of Christ her Son." If Jesus came to us by means of Mary, we can be sure that we will find Jesus in going to her (*Ejercicios*, p. 23). But scholar that he was, Fr. Brandsma immediately adds, in a filial prayer, his faith that Mary's greatness comes not from herself or from her personal merit, but from her Son. "O Mary, your image presents itself to us haloed in splendor and majesty. That splendor, in turn, flows from the Child Jesus you hold in your arms, the blessed fruit of your womb (cf. Lc 1: 42). Give us your divine Child. Look, we extend our arms to receive him and press him to our hearts" (*Ejercicios*, p. 24).

Mary's life like ours

In various episodes of Mary's life, Fr. Brandsma is not content to contemplate Mary until he sees how she relates to ourselves, how her religious experience was on the same line as ours. Mary's presentation in the temple by Sts Joachim and Anne, for instance,

134

should be seen as the need for ongoing consecration to the Lord's service. "A vocation is not something instantaneous, nor is our creation. God continues our creation, preserving us in being. Likewise, he continues our vocation, calling us constantly. 'I stand at the door and knock' (Apoc 3: 20) ... We must often make ourselves aware that God called us and continues to call us, so that we may always serve him with our whole hearts and that we may live consecrated to him ... We must begin anew each day. Always begin the day with Mary. Imitate her way of seeing God" (*Ejercicios*, p. 33).

The annunciation scene is applied to our own preparation for the coming of God into our lives. "Light passes through a crystal without breaking or tarnishing it. However, there is need for the crystal to be clean. Frequently our crystal is so clouded, so tarnished, with so little transparency! Where is our purity in the positive sense of consecration to God, of belonging uniquely and exclusively to him, preoccupied only about loving him? Is it not surprising that there is not more clear light in us? May holy Mary purify us ever more, disposing us more and more to receive divine grace ... 'Behold the handmaid of the Lord.' Let us frequently repeat these words with her." Practical as he was and unwilling to leave attitudes on a theoretical level, Fr. Titus mentions a practical means that obviously meant much him. "To recite the *Angelus* three times a day with greater devotion. Never to omit it, so that we might always live with the memory of this great mystery" (*Ejercicios*, p. 39).

The visitation, Fr. Titus intuits, is linked with the annunciation, with broad ramifications for every Christian's life. "As soon as Jesus took flesh in the womb of the Blessed Virgin, he urges her on to a work of charity ... The difficulties of the trip do not cause her to back away even for an instant ... The mystery of the dwelling of God in us must urge us on to practise acts of positive charity, of operative love." Again Fr. Brandsma links this mystery with an everyday possibility on part of all who celebrate the liturgy. The inner dispositions of Our Lady, so necessary for the true apostle, are vitally necessary for every follower of Christ. Thus the need to assimilate the values contained in the *Magnificat*: "Repeat the *Magnificat*, making our own the sentiments expressed in it. Always recite this canticle with special attention and meditate on it. The church prescribes it for us every day in the Liturgy of the Hours, at Vespers. Since we recite it all too routinely, we know it only superficially" (*Ejercicios*, p. 41-42).

Mary's suffering and ours

Because he had much to suffer throughout his life, Fr. Brandsma could identify with the place of suffering on Our Lady's earthy piligrimage. He had to leave the Franciscan minor seminary because of bad health—which hardly improved as he grew older. On account of his precarious health and his overextending himself, he failed his doctoral examination the first time he took it. He was held up in studies because one professor considered him too much of a rebel. His final, terrible ordeal in concentration camps would hardly have been supported had he not learned all through his life how to see God's hand in trial and suffering. And he saw that this, and no other path was followed by Mary. "We must be prepared to suffer with Jesus and Mary" (*Ejercicios*, p. 55). "[Mary] obeys the orders of St Joseph, she takes the divine Child in her arms with him and goes to meet privations and sacrifices ... She goes out towards an uncertain future, without knowing how long it will last. She first goes with him to Egypt, later to Nazareth, resigned and full of trust, to give us an example of resignation and obedience. Jesus is her strength. In our difficult hours, may she remind us of Jesus, guide us and protect us ... In our bitter hours let us recall the flight of Jesus into Egypt. Let us picture Mary and Joseph who suffer because they were specially beloved of Jesus" (*Ejercicios*, p. 5).

In all our needs and sufferings, scripture teaches us to have recourse to Mary. The episode of Cana shows us her maternal charity in action. "We must be convinced that we lack many things. We must acknowledge that we need the intercession of Mary to attain what we lack. We must beg Mary to obtain

136

from Jesus what is most necessary for us . . . We have here clearly depicted the care Mary has for us . . . In all trials and tribulations let us take refuge in Mary. Let us become devoted to Mary mediatrix of graces, and deepen the true meaning of this devotion." "See Mary as mother and queen of the apostles, and place our apostolate under her protection" (*Ejercicios*, p. 63-64). An integral part of Fr. Titus' vision of suffering was the joy that must accompany a life spent in the company of Jesus and Mary. As so many of his contemporaries, Fr. Titus stressed the grateful happiness that should mark the true son of Mary. "At feasts, we must maintain our joy so high and so noble that Jesus and Mary enjoy staying with us until the end of the feast. Our feasts should be a confirmation of our faith and of our love for God" (*Ibid*).

"We must travel the Way of the Cross with the Blessed Virgin in our everyday life, however not with complaints and laments, rather joyous and enthusiastic to prove the truth of the statement, 'My yoke is easy, my burden light' (Mt 11: 30). The cross is a blessing from which we should not flee. 'In the cross, strength; in the cross, salvation; in the cross, light.' In a religious community, we should find only happy faces, radiant with a happiness of a superior and intense order, and such a disposition should not be disturbed. The Blessed Virgin, our mother, is the queen not only of heaven, but also of earth. And we are the sons of this queen" (*Ejercicios*, p. 78).

Obviously, it cost Titus Brandsma to remain happy in the face of adversity. His arrival at a monastery was a distinct joy for his confreres; he had the gift of lightening many an evening recreation. In this too he was following a Marian trait: "Look on Mary as the 'strong woman' (Prov. 31: 10), prepared for suffering by long years of meditation on all that Jesus had preached. Consider that Mary is not surprised at what St John tells her, rather she immediately gets up and runs to share in his suffering" (*Ejercicios*, p. 65). His own long years of meditation on the value of suffering convinced him that it was the deepest proof of love. "With Mary and with John, let us kneel beneath the cross, in order to understand true love. Place ourselves in the hands of God in life and in death. With Mary contemplate the wounds of Jesus, especially that in his side, and hide ourselves in it. Renew our heart, making it a glorious tomb for Jesus" (*Ejercicios*, p. 69).

Titus could not have had a presentiment of how realistically he would be called on to imitate the Passion of the Lord in the atrocities of Dachau, but his convictions were strong: "'And I, when I will be raised up from the earth, will attract all to myself' (Jn 12: 32). Let us stay beneath the cross, so that the Blood of Jesus falls on us and purifies us. Yet again let us listen to those words on his lips: 'Behold your mother' (Jn 19: 27). This is the final proof of his love. With Mary let us approach Jesus and from his side drink of his pure Blood, which will transform us into new men" (*Ejercicios*, p. 89).

One of the resolutions he proposed for the retreatants is significant: "Flee from melancholy regardless of how difficult is the trial which we are suffering. Precisely on these occasions, make the Way of the Cross with Mary, with the scope of preserving joyous features and judge the sorrows of the world under a higher light—that in which they will appear to us as a sign of predestination and a motive of comfort" (*Ejercicios*, p. 79). He would have us fix our gaze on Mary: "Our Lady made the Way of the Cross with vigor and with love. 'Was it not necessary?' (Lc 24: 26): Our queen and mother knew that a sword of sorrow had to pierce her heart: that was her glory. She could not escape it. And we? Do we follow her? Our Lady points out the path of suffering for us. Later will come the resurrection and ascension. But first we have to merit our glory. This is what God wants. He has reserved a place and throne for us. We must work so as not to lose it. Let us say to Mary: 'Save our place, we are on our way'" (*Ejercicios*, p. 86).

But already in our present situation, Mary is working to transform us into worthy candidates for the kingdom. "Let us stay in the midst of the apostles. We are sons of God and of Mary. She is our refuge and our hope. We wish to pray with her to receive, at her intercession, the Holy Spirit, who transforms us into new and different men. We have continued to be the same in spite of the awful times in which we live. Would that finally we would be transformed into other persons! Our Lady brought to earth the fire which must inflame it. May it be enkindled and burn in us too, not beneath the embers, nor in the ashes. May the blaze of fire rise high!" (*Ejercicios*, p. 76).

Mary the sunflower

Like so many other writers, Fr. Brandsma had recourse to imagery to describe Mary's role vis-à-vis the Carmelite and the Christian. Often Mary has been compared to various types of flowers. For Bl. Titus, she can be compared to the sunflower. In what is a good recapitulation of his thought on Mary, he writes (*The Beauty of Carmel*, p. 67):

" The devotion to Mary is one of the most delightful flowers in Carmel's garden. I should like to call it a sunflower. This flowers rises up high above the other flowers. Born aloft on a tall stem, rich in green leaves, the flower is raised yet higher from among the green foliage.

"It is characteristic of this flower to turn itself towards the sun and moreover it is an image of the sun. It is a simple flower: it can grow in all gardens and it is an ornament to all. It is tall and firm and has deep roots like a tree. In the same way, no devotion is firmer than that to Mary. The fresh foliage, the green leaves point to the abundance of virtues with which the devotion to Mary is surrounded. The flower itself represents the soul created after God's image in order to absorb the sunlight of God's bounty. Two suns shining into each other, one radiant with an unfathomable light, the other absorbing that light, basking in that light, and glowing like another sun, but so enraptured by beams of the sun which shines on it that it cannot turn itself away from him, but can only live for him and through him. Such a flower was Mary. Like her, so may we, flowers from her seed, raise our flower buds to the sun who infused himself into her and will transmit to us also the beams of his light and warmth."

IN THE MOTHERLY WARMTH OF MARY

*Our Lady of Mt. Carmel in the life and writings of
Fr. Bartholomew Maria Xiberta, O. Carm. (1897-1967)*

Charisms are particular gifts. A person is gifted with one or several, but it is humanly impossible to embody them all. In fact, the gifts of nature and grace which characterize each individual usually follow on the general pattern of one's basic personality traits. A vigorously scientific theologian cultivates his gift of knowledge and perhaps wisdom. He will usually be wary of a childlike, tender, warm devotion to Our Lady, for instance, full of emotion and sentiment. Yet these two contrasting gifts coalesced magnificently in the figure of Fr. Bartholomew Maria Xiberta (1897-1967), an outstanding twentieth century Carmelite. The Spirit of the Lord graced him to the extent that two rather contrasting gifts not only coexisted in him but actually complemented one another.

On the one hand, Fr. Xiberta was recognized as a theologian's theologian. His acute mind—at the age of three he was already serving Mass, making all the Latin responses—dealt easily with the most abstruse theological concepts, to the extent that his works were often used as source material by other professors of theology. His expertise in medieval church teaching was recognized throughout the scientific world. At Vatican II Karl Rahner, S.J., personally presented Fr. Xiberta with an autographed copy of his volumes of *Theological Investigations* as a tribute to this pioneer on the subject of the ecclesial dimension of the sacrament of penance.

Yet, when he turned his mind and heart to Mary, he seemed to be another person. It may be that his warm, even passionate personality was able to make up for his scientific rigor by his effusive, open and tender love for God's mother and ours. Just as it could be said without fear of contradiction that he was the greatest theologian the Carmelite order has given to the church in many centuries, so those who knew him would have to agree that he was without peer in his love for Mary, mother and beauty of Carmel. Proud son of Catalonia, Fr. Xiberta could never forget what Our Lady of Montserrat meant for his people; on her annual feast, April 21, with typical simplicity he would—eyes brimming with tears—sing the popular hymn of Montserrat's patronness, *Rose d'Avril*, during the evening recreation session. As in the case of great people, he had no fear of the simple pieties of Catholicism. Holy pictures of Our Lady abounded in his breviary. They were no mere bookmarks; he often admired Our Lady's beauty and goodness depicted on them, and even during the celebration of the Divine Office would often sneak kisses at the image when he thought no one would notice.

Marian devotion in the concrete

Generations of students at St. Albert's International College, Rome, were all taught dogmatic theology by him; they remember him as the first one in chapel in the morning keeling or standing before the statue of Our Lady of Mt. Carmel, often fingering his beads, always speaking to her who was so close to his heart. He could not do enough to show his gratitude for such a mother, who called him to the family of Carmel. He once stated that one of the happiest days in his life was a July 16 feast of Our Lady which he celebrated in his native land with one other Carmelite. They sang every note of the Divine Office, including the three nocturns of matins at midnight, the two of them alternating, as if the choir were full of religious. Then during the day, his joy was consummated when he was able to spend the whole day celebrating the Eucharist and the Divine Office, hearing confessions and enrolling hundreds of people in the scapular of Our Lady. For Fr. Xiberta, who never took a vacation in the strict sense, this was better

142

than any vacation. How many times he could be seen running down Roman streets, having left an important theological meeting in the Vatican, anxious to be home at the International College to pray the rosary with the community before lunch. If the superior wished to make Fr. Xiberta extra happy, all he had to do was to ask him to sing the community Mass in honor of Our Lady of Mt. Carmel.

In his theology classes, Fr. Xiberta kept speaking about "the realities of our faith." He was not speaking about speculative, abstract truths. He meant the concrete persons of God, of the Blessed Mother, of the saints, of those who make up the church. Fr. Xiberta was one theologian who never let his theologizing hinder an effective and loving encounter with the subjects of his theological disquisitions. He seemed never to forget that an act of faith goes directly not to an idea or an ideal, but to the person of God. Our Lady was especially close to him because he considered that she personally invited him to be a member of his religious family of Carmel whose mother she was.

When he spoke of "Our Blessed Mother" it was with the hushed tones of one who experiences awe and reverence before someone whose love has been received and reciprocated. Just as he would speak of "the feast" and expect every Carmelite to realize that he was referring to July 16, so he often would speak simply of "her," taking for granted that Carmelites had Mary so much on their minds and in their hearts that they would immediately know who "she" was. Just as he would, naively but consistently begin counting the days before July 16 months beforehand, so he never tired of repeating simply "Mary is good." What he meant was that she so embodied goodness that she could not help—just as God cannot help—diffusing goodness wherever she gazed. "How good they are! They are above all good to us who have been called by them to religious life, and not to any kind of religious life, but to Carmel, that is, to the very home and abode of Our Blessed Mother" (*Fragmentos doctrinales*, Barcelona, 1976, p. 163).

While his occasional writings—letters, conferences, exhortations—are full of quaint, spontaneous and sometimes novel ways of expressing our relationship with Mary, Fr. Xiberta could not but speak and write from the background of a dogmatic theologian. Some have expressed surprise that he never wrote a tract on Our Lady, as he did on other dogmatic matters such as the Incarnate Word, the One God, the Triune God. The most basic reason may be that he was never asked to teach Mariology, and so he never had the opportunity to dedicate himself to something that would have been most congenial to him. Because of his abilities, he inevitably was assigned the "weightier" tracts. But another reason may be that the presence of the person of Mary was something so immediate and intimate to him, that he would have found it difficult to put it into logical categories. It may be that he who always was suspicious of psychology might have been "too emotionally involved" to write an objective theological treatise.

Based on solid theology

Whatever is the truth of the matter, Fr. Xiberta did put his talents to the service of serious, scientific studies on various aspects of Our Lady such as her Immaculate Conception (cf. *Carmelus* 1 [1954] p. 199-235). However, these studies are an exception to the rule. What absorbed his Marian interest most were the questions touching devotion to Our Lady within the Carmelite family. On occasion of the seventh centenary of the gift of the scapular (1951), he left no stone unturned to prove the validity of the scapular promise made by Our Lady to St Simon Stock. Any hint of doubt or criticism of the venerable traditions of Carmel regarding Our Lady and the scapular seemed to him to be a personal affront. He wrote an authoritative work on the vision to St Simon Stock (Rome, 1950), which was widely acclaimed at the time, but which subsequent historians by and large have abandoned, especially in its historical proofs. Until his death, Fr. Xiberta could never understand those who could say anything negative about the traditional devotion to Our Lady and her scapular in

144

Carmel. No small part of his final suffering was caused by what he perceived to be a losing battle.

This is not to say that his writings on Our Lady lacked solid theological foundation. Quite the contrary is true: Fr. Xiberta was a consistent man. He could never say one thing in dogma class and deny it in the life of devotion. He lived by the dictum which he shared with his students, "Theology which does not end up in chapel is of little value." In fact, he constantly taught that theology should be a great help for a solid spiritual life. Nowhere is this better seen than in his approach to Marian devotion. While he showed himself to be a maximalist on this question as on others, i.e., to say not the minimum but as much as possible about the realities of our faith, still his expressions of Marian devotion and love reflect the precision of a first class theologian.

Particularly in his talks to contemplative nuns, he stressed the deepest Christian truths as the basis of our devotion to Mary. Firstly, Mary would be a no-body without God's unique action on her. Just as Christians are made sons of God and so are immersed in a divine life through baptism, so Mary was incorporated into Christ by the *gift of divine motherhood.* "The eternal Word descends on Mary; he takes on that flesh which Mary's natural function was giving life to, and he makes it his own flesh, filling it with the fullness of his Godhead. The miraculous action of the heavenly Father joins with the motherly activity of Mary. The result of this contact—of the divine and human—is the Holy One, who shall be called Son of God" (*Talk 1* in *Charlas a las contemplativas*, Barcelona, 1967, p. 3). Fr. Xiberta does not see Mary's dignity based on some secret force of attraction she exercised over Christians, but on the objective fact that she joined the Father in producing the Savior of the world, Christ Jesus.

She is such an important person because she was so possessed by God that she was able with the Father to make up the one total origin of Christ, the Word of God in human flesh. "Not that Mary was in contrast to the Father, as merely providing her natural capacity to his divine power. No woman by her

145

natural power could engender God, not even Mary. God himself had to intervene. Just as it is God alone who can raise man to the level of being his son, so only God could make Mary provide the motherly contribution to the formation of a person who was simply God in the fiesh. This is why: Mary, possessed by God in order to become the mother of God, is inserted—let us say it in these terms—into the divine family and contracts special relations with each of the three divine persons" (*Talk 2* in *Charlas*, p. 6-7).

The theologian sees this special and unique grace granted Mary as closely linked with her virginity. But virginity must be taken in its broadest sense. It is a gift by which "the soul has all its faculties detached from creatures and applied to God. All its faculties, that is, understanding and willing, mind and heart, thoughts and affections" (*Talk 3* in *Charlas*, p. 9) "Mary was an 'untilled field' because no human contribution but rather the Holy Spirit and the power of the Most Hlgh could communicate to her the fruitfulness directed towards the engendering of a divine fruit, the Incarnate Word" (p. 11). But even more important, Mary was a virgin interiorly: her consecration to God's service made her available to his will in her regard. "Her whole being was inundated by the divine light of her Son, like the woman clothed with the sun of the Apocalypse (12: 1). This divine light did not bathe her only outwardly, like an opaque object, but rather penetrated the most intimate part of her being, just like a very pure crystal which is penetrated by the sun's rays" (p. 12).

Mary leads to God

The basis of all devotion to Mary must be firmly anchored in these truths. Fr. Xiberta literally bristled when he heard a reputable spiritual director telling those he was counselling that they should downplay devotion to Our Lady in favor of a direct approach to God. He prepared a talk aimed at proving the Catholicity of just the opposite approach: *adoration of God is greatly enhanced by a fervent and enthusiastic devotion to Mary*. He begins from God's side.

146

He is the beginning and end of all things. "The activity of God provides the totality of being and not just some part, as for example the order, the beauty or some particularly striking aspects. The activity of God does not end with his giving existence to things; rather it continues in their preservation, without which they would revert to nothing." He even continues to have impact on free creatures and without it they would be inert (*Charlas*, p. 17).

Man's response to this activity is adoration, the first impulse of worship. But this adoration, in all religions, has been offered God by man by means of external gestures and objects. So for instance by sacrifice man aims to transfer from his own use the material goods he offers to God, symbolizing God's ultimate domain over all things. The epitome of religious sacrifice is found in the Eucharist, in which we offer Christ to the Father, as a symbol of our own consecration to God. Creatures, shot through with the glory and goodness of God their Creator, are at our service. "When we contemplate them we become aware of how much God loves us and to feel loved is the best incentive to correspond" (p. 20).

But in what creature more than in Mary does the grandeur of God stand out? She who was greeted as "blessed among women" (*Lk* 1 : 28) is replendent from within with the interior beauty that in the final analysis is far more important than any material magnificence. "Mary is the most precious gift of God's goodness. Among creatures is there a greater gift than the love of a mother? In giving us Mary, God had the love of the mother of God also become the love of our mother" (p. 21). "There is nothing in Mary that keeps us at a distance from God. Since she remains rooted in God, when we praise Mary, we likewise fully praise God." Fr. Xiberta's conclusion: "We should not go to God by way of a slackening of Marian devotion, but rather by fostering it with the greatest intensity. What should always be found in our devotion to the virgin is to see her always united to God, as befits her dignity" (p. 22).

Mary, then, is not only for God, she is also for us. Because she engendered Christ, who came only "for us and for our salvation," she is intimately linked to us. By taking on flesh, Christ Jesus already brought back human nature to God's domain. This flesh he took from Mary; she could not but enter into the whole process of our redemption. Christ did not redeem us just on the cross. His whole life, beginning with his conception in the womb of the blessed mother, was redeeming us, weaning every stage of man's development from subjection to the evil one. In the Mystical Body of Christ, which provides us with a share in God's life, "Mary has the place of the neck, by which all grace vitally passes on to us" (*Talk, Charlas,* p. 25). Mary becomes queen of the kingdom of her Son, but alluding to St. Therese, Fr. Xiberta is quick to point out that she is always more mother than queen. "The place assigned to her in the plan of divine providence is more suited to shine bright with love rather than with magnificence, to give more luster to mercy than to power. The greatness of Mary as queen is without limit, but the limitless measure of her love is even more evident. Mary is the woman clothed with the sun and crowned with twelve stars (*Apoc* 12 : 1), before whom it is right to be overwhelmed by sentiments of due reverence and veneration. However, that person penetrates even deeper into the mystery of Mary who considers her as the sweet mother before whom he can spontaneously give free rein to confidence and love" (p. 27).

This vision of Mary gives Fr. Xiberta the means to interpret Christ's words about his mother during his public ministry in an eminently positive sense. When Christ exclaimed, "Whoever does the will of God is my mother..." (*Mk* 3 : 35), the obvious explanation is that Christ puts spiritual values above any other, even that of physical motherhood. In his meditations Fr. Xiberta intuited a possibly deeper meaning: "Whoever does the will of God, I will accept him like my own mother, not in that she generated me in the exercise of her motherly function—since this is something that cannot be communicated—but rather in the place she occupies in my heart.... If you fulfill the will of God, listening to my words and putting them into practise *as did my mother*, you will form

148

with her the one object of my love" (*Talk 6* in *Charlas*, p. 29).

Sons of Mary's sorrow

In Fr. Xiberta's view, we are so precious to Mary because we cost her so much. He often reverts to the truth that we are *sons/daughters of the sorrows of Our Lady*. Mary may have conceived her Firstborn in the joyous atmosphere of the angel's announcement; we, on the other hand, became her children while she was gazing at her crucified Son under the cross on Calvary. If the battle against the reign of the evil one cost Christ his very life, it could not have left his mother, co-redemptrix, exempt from suffering on our behalf (cf. *Talk 9* in *Charlas*, p. 43-47). Fr. Xiberta does not leave all this on a theoretical level; he meditates aloud, measuring the depth of Mary's anguish. "When we know that someone dear to us is suffering, love spurs on our imagination. Then, by means of that imagination, there falls on us something like a crushing burden—all the real, possible and imagined sufferings. All this increases our sorrow, colored by the uncertainty of what is really happening to the person we love. Without doubt, Mary's imagination could not go beyond what Jesus was actually suffering. . .." (*Talk 8* in *Charlas*, p. 40).

What moved Fr. Xiberta most was the fact that, as a mother, Mary would have but to plead with the Father to have such a bitter chalice pass from her and her Son. She and her Son would receive the same reply. "In this way the heart of Mary was crushed under a double weight: the one caused by the torments of Jesus, and the other by fear of seeing us condemned. Mary loved Jesus, but she also loved us who are her spiritual sons. Having to choose between these two loves as mother, in a certain sense her love for us prevailed. And so Mary agreed that Jesus fulfill his passion and death so that we might be saved. What will the love of Mary for us not be, if it induced her to accept the death of Jesus, her other Son?" (*Talk 7* in *Chartas*, p. 32).

149

When hearing confessions, Fr. Xiberta would habitually ask two simple, direct questions: "Do you love Jesus? Do you love Mary?" Absolution was forthcoming upon an affirmative reply: an approach worthy of an abstruse theologian, whose speculations exasperated lesser minds. He was able to cut through to essentials, which for Fr. Xiberta were a loving commitment to Jesus and to Mary. Never Mary without Jesus. He who wrote his weightiest and best known treatises on the Incarnate Word could never forget that the "enfleshed" part of Christ Jesus came directly and wholly from Mary. Jesus had no earthly father; thus everything human in Jesus derived from Mary. How could he miss her when he saw Jesus?

For Fr. Xiberta the Carmelite way was no highly technical, complicated road to God. His basic intuition was that "Until the end of the world, Carmelite life will be a losing of self in God in the motherly warmth of the Blessed Virgin" (*Talk 4* in *Charlas*, p. 15). In terms redolent of St. Therese, he stressed the God-inspired origins of authentic holiness. Basic is to let God and Mary love us. Theirs is the initiative; ours must be humble, joyous acceptance. "Let yourself be loved deeply by Jesus and Mary. Let the love that they reveal to you now be an anticipation of the love they have prepared for you from all eternity" (*Fragmentos doctrinales*, p. 164). "The first thought that you must very often consider is how much Jesus loves you. When you are well recollected in the depths of your heart, look and see whether it is not true that Jesus has not given you a thousand proofs of his special love. And when you feel yourself to be so loved by Jesus, be proud and throw yourself completely into the arms of Jesus. And when you are well embraced by Jesus, ask Our Blessed Mother to press you together tightly and always keep you united with unbreakable bonds" (*Fragmentos*, p. 299).

Because he himself had such a great heart—he took the objection of even a neophyte student just beginning the study of theology seriously and gave him as much time as he would to the pope's theologian, who on more than one occasion consulted Fr. Xiberta—he could appreciate the infinite ocean of love stored up in the heart of Christ for each person. He never tired of repeating how Jesus kept heaping his gifts of love on him every day of his life—and at the top of his list of gifts was that he enjoyed all of them in the house of Mary. What if at times the presence of Jesus and Mary is obscured "knowing that they are good and that they love us? Certainly, they do love us. Fifty years now that they love me and feed me my daily bread, that bread kneaded in the house of Mary" (*Fragmentos*, p. 142).

The spiritual life begins and ends not with human effort or virtue, but with the goodness and mercy of Jesus and Mary. "I wish always to insist on the same point: let's not lose time looking at ourselves, not even to seek out reasons for humiliations. Let us begin to gaze at Jesus and Mary in order to admire their goodness. And when we are well penetrated with that goodness, only then let us think of our miseries which bring the divine goodness into even sharper light" (*Cartas desde el Carmelo*, I, p. 485). Reflecting the more traditional thrust of medieval spirituality as contrasted with the more "modern" approach propagated by the Jesuits, Fr. Xiberta saw man's holiness coming from above rather than resulting from man's efforts and virtues. His quaint way of putting it: "What is Carmelite life if not always listening to the voices of Jesus and Mary? Why do we have silence and solitude if not so that we lose not even a single word of theirs?" (*Fragmentos*, p. 356).

A fitting response is joy

His numerous calls for joy in the spiritual life were based on this: Jesus and Mary continue to be the same loving persons, interested in us, even when we do not deserve it. "Religious life should be full of joy. We serve Jesus and Mary. What more do we want? Even if we are bad we have a new motive for joy because, our badness notwithstanding, Jesus continues to love us" (*Cartas*, p. 494). This means that in adversities, even of a spiritual nature, joy is the order of the day. "Having Mary as mother, even if the world should collapse in ruin, there would be no reason for sadness. To gain or lose merits interests me very little. What I desire is that Jesus and Mary be content" (*Cartas*, p. 495). In terms that reflect the Little Way of St. Therese, whom Fr. Xiberta on occasion cites explicitly, he insists that whatever Jesus and Mary send us is for our good, our real good. "We must not be demanding of Jesus and Mary. We should be content with whatever they give us. If they leave us in dryness, we should not complain. They do too much as it is, keeping us in their home. Always say this to Jesus when you feel you are in aridity. Don't hanker after any consolation except that which Jesus and Mary give you on their own initiative" (*Fragmentos*, p. 170).

He had seen the frustration of several religious because of their gnawing tensions. His faith was in the presence and power of Jesus and Mary, who were better than any help—physical, psychological or social—that could be offered. "The important thing is to remain always in a spirit of trustful repose in the hands of the Lord and of Our Blessed Mother so that sentiments of anguish do not dominante our souls" (*Cartas*, p. 155). At times he was accused of being too much of a legalist, insisting as he did on regular observance. But the way in which he understood the regular life in community was the way of supreme freedom: "I would like to remind you that all religious observance is not principally a means of earning merits for eternal life. Rather it is to honor Jesus and our Blessed Mother" (*Fragmentos*, p. 207). Or putting it more forcefully still: "I would not want to give you bad advice, but I am convinced that we should not long to be saints, but rather to be pleasing to Jesus and Mary" (*Fragmentos*, p. 158).

Too many lives in the Spirit have been blunted because of an inordinate concern with creatures and especially with oneself. Holiness is not minute nit-picking of one's faults and failings: "If a person is concerned with creatures, above all if he is concerned with himself—whether I am now this way or that, whether they are doing this or that to me—then he will never succeed in living in intimacy with Jesus and Mary" (*Fragmentos*, p. 157). In other words, religious perfection is not self-fulfillment, but making

Jesus and Mary content. "The concern to raise us to perfection belongs to our blessed mother. We must live with the desire to provide joy for Jesus and Mary, not to succeed in becoming saints. This is why we seek every moment to do what appears to be more perfect, but only in view of making Jesus and Mary content" (*Cartas*, p. 490).

Simplicity and joy—two attitudes so much appreciated by today's troubled world—could be called Fr. Xiberta's hallmarks. They result uniquely from the conviction that he is so intensely loved by Jesus and Mary. "To sum up: always walk in holy simplicity, knowing that Jesus and Mary are thinking of us. To live with them, to talk to them continuously; to explain everything to them, to love them, and to do nothing more. It seems to me that this is life in Carmel. In this case, everything that you do is good, even if it comes out badly. And always live in holy joy. Our life is the life of little children who think neither of their meals nor of their health, only of enjoying the goodness of dad and mom" (*Cartas*, p. 492).

Carmel, then, adds this coloring to growth in the Spirit: to become more Christlike, stay close to Mary. She invariably leads to her Son, and continues to say today as at Cana, "Do whatever *he* tells you." "It is clear that the best way to invoke Mary is to put her alongside her Son (by whose side will Mary be if not her Son's?) He is the second person of the Blessed Trinity. Realize that in our sacred order we have always sought to place Mary at the side of Jesus, not to confuse them, but so that Mary introduce us to the presence of Jesus" (*Fragmentos*, p. 179). Mary's *Magnificat* was proclaimed to exalt God's wondrous deeds; her function in Carmel is the same: to allow us to act in a way befitting sons and daughters of God. "We have reason to sing our *Magnificat*, because the Almighty has done great things for us: Great things like those he did for Jesus, like those he did for Mary, that mother of ours, so incomparably good. The Holy Spirit descended on her and in this way the Son who was born of her was not a pure man, but the God-man. The same in us: the Holy Spirit descends on us and on our activities; if we do

153

not place obstacles in his way they are no longer purely human activities, but divine and human. How stupid we are when we strive to perform purely human actions, like complaining, lack of charity, failings against silence, lukewarmness. . ., when at every moment we could be performing divine-human acts like faith, hope, charity and the whole life of observance" (*Fragmentos*, p. 140). Even when human limitations and weaknesses did not allow of a perfect following of Christ, Fr. Xiberta refused to get bogged down. He was too convinced that Mary was a mother who never gave up on her sons. "As I look on my poor soul, I sometimes think that the blessed mother brought us to Carmel precisely because of our weakness. She did not want to entrust us to anyone. She took us *into her own home* so that she herself might be with us and concern herself personally with our lives" (*Fragmentos*, p. 177-179).

Mary and contemplation

Carmel's contemplative vocation is intrinsically linked with devotion to Our Lady. She who pondered the events of Christ's life in her heart is the model for every Carmelite in his efforts to live out his charism. Nowhere did Fr. Xiberta find this better expressed than in the hymn at Lauds on the July 16 feast. How often he repeated the simple but deep truth:

> Let us ascend to the heights of Carmel.
> Our virgin mother is calling us from there,
> Seeking to nourish us with graces.
> It is there we contemplate the beauty
>   and glory of God.

Mary's contribution to Carmel's mission is essential. Fr. Xiberta felt he found its kernel in a medieval Carmelite writer: "A phrase of Ven Arnold Bostius, O. Carm., summarizes the whole activity of Mary in favor of Carmel: *Amando se constringit amari*: loving us, Mary forces us to love her. Not the opposite: in loving her, we force Mary to love us" (*Talk 33* in *Charlas*, p. 195).

154

He wrote a short article on this sterling insight. "Mary is the first to love. She begins the tender idyll which will develop in the depths of our souls. She continues it, always taking the principal part. Man enters into this devotion, already won over by the excess of love that Mary shows him; and he remains there, enjoying her love, and calm with the pleasant serenity that the promises of Mary inspire in him. He runs in the footsteps of Mary towards the eternal goal which he will know how to achieve, supported by Mary." He applies this to Carmel's preferred Marian devotion, the scapular: "Here we have the secret of the mysterious effectiveness of the devotion of the scapular. Mary generously spreads her love, the sweet, sublime love of a mother. And souls, won over, repay love with love. And so they do good and flee from evil. And so, free from the paralyzing fear of the future, they go on their way secure, confident, fearless, towards the open doors of the heavenly fatherland" (*Amando si fa amare* in *I Trionfi della Bruna*, June, 1951, p. 5-6).

For Fr. Xiberta, Carmelite communities were "the personal property of Mary, that is, the garden where Mary finds her delights. Do your best, then, to make sure that Mary is content" (*Fragmentos*, p. 223). The basically contemplative attitude of this faithful son of Mary is confirmed in this, that he never thought that he had come to Carmel to enhance it with his talents and graces, but rather that he was introduced to an order adorned and graced by Our Lady. Grateful hearts should spend their lifetime on earth rejoicing over so much unmerited and unsuspected goodness. "For us Carmel is the place in which we find prepared beforehand all kinds of graces on which our souls are abundantly nourished. 'I have brought you into the land of Carmel, so that you might eat its fruits and the best it has to offer' (*Jer* 2 : 7). By the name 'Carmel' the prophet designates an extremely fertile and beautiful land. ... This name is applied to the benefits that Mary gives us, transplanting us to her land, which is certainly exceedingly fertile and beautiful, and in which we can have as many spiritual fruits—delicious and superabundant—as we want" (*La Fiesta de la Virgen*,

p. 143). Citing the liturgical text for the feast of July 16, about which he provided an extended commentary in book form, Fr. Xiberta believed that Mary forged a pact with Carmel, a pact of goodness and fidelity: "Israel lived trusting in the word of God. In a much fuller way the Christian lives trusting in the new pact irrevocably sealed with the blood of the Son of God. ... This Christian hope is nourished in us in an extraordinary way by the promises Mary made to Carmel. Nothing should strike fear into persons consecrated to Mary. Mary has gazed at Carmel and her gaze is a foretaste of all graces:

> Why hesitate?
> Where the Virgin Mary gazes,
> There heavenly graces abound.

Personal lack of worthiness was never a major hurdle for Fr. Xiberta because he was too busy admiring the greatness of Mary's motherly love. "We must live happy in Carmel since we are the order of Mary. What more could we hanker after in this world than to belong to our Blessed Mother? ... Our Blessed Mother saw us so weak that she picked us for her house, not to adorn it, but rather as sick people whom she would look after. Because when we see ourselves needing to acknowledge our unworthiness, our carelessness, our continued imperfections, what we have to do is to admire the incomparable goodness of our Blessed Mother. Knowing full well what we are, still she chose us" (*Fragmentos*, p. 169).

Carmel is Marian by nature

Carmel is not faithful to its original charism if it does not foster love for Mary, "one of its prime obligations. Our Lord God has marked out for us the mission of glorifying his Mother. And if we don't do this, what on earth shall we do?" (*Fragmentos*, p. 175). But this love for Mary does not consist in flashy or spectacular manifestations, but in the cultivation of the spiritual life. "We should be proud that Carmel is the order of Mary. I believe that the Lord refuses us other things about which we might be proud on a human level, so that we might feel all the more intensely pride in belonging to Mary. The Lord God destined Carmel so that in it our Blessed Mother might receive a little of the glory marked out for her as queen. Not the glory of a fireworks display, but the intensity of the interior life is what will give our blessed mother the glory she deserves" (*Ibid.*).

Mary is inviting us not to any kind of spiritual life, but to one that reaches the heights of Carmel. "Carmel is the mount of contemplation. . . and Mary invites us to ascend to the summit, appropriating to ourselves the most sublime degree of the spirit of contemplation. . . Mary promises us to strengthen our hearts and to protect our arms" (*La Fiesta*, p. 163-164). For this reason Fr. Xiberta did not hesitate a moment to write: "The day that Carmel ceases being wholly Marian, that day it would lose its reason for existence" (*Fragmentos*, p. 176). And the reason is again not because of what we contribute, but because of the greatness of the gift: "Yes, it is true; our love for Jesus is not a calling, it is a reply. I ask you for the love of God that in our beloved Carmel the souls called there by Mary be perfected around Jesus. This is what Mary hopes by the goodness which she grants us so generously and abundantly" (*Cartas*, p. 444).

The intimacy and familiarity that Carmel enjoys with Mary can be summed up in its official title: Brothers of the Bl. Virgin Mary of Mt. Carmel. "No, the order does not exaggerate in its appreciation of this title as its most notable adornment. This is no empty word: rather, the name designates the constitutive characteristic" (*La Fiesta*, p. 139). The exclamation marks that Fr. Xiberta uses when he cites the words of the liturgy, "You are our sister," betray the depth of feeling and conviction with which he pronounced these words. "An ancient writer, in order to prove that we are correct in calling ourselves brothers of Mary, notes that our holy Rule copies the life of our Blessed Mother" (*Fragmentos*, p. 164). Titles were not honorific adjuncts for Fr. Xiberta; they denoted personal bonds that touched the heart of the matter. "The contemplation of our blessed mother— so beautiful in her person, so beautiful in her mercies—is really always new. How great to have her for mother and for sister! Many are called her sons, but brothers of Mary, no one was so daring as to call themselves in this way—only we Carmelites. This being able to call Mary not only mother but also sister—the elder sister—and friend, even friend!... As if it were an I-thou relationship" (*Fragmentos*, p. 355).

The scapular devotion

Following the tendency of his optimistic disposition, Fr. Xiberta spent very little time destroying "myths." Although he could be critically severe on a scientific level, his propensity was to allow the gifts of God and of his mother to take hold of him. To appreciate them correctly, he wanted to know about them even in detail. Theologian that he was, he saw the excellent fruits that the scapular devotion had produced. He valued the efforts of his Carmelite forefathers to make the devotion one of the leading Marian devotions in the Catholic church. As he saw the devotion intimately linked to the vision of Our Lady to St Simon Stock, he left no stone unturned to prove the authenticity of the vision. But Fr. Xiberta was too wise to stay on a merely external level. He who delved into the inner nature of the deepest mysteries of our faith could not fail to reflect on the spiritual meaning of the scapular devotion. Unfortunately, because his historical review of the vision to St Simon Stock is not fashionable among some critics, his valid and theologically rich doctrine has also been neglected.

The scapular is best seen as "Mary's sacrament." "Ah, the habit of the order of Carmel, external sign of brotherhood with Mary, converted by her into a pledge of eternal salvation! Rightly the holy scapular has been called the sacrament of Mary. It is truly an outward sign of the invisible protection of Mary" (*La Fiesta*, p. 141). "Our alliance with Mary, on our part, does not consist in the material wearing of a symbolic vesture; nor on the part of Mary, in the promise to attend to our temporal needs and to procure for us at the final moment a tardy repentence. Mary signs no alliances of such low quality. The alliance which Mary extended to Carmel has as its immediate end that of leading us to the fervent practice of justice and holiness" (*La Fiesta*, p. 168). How many of his rich insights Fr. Xiberta gathered from the texts of the liturgical rites. In this too he followed the venerable spirituality of his Carmelite family: to base his spirituality on the church's official prayer. This was his guarantee that he was not just projecting self into his ruminations. "I give up all the prerogatives that other orders have for this one alone: to belong to the family of Mary. However, what responsibility, what an obligation, to strive not to be out of tune with Mary, the Immaculate one. Let this thought be a stimulus to become holy ceaselessly. Wearing the vesture of our Blessed Mother, strive to clothe yourself with her virtues as well. Keep in mind the *Magnificat* antiphon for the octave days of our Blessed Mother: *Glory of Mt. Carmel, those who are adorned with your vesture clothe with your virtues as well*" (*Fragmentos*, p. 194-195).

To clothe her child is one of the most spontaneous concerns of a mother. Mary has not ceased to do just that since she cradled her Firstborn in her arms: "Our Blessed Mother covered the little body of Jesus with swaddling clothes and this was a symbol of what she would like to do for the mystical body of that same Jesus. She has sought to do this particularly with us, covering us with the clothing of the holy scapular, poor as that of Bethlehem, however full of the same love. We must be extremely happy to have a mother like that" (*Cartas*, p. 255). But here too the greatness of the gift is measured by the maximum generosity on Mary's part and by the utter simplicity required on man's part. "Why I think the scapular devotion is one of the best and an unsurpassed expression of the Catholic spirit is precisely this: we have nothing else to do than to say to Mary with all our hearts, 'Mother,' and then to wait for her to do great things for us, as befits a grand lady. There is nothing less Catholic than to conceive religion as an exchange between God and man: I give so much and he repays me so much" (*Cartas*, p. 229).

The scapular devotion aims to nurture an unlimited trust in Mary's faithfulness, analogous to every Christian's trust in the faithfulness of the Lord. "The trust we place in the scapular is a particular instance of trust in the suppliant omnipotence of the mother of God. However, an incomparably great trust, because it relies not on our devotion but on the fidelity of Mary. A limitless trust that the virgin will obtain for us graces that are so efficacious that they mellow and overcome our hearts, regardless of how hard and rebellious they are. No, the Carmelite scapular is not a substitute for good works, but rather a powerful entreaty for heavenly aid necessary to practise good works. And why not have a trust without limits? What saintly father or theologian teaches that trust in the protection of Mary should be limited?" (*Enciclopedia del Escapulario del Carmen*, p. 240).

Symbol of consecration

The Catalan friar never could understand those who shrugged off the scapular as unimportant, especially in comparison with other elements of the faith. The reason: the scapular is an outward symbol of the core of Christian living, namely, consecration. "Devotion to Mary, experienced in all its fullness, is not limited to offering acts of homage on given occasions, but rather it constitutes a permanent thrust of the most intimate affection of the Christian heart. To be devoted to Mary does not merely mean to follow one of many pious practises which are freely added to the observance of the precepts of the Christian life. It embraces the whole person; it constitutes a kind of personal character which is connected with the personal character of the Christian. On the other hand, we do not expect of Mary merely this or that particular grace, but rather constant protection. The person truly devoted to Mary assumes in her regard the position of a son towards his mother: he gives his whole being over to her. These characteristics of devotion to Mary are epitomized in a single word: consecration, that is, a total and exclusive commitment by which the consecrated person belongs completely to the person to whom he is consecrated, not for some determined moment, but permanently.

"Consecration in the primary sense is made only to God, because total and exclusive commitment belongs to the worship of adoration. But in a subordinate way, it also is made to Mary insofar as she is the mother of God, co-redemptrix of the human race and mediatrix of all graces; in one word, because Mary exercizes a universal function in the economy of salvation.

"In order to have a concrete expression, consecration requires a sign of permanent devotion. The very act of committing oneself will be expressed with a formula, which can then be repeated at regular intervals. But by nature consecration is above all a state, a character; and so, something permanent. . .. These outward symbols of consecration are. . . a sign of one's commitment to Mary, and at the same time of her love and protection, and this always, day and night, alone and with others, in life and in death; a bond of union with Mary even when a person cannot think about her at the moment. . .. The most effective memorial is the scapular, made in such a way as to be worn continuously. It is there every moment to remind us that we belong to Mary" (*L'abitino del Carmine* in *Il Monte Carmelo* 25 [*1939*] 225-229).

A garment is a most suitable symbol of Marian devotion because of Mary's maternal role. "With what solicitude and tenderness a mother dresses her children, with what love she provides for their clothing. In the Old Testament, Jacob showed his love for Joseph by giving him a coat of many colors. Similarly, in order to make clear the loving union between Jesus and Mary, pious tradition aptly recalls the seamless garment which Mary made for Jesus, and which her divine Son wore even to Calvary. A garment, therefore, is an ideal symbol of consecration to Mary, for if consecration means total giving on our part, it means still more Mary's boundless motherly love for us. . ..

"In receiving the scapular, the faithful are not accepting some human creation, but precisely the garment bestowed upon them by their heavenly

161

mother. The two great promises connected with the scapular, together with its long history of graces and miracles, express for us in a concrete way Mary's function as our mother. The promises of the scapular are the embodiment of what can be hoped for from Mary by those who give themselves totally to her, and who place themselves under her protection. For whoever wears the scapular, trusting in the great promises of final perseverance and liberation from purgatory, even as he makes a complete offering of himself to Mary, so he will know the protection of Mary, mother of goodness and unfailing power. Thus the scapular is the symbol and means of consecration to Mary, consisting in an offering of ourselves, and in the motherly protection of the Virgin Mary" (*The Carmelite Scapular* in *Carmel in the World* 15 [1976] 158-159).

Sign of humility and hope

Fr. Xiberta addressed himself to the question: why are Catholic hearts attracted to such simple, unsophisticated devotions as the scapular? His answer is worthy of the great theologian that he was. He recognized two basic Christian attitudes as the basis of the ordinary Catholic's understanding of the scapular: hope and humility. "Our relationship with God is just exactly the opposite of a mutual exchange of goods. ... God does not love creatures because he finds them good, but by loving them he renders them good. The liberality of God towards man is mercy and mercy is exercized only where there is wretchedness. The ultimate foundation of our salvation is not to be found in anything that we have given God, but in the fact that God, when we were still sinners, loved us and called us to share in the grace of his only begotten Son (*Rom* 5 : 8), and he continues his work until he will bring it to perfection (*Phil* 1 : 6). ...

"Good works! Undoubtedly they are indispensable to salvation. ... 'God who has made us without our cooperation will not save us without our cooperation.'... Still, we must remember that the works themselves are the fruit of grace, for the goodness of

God has gone so far as to concede that in our relation with him there should also be a place for justice. The function of good works is totally subordinated to that of grace; their perfection, although real, is the perfection of a creature... It is for this reason that the church teaches that in the decisive moment of death we should approach the divine judge with the humble prayer of the psalmist: 'Enter not into judgement with your servant, Lord, for in your sight no man can be justified' (*Ps* 142 : 2)."

"And then perseverance. Not those who begin but those who persevere to the end will be saved (*Mt* 10 : 22). But in ourselves we have no assurance, no guarantee of arriving. After so many sad experiences, who can have confidence in himself?... He who thinks he stands firmly, admonishes St. Paul, should beware of a fall (*1 Cor* 10 : 12) and in fear and trembling should he work to earn his salvation (*Phil* 2 : 12). Perseverance is a great gift that can only come from God, who is omnipotent to sustain those who stand resolutely and to lift up again those who have fallen" (*Rom* 14 : 4).

"Behold the truths which the scapular inspires in the depths of the soul, truths which the Christian people know and understand, perhaps without reflecting: behold, too, the profound significance of the feast of Our Lady of Mt. Carmel which returns radiant every year in July, causing to vibrate in our hearts most vivid sentiments of humility and hope" (*The Scapular, Devotion of Humility and Hope* in *Mary* [1953] n. 4, p. 109-110).

The July 16 feast

It is fitting to close this sketch of Fr. Xiberta's devotion towards Our Lady of Mt Carmel referring to the July 16 feast. He never tired of recommending a loving reflection on the liturgical texts of the feast in order to savor the graces that the church understands us to receive though devotion to Carmel's mother and queen. In his letters he presupposes that Carmelites prepare for the feast to make it the most solemn celebration of the year. As students we teasingly asked him was it right to celebrate July 16 with more solemnity than Easter itself. "Listen," he replied, "you have to make distinctions..." but he would never retreat from his statement that July 16 should be the unsurpassed Carmelite celebration. "I suppose you are practising the chant for the office, so that day will be more splendid than any other day of the year. But I would want them to change the rules of Gregorian Chant for our blessed mother, because they always have us sing softly; on that day I would want to be able to shout at the top of my voice. How can you sing *piano* that *Quam pulchra es... How beautiful you are, how gracious, O delightful one?* How can you say all that to Mary in a subdued voice?" (*Fragmentos*, p. 354).

It is Mary who brings us Jesus today as at the incarnation. "We receive the Body and Blood of the Lord today (i.e. July 16) as a banquet—in intimate union with Mary. Approaching holy communion, we remember that that Body and Blood are the fruit of Mary, formed from her pure flesh by the action of the Holy Spirit, nursed at her breasts, lovingly fondled in her arms, heroically offered by her for our redemption. The Body and Blood which we receive, truly, really and substantially, are the first and supreme gift that Mary gained for us. From it derive all the other gifts which are granted us through the centuries, as a result of the economy of grace established as a substitute for the Old Alliance, an economy based on the communication of this Body and Blood" (*La Fiesta*, p. 171).

How better capture the simple, tender, childlike affection of this mighty theologian for our mother of Carmel than in his own experience. He never showed us more of his heart than when he exclaimed (*Fragmentos*, p. 352): "The Feast of July 16 is not just any kind of feast; it is much more. It is the finest day of the year, the day closest to that one without sunset in heaven. It is the day when we experience what we will be doing in heaven: being close to Mary under her white mantle, contemplating the infinite beauty of God, of which the blessed mother's beauty is a reflection. To enjoy her, talking to her on a one-to-one basis and... listening."

9

MARY'S SEER AND BUILDER

Fr. Malachy Lynch, O. Carm.
and the restoration of Our Lady of
Mt. Carmel's Shrine at Aylesford

Visionaries usually do not make good builders. Poets and mystics, who have a special gift of seeing things at a deeper level and in novel relationships, seldom are also blessed with the practical gifts. This is just what makes the personality of Fr. Malachy Lynch, O. Carm. (1899-1972), so fascinating. While on the one hand he embodied the man of faith from the Wicklow hills of Ireland, for whom the world of the spirit was the "real" world, on the other hand he is more responsible than any other person for the restoration of the venerable friary of Aylesford in England. Aylesford has become—inspired by his vision and courage—not just an interesting historical relic from the past of Carmel, but a vibrant Marian shrine which on a given summer Sunday attacts thousands of pilgrims.

In 1949, when The Friars was reacquired by the Carmelite order after an absence of 400 years, Fr. Malachy was a reluctant choice to be superior of the new foundation. He was doing amenable and zealous work in Wales, where he had restored a small local church dedicated to Our Lady. It was obedience that brought him to Aylesford. This in itself was the definitive proof that the restoration of Aylesford was not his doing—it had not been, he insisted, his inspiration nor his choice. It was Our Lady's doing. The all-pervading conviction of Fr. Malachy was that this initiative was not from below, but from on high. People wrote to thank him for the help he had given them, many times by means of the *Pil-*

grim's Newsletter from Aylesford, which became The Friar's link and lifeline, since the ideal was to build the shrine from the alms of pilgrims and benefactors. Fr. Malachy disclaimed personal credit:

"Everything we do here is Our Lady's work. There can be no other motive. It is just common sense. It is very simple and unsophisticated. You do what you can. If you have no money for materials, she sends it; if your health goes, she restores it—incredibly; if you go on missions for her, she pays your fares and lodges you royally. All this happens quietly without any fuss or complication—sometimes it has happened before you know. . .. The rebuilding here is a test case. We are in a desert; we have no income, yet the work of restoration goes on, and at what a cost! Help always comes and it is nearly always unexpected and astonishing" (*Newsletter* n. 11, February, 1953).

Our Lady's initiative

Beginning with the very purpose of Aylesford, Fr. Malachy saw Mary behind all that happened. She was constantly sending signs to counteract and conquer the negative signs and difficulties roused by the envious evil one. When the Carmelite order had the good fortune, under Prior General Kilian Lynch, to purchase The Friars, the embarassing question became what it would be used for. Answer: an international house of studies of the history of the order. Quite unexpectedly, another purpose emerged:

"They [the major superiors in Rome] had not discovered that Our Lady was *making history* and writing a new and vivid chapter herself. Pilgrims continued to come; one day 1,200 came with two hours notice for tea! The sisters were not intimidated and it was done. Some day we will be given credit, quite wrongfully, for making Aylesford a place of pilgrimage. The first pilgrimage came very soon after we had taken possession. A legionary from Ealing wrote saying: 'We are bringing our legionaries to Aylesford. Will you meet us at the bridge at three o'clock?' We did, and 400 Legionaries led by Dom Ambrose Agius,

OSB, descended from coaches and moved across the bridge as if it had happened often before. And of course, it had; many thousands of pilgrims in the same spirit had come across that ancient bridge in the days when England was Catholic. That was how the first organized pilgrimage began; it was not *our* doing. Everything that has happened at The Friars has that quality. We can regard it quite impersonally, but it is not difficult at all to know who is behind it all" (*Newsletter* n. 6, October, 1951).

Faith in the initiative of Our Lady in the upbuilding of her former shrine in Aylesford extended, in Fr. Malachy's vision, to all aspects of the matter by what he called "indirections." Quite often things took a different turn than that first planned. This was true most prominently in the reduction of first plans to build a large church to the more manageable outdoor shrine with several interlinking chapels as it stands today. How often the purpose of Allington Castle—just down the Medway River from Aylesford—has changed over the years since it was acquired in 1951 to house the Secular Institute of Carmel, which had outgrown its original lodgings at Aylesford. The very *raison-d'être* of this Institute is a concrete instance of how Our Lady manages:

"On the Feast of all Carmelite Saints, just a fortnight after our return, the Institute of Our Lady of Mt. Carmel was founded and the first three sisters were clothed.... The sisters were certainly valiant and necessary. Everything was just as unexpected for them as for us. They accepted the situation and the circumstances and discarded at once their conventional ideas. Nothing daunted them: they were ready for anything, and that was the spirit which grew with experience. They learnt that God's presence is not apart from his will, and to fling oneself into God's will is the highest wisdom. They had come to do Our Lady's gracious will at Aylesford. Hers was the initiative; they had only to watch for signs of it. It was obviously her will to restore her ancient shrine and glory. They had come into a desert hoping for something—they knew not what— prayer and quiet and the contemplative life. They soon found a life of ceaseless activity.... You can

167

plan your contemplation and create a conventional setting and end up by becoming only an artificial mimic. It is possible to be busy and yet never lose the sense of God's presence if you are busy doing God's will. And doing God's will indicated by Our Lady issued quickly in detachment" (*Newsletter* n. 6, October 1951).

Vision of faith

The basis of this vision is faith in eternal life as the real life to which man is destined. Our Lady and the saints are more surely alive than anyone on earth because they can now no longer lose that life which we still conserve in vessels of clay. Fr. Malachy saw this as the prime vocation of Carmelites, to be prophets in the sense of *seers*, those persons who are "seeing always the unfolding pattern of God's wonderful providence and its shining logic." What today we call "salvation history," the first prior of Aylesford intuited as the omnipotence of God able to realize his purposes beyond our wildest dreams. For this positive vision the most sane and predictable conviction is that God invariably wills what is best for us and for the world. Our Lady is part of this will of God for us, and is particularly to be found in a place like Aylesford. Fr. Malachy took seriously complaints by non-Catholics who objected that his otherwise interesting newsletters gave too much prominence to Mary to the detriment of Jesus her Son. He replied:

"She is alive now in heaven, in a state of life beyond imagining, flaming in the breath of the Holy Spirit. She did not become an angel in another life; she is still and ever will be in eternal relationship, the mother of God. We shall see her in that life we call heaven and be glorified by the sight of her. If she is not alive, neither shall we be after the few short years of this precarious life here. But Our Lord is risen from the dead and surely he who made the commandment 'Honor thy father and mother' has not left his own mother dead in the dust. All this is simple and obvious. Otherwise there is no Communion of Saints. We have communion with nobody and we are praying into a void."

But he goes a step further and addresses himself to the problem of how a human being, even perfect as Our Lady was, could pay attention to all the people throughout the world who invoke her.

"That clamor of a multitude 'We have no wine' never ceases; but there is that mysterious partnership 'What God has joined together,' etc. From him comes this unimaginable power. This power of Our Lady over her Son has puzzled even the saints. 'What is that to you and to me?' It is a rhetorical question and we know how extremely much it was 'to you and to me.' If you ask, if I ask, but if she asks! I suspect she does not have to ask. She is not just there to hand on our petitions. That is too human a way of regarding her. She is in herself the supplication of all humanity. It is as if all the needs of humanity, bitter and sweet, were cryng out in her. Dante, who is the Christian thought of the Middle Age, sees her coming to the help of one who did not ask her. She was not asked at Cana. Hers the quick-eyed charity, the intuition of a woman, the daring initiative; don't we know it well" (*Newsletter* n. 24, January, 1956).

Although wary of professional theologians, Fr. Malachy's theology was redolent of the age-old faith of his forebearers who shaped theology even more than they were shaped by it. Mary was nothing without the breath of the Holy Spirit that made her all she is.

"Since the church is Christ to us, 'He that heareth you heareth me,' it is Our Lord who through his church has given his mother this year (1954) in which to work his will of mercy and pity on a distracted age. . .. The Holy Spirit it is who kindles the living flame of all devotion, and devotion is love in flames. In the last age *frigescente mundo*, he inspired in men's souls devotion to the flaming loving heart of Christ. In this 'Age of Mary' he is kindling in men's hearts a strong and ardent love of the mother of God. In that last age a revival, in this age a rebirth; in the beginning the Holy Spirit chose Mary for the birth of Our Lord in this world. Now for the rebirth in men's hearts. Where birth and life are concerned you need a mother. That is God's way.... To reject her is to reject the work of the Spirit."

Because of this straightfoward and insightful belief in God's ways, he smarted under the attacks of those who wish to "purify religion" of such human accretions as Marian devotion. He foresaw that on this earth victory will not always seem to be achieved by believers; but eternity is God's. His mills grind slowly but surely. He hammers home the point that Mary, far from attracting men away from God, actually bridges the gulf:

"The Blessed Mother does not widen the gulf; she bridges the gulf between us and God. Last Sunday a Welsh convert priest told us the story of how years ago she led him to the fold; and how in language full of imagery they celebrate her in Welsh literature. 'I saw Mary with a halo round her head digging a trench between every soul and hell.' Mediatrix—minister of grace—formal language this, but the Welsh line says more. It was Welsh to describe the Immaculate as 'whiter than snow on Snowdon.' Though many centuries divide us we cannot but sense the reality of this cry to her of one in pain. 'Great is my burden for health, Mary. Greater than the greatest burden in the world. I am a man smitten by sickness. Who has borne pain like pure fire. Great is my pain, O Mary of my island'" (*Newsletter* n. 14, January, 1954).

Our Lady and the saints, because they are supremely alive, are also active. It was in the context of his visit to Fatima, where he was impressed by the simple, deep faith of the native people, that he wrote:

"The saints, even the most distant in time, are contemporary. They are not just sitting down in heaven like a lot of Buddhas contemplating themselves. If *we* are ministers of grace, one to another, they too are ministers and have more grace and life to minister than we have. That they are alive and so doing we know from experience. The more a Catholic people lives in communion with the saints, the more they are detached from purely worldly consid-

170

erations. They don't make them the end of all their striving. Sometimes as in Portugal they are careless of all but the supernatural, of almost everything we regard as essential to living. They don't envy us our motor cars or our gadgets. ... When you see hundreds of thousands of pilgrims at Fatima, waving good-bye with their handkerchiefs to Our Lady, represented by a very indifferent statue all decked out in flowers, even we—until we understand more fully— think it is extravagant and too much. It is a mystic who has said, 'where love is, there is vision,' and to these simple but profound souls Our Lady is revealing herself through this simple means. When you understand this, you realize that Our Lady is as near to their love as she was to the children who saw her over the Cova" (*Newsletter* n. 33, November, 1957).

Person-conscious

Person-conscious would be a thumbnail description of Fr. Malachy. While tradition, the scriptures, church teaching all were to be revered, even more so were living persons. He showed this in his everyday dealings with people, but especially in his appreciation of heaven's citizens. Because they were more surely and definitively alive than we, Our Lady and the saints were of prime import to him, but not in a sentimental sense having to do with a mere pleasant feeling or memory of our forefathers in the faith, but rather as *presences*. Although he was intent on filling Our Lady's shrine with worthy and only the best art work, still he got to the heart of the matter when he wrote:

"What Our Lord looked like or Our Lady and St Joseph, we shall not know this side of eternity. It is more real to think of them as *presences*. Presence has to do with the soul and the rational nature. You say people were present to you but you do not say a cat was present. Have you ever noticed that some people seem to carry life with them, and some death? I have known one great priest who seemed to fill a room with his presence and everyone within it seemed to become more alive. ... Our Lord's *presence* must

171

have filled the whole world just as now it fills every church where the Holy Sacrament is reserved. You sense Our Lady's presence in this way at Lourdes or Fatima. You feel it very strongly at Aylesford. What is it? It is a mysterious contact with life. We who are bleak and wanting receive life. It is an enlarging, an unexpected freedom given of another world, a secret discovery and everyone's secret to himself. Even if we were to see Our Lady and St Joseph, we could not communicate our vision except in stammering speech. It would remain almost completely our own. My secret to myself" (*Newsletter* n. 25, May, 1956).

Mary is quite the opposite of what is so often thought about her, as detracting from the love and devotion and commitment that should be reserved for God. Just as the mystic Juliana of Norwich spoke of "the marvellous great homeliness of the Incarnation," so Our Lady always brings Christ closer to us by showing us in her concrete person the human side of Christ Jesus, which she provided for him in an exclusive way:

"She it is who makes it possible for all men to be *at home* with God. And so we may say in a homely way that she will have a *free hand* this year (1958 Marian celebrations). Not that she has not always had a free hand. She was not forced to be the mother of our Redeemer. She is the woman of terrible and daring initiative upon whom Gabriel the Archangel waited for her consent. It is the witness of the centuries that this daring initiative has not been taken from her.... Her quick-eyed charity will be crying out to Our Lord, 'They have no wine.' They have no faith; they have no hope."

Mary must not be allowed to become a problem or a theological arguing point. We do have statements—statements that are binding on Catholics—about her, which have to do with the core of our faith; but even more important is her loving and loveable person.

"Some, not many, are uneasy about this homely way of writing about the mother of God. They think it too popular and extravagant, if not maudlin and sentimental. They would wrap her up in theology

and would proceed always by way of definition.
Now the definitions of the church are clear and accurate and necessary and the church is strict and dry in
her definitions that we may be wild and free in our
devotions, in order that the pilgrims of Fatima may
be able to wave their handkerchiefs to Our Lady. . ..
It is the saint and theologian Bernard who is most
warm and indeed popular in his writings about Our
Lady. It is this great saint who says you can never
say enough about her. . .. She is more than the sum
total of all the conclusions of the scholars and theologians. She is a woman alive. He that sees her forgets to live or die. And she—herself, as they call the
'Woman of the House' in Ireland—it was who said to
Bernadette at Lourdes 'I am the Immaculate Conception' as if she would say, I am not just two big words
that you cannot understand, Bernadette, I am the
woman of the house of God, the house where all men
are at home with God. And Bernadette was glorified
by the sight of her. Similarly in the Apocalypse it is
not a flaming scroll in the skies which St John shows
us but a great wonder in heaven: a woman clothed
with the sun crowned with the stars and the moon
beneath her feet."

Mary is the living proof that God deals with us
not in abstractions but on a person to person basis.
Places like Aylesford are needed to localize Mary's
presence: not as mere projections of human needs
nor of religious maternal dimensions, but as a gift of
God and a masterpiece of the Holy Spirit.

"The misunderstanding not difficult to understand is that she is in some way in competition with
her Son. How on earth could such a thing be when it
is her very purpose to give him to men? . . .. All true
devotion is the work of the Holy Spirit of God in us,
and in this way only she is the gift of God. Implicit
in the gift of faith is our relationship to and with Our
Lady through the power of the Holy Spirit. This
relationship grows into a strong and powerful love.
By grace you grow in the knowledge of her, you
know her, She *becomes* more vivid and alive *to you*.
You are given the power to answer her terrible love
of souls. This is true devotion because it flows *from*
grace. Let no one slander the Holy Spirit of God.

He knows what the world needs, what every child of Adam needs. Then how could we refuse such a gift of God, how could the world reject it? Incredibly, she was rejected at the reformation: at Aylesford her church pulled down and the stones scattered! You would restore it to her. Perhaps that is why she is so vividly alive to us when we see her at her work and sense her presence and know her power" (*Newsletter* n. 34, January, 1958).

Our Lady's presence makes itself obvious especially in moments of trial, when a deep, tender, lasting love of a mother is needed. It is then that she shows herself to be, in the expression of the liturgy, "Terrible as an army set in battle array." How many times Fr. Malachy reminded his readers and listeners of Our Lady's concrete and constant proofs of protection, even in the most dire of circumstances. Even though the early mystique of Aylesford precluded radios and television, world-shattering events like uprisings in Poland and Hungary (1956) were amply documented in the newsletters, from a faith-filled and hope-filled vantage point. Fr. Malachy on many an occasion cited the prayer Pope Pius XII had composed in honor of Our Lady of Mt. Carmel when he salutes her as the "Victorious Queen of all the battles of God."

"O Virgin of Carmel, patron of those who go down to the sea in ships or trust their lives every day to the uncertainties of wind and wave, from the bridge of the Barque of Peter, when we hear the roaring of the hurricane and see before our eyes the anger of the sea which threatens to engulf our Barque, we lift our eyes in sure trust to the Virgin of Carmel. *Respice stellam: voca Mariam.* Look for the morning star; call upon Mary. We implore her not to forsake us for Satan is ceaseless in his attacks and violence. Since the onslaught and fury of the forces of evil is always increasing, we mainly rely upon her most powerful help. Never shall we despair of victory while we put ourselves under her most powerful patronage" (*Newsletter* n. 39, November, 1959).

174

The Marian roots of Carmel—and so of Aylesford—are characterized by a predilection for man's
response to the glory, power and graciousness of God
and of his Mother: prayer. The purpose of Aylesford's apostolate was spelled out specifically: prayers
for 1) lapsed Catholics, 2) the renewal of a living
Spirit of faith and the apostolate of all Catholics, 3)
the restoration of Our Lady's Dowry (*Newsletter* n. 8,
February, 1952).

The prayerful atmosphere which drew many of
the early pilgrims to Aylesford was realized in many
different forms over the years. Monthly all-night vigils of prayer and penance were introduced not long
afterwards. The Rosary Way of the fifteen decades,
adorned with exquisite outdoor shrines in ceramic by
the Polish artist Adam Kossowski, became a staple of
Aylesford, showing concretely that the various pieties
of Our Lady like the scapular and the rosary are never in competition with each other. Specific intentions for prayers were never lacking, given the per-
sonalistic approach of Fr. Malachy. He marvelled at
the strength of the Polish faith in Our Lady, whom
King Casimir had proclaimed Queen of Poland 300
years previously:

"The devotion of the Poles to Our Lady is a truly
astonishing thing. It is a most noble work of grace
that marks them, everyone. It is the work of the
Holy Spirit. To them she is never the subject of argu-
ment or doubt. She *is*. She is Poland in a more than
legal or even mystical way. One of them said to me
the other day about praying to her or with her, 'We
pray, we thank, we accept.' A queen suffers with her
people. *She* knows 'it is a short pain and a long joy'
and 'they accept.' Our Lady of Częstochowa with
her scarred face is marked with the wounds of her
country's history. That face is said to be the truest
likeness of her. A copy is venerated here and this
year we are expecting many thousands of Poles to
come and find her. She has been called 'the hope of
the half-defeated'" (*Newsletter* n. 25, May, 1956).

"The feet of the maid who walked in Galilee and climbed to the hill country of Elizabeth will surely walk upon the head of the serpent of sin. Her patience is as terrible as the patience of God. Her triumph will surely come in all the lands where Satan has been given, mysteriously, to reign for a brief hour. The vision of St John in the Apocalypse: . . . 'a great sign in heaven—and behold a great red dragon. . . and the dragon stood before the woman who was ready to be delivered that he might devour her son.' Poland has drawn the attack of the red dragon because of the woman who is their queen" (*Newsletter* n. 27, September, 1956).

Rebuilding Mary's shrine

Although the faith risks everything on the reality of the world of the Spirit, still it values the anticipation of eternal glory in the concreteness of human life on this earthly pilgrimage. Fr. Malachy's deep sense of faith could not neglect the here and now, already reflecting the eternal and true. His appeals were stark and to the point. Restoring the spirit of a nation to the correct faith perspective had to be something for men, not angels. It had to be concrete and it had to cost, as anything of value does. The restoration of Mary's desecrated shrine was but one concrete way of localizing Mary's material presence of charity and mercy.

"For the rebuilding of this church and the means for it, I have no fear at all. It is the right thing to do. It is the beginning of the real restoration. Until that old sanctuary of Mary is covered again and in use there is a continuing sacrilege. It was given to God forever. His angels are guarding it still. We must recover it from the wild. These great foundations are crying out to us in every stone. I think of Chartres in the ages of the faith: how men, women and children gathered to build that great church in a corporate and loving act and gift to the mother of God. The priests were there, too, to offer masses, to encourage and to shrive, because no stone was laid by anyone in sin. Every age may not be an age of faith,

176

but every age is an age for faith. The new Aylesford will be built by faith. We have the same mighty faith which gave Chartres with its sculpture and its glass to Our Lady. This church will be in scale and it will surpass our expectations. She will add her gracious touch—as ever" (*Newsletter* n. 17, September, 1954).

In his numerous appeals for help. Fr. Malachy never apologized for being a mendicant, a beggar: he acknowledged this to be his vocation. The newsletters are full of practical ways in which people could help in the restoration of Mary's shrine. By the very fact of receiving the newsletter, they were members of Our Lady's Building Company, of which the mother of God is director and Fr. Malachy the secretary. How many times he found himself with an overdrawn account in the banks... and so his desperate appeals to Mary's friends and helpers. When Allington Castle was in danger of being lost and much pressure was put on him to sell, he appealed to his readers in horrified tones: "I was under great pressure to advise the General to dispose of Allington but this seemed a dreary and unnecessary course to me. It was nothing less than horrifying. It is in the same marvellous pattern of God's providence as The Friars. It seemed too strange that it should be of no further use. Also Our Lady was installed in the midst of its towers and battlements on Easter Sunday, 1951, which was also the feast of the Annunciation. She is the one who turns sorrow into joy, but not joy into sorrow. It would have been a great sorrow to take her and her Son from that strong place. That could not happen. ... We have established there the apostolate of 'The Open Door'" (*Newsletter* n. 37, June, 1958). His suggestion was that convert Catholics in particular contribute something "in thanksgiving for the faith." But in the interminable process of restoring both Aylesford and Allington, Fr. Malachy had recourse to every means at his disposal: raffle tickets, "stone certificates" by which people could buy individual ragstones to rebuild Mary's shrine, covenant agreements with the government tax office, and many more. At times he apologizes for one thing: not placing enough faith in Our Lady and being too cowed by threats from bank managers.

His constant theme is: give a small gift to Our Lady and she will never be outdone in generosity. He was particularly intrigued by the French proverb about Mary: "If you give her an egg, she will give you an ox," and he testified:

"That is Our Lady's way, and it is open to you to try it. If you give her a small thing, often a worthless thing, it will not go without its great reward. Years ago in Wales we had been praying for an alternative to our small college at Aberystwyth. We thought the answer was long delayed. In the end it came, not one great mansion but two, and you know how first she gave us back The Friars after the long centuries, and not only The Friars but Allington Castle, the castle of the despoiler; and does not the liturgy of Carmel say that the spirit of Carmel is a *double* spirit, and that those who wear her holy scapular are *double-clothed*. They shall not fear the cold or snow" (*Newsletter* n. 8, February, 1952).

He wants to impress on the people that Aylesford is theirs. They have contributed to its restoration in ways big and small. The Carmelites are mendicants and can own nothing; they are but administrators. The People of God are the only true proprietors of the renewed Marian sanctuary.

"You who are members of Our Lady's Building Company... *you* are the builders, not only by your alms but also by your prayers. I am sure that all of you, particularly those who have given their hands, will be forever blessed. From the beginning I have regarded an alms or help of any kind as giving you ownership with Our Lady and part in the apostolate of Aylesford. You have Our Lady's seal, the old Seal of the Prior of Aylesford, on your certificate as proof of this. This is not make-believe. It is more real than any ownership can be in this passing life. It goes with you into eternity. We mendicants can own nothing, so that what you give to Our Lady is yours. That is as it should be. Because of this Aylesford is not a place removed and out of this world. Rather is it the supernatural which guards the earthly sanities. Sanity is a word which surely must come from 'sanare,' which means 'to heal,' and Aylesford in this sense is a healing place." (*Newsletter* n. 56, September, 1961).

He goes on to a moving explanation of how he believes sanity is the normal thing for Catholics who want "to grow up under the shadow of the altar, mixing heaven and earth. . .. It is sanity to want to have community with others in the largest society that is, bound together in bonds of grace. For Our Lady's Building Company we must have vision. . .."

To the end Fr. Malachy refused to be content with what had been achieved. A seer, he saw constant possibilities. He wished to provide a place where Catholics could do what they should be best at: being families and a family. He wished to build a City of Mary around Allington Castle, giving especially larger Catholic families the possibility of a healthy and inviting atmosphere. His vision was not shared by many others, who could see only debts and additional headaches. But Fr. Malachy's basic, Catholic sense never left him. When his weekly Sunday sermons to thousands of pilgrims at afternoon devotions mentioned that the stones were shouting out to be put back in place in Mary's shrine (with a regularity that made it possible for novices to take their cue to light the charcoal for benediction which would soon ensue), he was merely living out his vocation as a Carmelite friar, who would lose credibility if he ceased preaching Our Lady.

"The Carmelite Order. . . exists to honor her [Mary]. It has never seen her otherwise than with her child in her arms, the woman of prophecy, the quickest and most homely summary of the Incarnation. The church is Christ to all men and Carmel's rule and life has long been recognized by the church, which means recognition by Christ Our Lord; so you see it is Our Lord who, having an order which fulfills his own commandment, honors his own mother. Also the vocation of Carmel is the vocation of the mother of God, to give Our Lord to men as graciously as ever she did. It is as simple as that and that is why there is so much about her in the Newsletters. If you wonder when you come to see Aylesford, when you read the haphazard chronicle of her doings, well she is the cause and sufficient explanation of it all. She is not an enigma. She is very clear and in all she does you cannot but see her touch" (*Newsletter* n. 24, January, 1956).

The scapular

The Newsletters in fact are full of people, happenings, situations in which these truths are verified. The larger part of the letters contain testimonies of how Mary does act as mother, does favors even without being asked, performs miracles. Aylesford was the scene of what many believe to be true healing miracles—a youngster, Pauline, being cured of leukemia—but even more importantly miracles of the spirit—the father of another leukemia victim, Peter Corless, being brought back to the faith even when the youngster subsequently died of the ravaging disease. Many times Fr. Malachy apologizes for not having enough space in the Newsletters to print at least a sampling of the numerous letters he received from grateful people who regained their health and sanity and holiness at Aylesford. A book could be written just with these testimonies. Because she is the mother of our Savior, the one who saves man, Fr. Malachy ceaselessly centers on Our Lady as heralding this victory of her Son and being its instrument. And this is the context in which he sees the scapular:

"The scapular is Our Lady's consecrating cloak or mantle, clothing us with grace, binding to us her great power. Through it she awakens in us our weak faith. I am firmly convinced that if all who wore her scapular made a simple act of courtesy to Our Lady every morning by kissing the scapular, saying to her even with a half-will 'Use me today,' that she would do so in the most unexpected and fruitful ways. Instead of your scapular being something you wear without meaning, it will become the vital link with Our Blessed Mother of Carmel and be an immense means of grace. We must bind unto ourselves her great power after the manner of St Patrick: 'I bind unto myself this day the power of God.' So too we may bind unto ourselves in this evil day the power of

Our Lady. It is the Holy Spirit of God who is giving
her to us in this age. She can give God back to the
world. That is her vocation until the end of time"
(*Newsletter* n. 28, November, 1956).

From its beginnings, the apostolate of Aylesford
was irrevocably linked to the scapular devotion.
Some of Fr. Malachy's most pointed complaints were
aimed at the neglect of the scapular. Not only did
one tradition claim that Aylesford was the venue of
Our Lady's appearance to St Simon Stock, but the
restorer of Aylesford exalted in the fact that of all the
Catholic pieties, the scapular was one which had its
origins in England. But even more importantly it
was a simple, humble, effective sign of the Catholic
faith. Its symbolism is rooted in the gesture of clothing, which is universal, traceable even to the Old Testament.

"The Scapular is the only great piety of the
church which had its origins in England and is cen-
tred on Aylesford and St Simon. It is the continuation of the most ancient gesture of consecration
known to man. Elijah, the founder of the order of
Carmel, consecrated his successor by throwing his
cloak over his shoulders. When Elijah was taken
away from the earth, his mantle fell upon Elisha
again to give him the spirit of Elijah. The hermits
came to Aylesford wearing a habit which symbolized
the mantle of the prophet. It was this mantle which
Our Lady touched on St Simon making it her sign of
salvation to all who would wear it. From that day to
this it is Our Lady's consecrating cloak thrown over
her children giving them her spirit and investing
them with power. Secular institutions still invest of-
ficials with authority, and 'invest' means 'to clothe,'
and the mantle or cloak of office is still used by them.
How much more full of meaning is the scapular!
Simply it is Our Lady putting her cloak over her children. Millions in every country and in all the generations since St Simon have been invested by Our Lady.
'I have spread my garment over you, I have spread
my garment over you, I have sworn a pact with you'"
(*Newsletter* n. 9, July, 1952).

The scapular devotion is not pabulum for those who are too simple for the more substantial food of the faith. Fr. Malachy sees it as intimately linked with the whole spirituality of Carmel. It is the exterior binding of oneself to a life of prayer and sacrifice that the Carmelite rationale presupposes, and precisely because it is linked intrinsically with Our Lady:

"We may say that the heritage of our Blessed Lady of Mt Carmel is the gift of contemplation and prayer which issues in zeal for souls. The same Holy Spirit who sanctified Elijah wrought greater mysteries in the soul of Mary, in whom all his gifts came to perfection. Uniquely in her soul were the gifts of knowledge and wisdom. 'The God before whom I stand' was always present to the spirit of Elijah, but how much more to Mary. She was the mother of the Word Incarnate, who was never separated from him by sin. He lived in her and she lived in his presence always. We are honoring the choice and work of the Holy Spirit when we honor her. She is his gift to us as she was the gift to St John given from the cross. . ..
"It is not easy for those without the faith to understand Our Lady, precisely because she is a gift of God. We give a natural love to our parents, but the love we give to Mary must be supernatural, and we cannot love her at all in this way unless the power to do so is created in us by the Spirit of God. . .. We must pray that this gift be given to all men. . ..

"To a world half way to dissolution she has been proclaimed glorious and triumphant—star-crowned, clothed with the sun, the moon beneath her feet. We need her power and the scapular is the great means by which she gives it without measure. . .. The scapular binds us unto all the power of Our Lady—power in temptation, power in the apostolate, power over the souls of men for their healing" (*Leaflet* for the 7th Centenary Year of the Scapular, 1951).

No official prayer formula is attached to the scapular devotion. Its fundamental symbolism is the gesture of clothing a person. However, Fr. Malachy proposed a simple formula which would capture a whole spiritual approach. He incessantly preached the "Use me today" apostolate. Leave oneself in the hands of Our Lady day by day, and in her motherly charity she will find any number of ways to make use of one's talents, graces and presence. The Newsletters are full of examples of how Our Lady uses others for most unexpected purposes.

"If every morning you kissed her scapular, saying to her, 'Use me today,' she would. Put it in the center of your will and she will use you as 'a living tool of God.' This is very simple. Even children will understand it and practise it. What wonderful apostles children can be. They are the world's greatest realists. If all the Catholic schools and particularly the convents would take it up and teach the children in this way and lead them, we would see Our Lady working wonders of conversion in all. There would be a great awakening. It is simple as that" (*Newsletter* n. 27, September, 1956).

Children and tertiaries

There is no dearth of instances in which children were responsible for bringing their parents and elders back to the faith. Fr. Malachy found children enthralled when he described the meaning of the scapular. He saw the affluence of children at Aylesford in school groups and especially on the annual Childrens' Day, led by the bishop himself, as signs from Our Lady that the new generation of Catholics would be a generation convinced of Our Lady's role and message. In his usual catholic vision he notes:

"I am more and more convinced that the children are the apostles to be used by the blessed mother of God in this haggard and despairing age. Two years ago the Marist Sisters from Fulham brought their school here to give a recital of psalms and passages from the New Testament. It was most moving and unforgettable. At Craiglochart Sacred Heart Convent near Edinburgh I heard a Recital of the Passion done by the whole school. The Passion was illustrated by colored slides. There was a power of innocence and impudence in the children's voices that was more terribly moving than any adult performance. It was quite shattering. Children never

fail nor miss. They can't. They have baptismal innocence; hence their power over the human heart."

Another school group from Annecy Convent at
Seaford, at the end of a full day at Aylesford, went in
procession to the Lady Altar and very simply and
informally made an act of consecration and this is
what they said to Our Lady:

"We are here today at Aylesford to honor you as
Our Lady of the Scapular, and to give you this small
offering towards the new church to be built here in
your honor. . .. We choose you this day as our queen,
for our mother you already are, and we consecrate to
you all our future lives, that we may each of us fulfill
God's will. . .. All of us here are hoping and praying
that, one day in the not too far distant future, Aylesford will be to England what Lourdes is to France—
the center of a great devotion to you and the place
which will be recognized as your special 'home' in
this our country, the *Dowry of Mary*" (*Newsletter*
n. 36, April, 1958).

The connection between Lourdes, Fatima and Aylesford was a favorite topic of Fr. Malachy. He often
recalled that Our Lady appeared to Bernadette for
the last time as Our Lady of Mt Carmel (a fact corro-
borated by an aunt of the saint), and it was the time
Bernadette was so overwhelmed by the beauty of Our
Lady that no statue or image could ever satisfy her.
And Sr. Lucy, the seer at Fatima, assured Fr. Malachy
and especially his brother, the Prior General Kilian
Lynch, that the message of Fatima was intimately
linked with devotion to Our Lady of Mt Carmel.
What encouragement, then, when Fr. Malachy during
a semiprivate audience with Pope Pius XII could report: "He spoke to me most encouragingly of Aylesford and blessed again all our endeavors! He has giv-
en to Aylesford indulgences and privileges granted to
Lourdes and Fatima, which is more than we dared to
ask" (*Newsletter* n. 14, January, 1954).

Another area of constant commitment by Fr.
Malachy was the Third Order, which received such
an impetus from the Aylesford mystique, an impetus
which has made it one of the strongest groups in the

Carmelite order to day. He was as direct and challenging as ever:

"A tertiary belongs to the intimate family of Our Lady. It is not an organization though it is an organism as a family is. You would be surprised if I asked you 'what are the rules of your family?'... A rule by itself can create an organization but only divine charity can create the spirit of the family of Carmel. If you begin by reading the rule you will probably be put off.

"If you are baptized and living in the grace of God, the Holy Spirit of God is working in you and through you but not without you.... The desire to belong to the family of Our Lady comes from the Holy Spirit.... It is a grace and a vocation, and if you are bound in kinship with Our Lady, it is a very special grace.

"Devotion has been defined as 'love in flames.' Devotion to Our Lady, if it is true—that is, if it is from the Holy Spirit—must be a flaming thing. Our Lady is flaming with his breath. She is 'terrible as an army set in battle array,' terrible in the power of her grace. It follows that her impact through us, her family, on the world must be one of flaming love. 'Put me as a seal upon thy arm for love is stronger than death....' It is not the purpose of the Third Order to make you a religious in the world. It is the Third Order *Secular*. You remember how Our Lady after the Word was made Flesh went in *haste* to the hill country to do an act of kindness, and how the Baptist was sanctified through her coming to Elizabeth.... The grace of God will be urging *you* as it urged her *to do something*.... The Family of Our Lady, with Our Lady and Aylesford, could bring England back to the faith. Actually our tertiaries are beginning to astound us by their devotion and zeal" (*Newsletter* n. 25, May, 1956).

Final prayer

A catholic vision is eclectic by nature. Fr. Malachy in his ardent zeal could not but see grace provided by God's mother everywhere—even from unlikely persons and places. He never tired of passing on to his readers and listeners whatever had been offered to him as a grace. Particularly when it had to do with Our Lady, he loved to share the best with others. Favors, interventions, prayers: the newsletters are full of the mercies of the Lord at the hands of Our Lady. Typical is a prayer to Our Lady of Mercy, written in a Siberian prison camp by four Lithuanian nuns—"in banishment yet living in the whole world of God. Millions could envy them" (*Newsletter* n. 48, April, 1960):

> We have gone astray. We are weary and cold.
> Mother of mercy, once again you have not left us alone in the days of sorrow and affliction.
> Again from heaven you descended in the brightness of refulgent light to visit our blood-stained land.
>
> Mother, to whom shall we flee, to whom shall we appeal in abandonment, afflictions and distress?
>
> Cast your glance, O Mother, at our hearts, bruised by sorrow and longing; at our lips, blue from hunger and cold.
> Bring us back to the land that heaven itself has given us; to the land adorned with churches and wayside crosses;
> To the land you have loved from the very beginning.
> Allow us to see again the pictures and shrines abounding in grace.
> Permit us to sing again the hymns of gratitude and love to merciful Jesus and to you, O Mother of Pity,
> To you who have promised the remission of all transgressions.

10

THE PERFECT DISCIPLE OF HER SON

Marian devotion according to
Fr. Kilian Lynch, O. Carm. (1902-1985)

The Carmelite order has had its share of saintly priors general: St Simon Stock, Bl John Soreth, Bl Baptist of Mantua. Besides the latter two, it has had many others who worked strenuously for reform and renewal: names such as Nicholas Audet and John Baptist Rossi (Rubeo) immediately come to mind. It has had its prophetic figures like Nicholas of Gaul who with his *Fiery Arrow* cried out an unpopular but empassioned call for a return to the origins. Fr. Kilian Lynch (1902-1985), prior general during the critical post-World War II years, will long be remembered for his commitment to the whole order. A man willing to take risks with both personnel and foundations, he helped the order to concretize its identity in many quarters.

To grasp the spirit of Fr. Kilian's stewardship, there is hardly a surer guide than his vision of Mary in Carmel. The person who judged him too distant and reserved, needed only hear him preach on a Sunday afternoon at the Marian shrine in Aylesford to experience the warmth and depth of his spirit. Whoever deemed him too authoritarian, needed only a deeper acquaintance with him to realize that what he wrote about Mary's humility and obedience and simplicity was the mirror of his own spiritual stance. Anyone who felt he was too unfeeling in his dealings with others, could have discovered the truth in his unabashedly tender devotion towards the mother and beauty of Carmel.

Fr. Kilian's brother, Fr. Malachy, had proclaimed in his sermons: "The saints are alive!" The younger Fr. Kilian applied this in the very first place to Our Lady. Mary was not a beautiful image, she was not the ideal of Christian womanhood, she was not a symbol of the heights to which mankind is invited. Mary is a living person, anticipating even in body the glory that is reserved for others at the final resurrection. In season and out, Fr. Kilian shared this deepest of convictions: Christ Jesus left us Mary as our mother with his dying breath. She is the last of his immense treasury of gifts. Mary, being mother, never deludes, never takes advantage of, never abandons, never forgets.

"A mother's love is the most practical thing in existence. It is never satisfied with words, but is always pouring itself out on someone. Mother-love is also capable of the greatest sacrifices; it is born in suffering and time serves only to increase its generosity and service. If this is true of the mother-love we have all experienced, what must be said of the love of her who became the Mother of Sorrows and the Queen of Martyrs for love of us? When we see her with the sword of Simeon plunged deeply into her heart, how can we ever doubt that her love for mankind is as practical as that of her Divine Son?

"Since she became the mother of men, she has never ceased to show herself a mother to all who have gone to her for help. He who is mighty has done great things to her; and she in turn, who is mighty through the power of her divine motherhood, has done great things for those who have sought her intercession. She has been the cause of our joy and will continue so to the end of time. When the very existence of her order was in danger, St Simon could think of no one more powerful than the mother he had always loved with the tenderest affection. She had given so many proofs of her love in the past that he knew she would not send him away empty-handed. ... To St Simon and to all Carmelites she repeats the words of Isaias: 'For a small moment I have forsaken thee, but with great mercies I will gather thee. ... For the mountains shall be moved and the hills shall tremble, but my mercy shall not depart from thee, and the covenant of my peace shall not be moved: said the Lord that hath mercy on thee. O poor little one, tossed with tempest, without all comfort, behold I will lay thy stones in order. ... And thou shalt be founded in justice: depart far from oppression for thou shalt not fear; and from terror for it shall not come near thee' (Is 54: 7, 14)" (*Mary's Gift to Carmel*, Aylesford, 1955, p. 13-14).

Fr. Kilian, with an outstanding doctorate from the Gregorian University, cited the words of the prophet Isaias in an accommodated sense, of course. But for him the scriptures were encounters not only with God's loving and saving dealings with men, but also revelations of God's own nature. Mary was so filled with God that she reverberated the same traits which scripture applied to God. Fr. Kilian explains:

"Our Lady is the 'Virgin Most Faithful:' she will keep her promise and, since she is heard because of the great reverence due to her as mother, her Son is bound to hear the prayers which She pours forth in our behalf. Her love for us is invincible for it was cradled in the Sacred Heart of her Son. It is stronger than death itself, and the waters of contradiction and ingratitude can never extinguish it. She knows us better than we know ourselves. She sees us tossed, without any comfort, on the billows of life, and in her great and tender mercy, she has stooped down to bring us peace. ..." (*Ibid.*)

Until the end, Fr. Kilian kept studying, reflecting, reading, meditating. A more appreciated gift could not be given him than a recent book, particularly about the faith. He was delighted with literature on Our Lady, of which he never had enough. His well-rounded appreciation of Our Lady enabled him to combine keen theological precision with the affective tonality which cannot be long absent from Carmelite spiritual writing. His sermons on Our Lady reflected this gift of solid orthodoxy coupled with warm, filial devotion. The result was a solid rooting of Marian devotion in the outstanding realities of Christian faith: in Christ's redemption, in the sacramental system, in the sign of predestination, in the commun-

189

ion of saints, in man's cooperation in his own redemption.

"Those who shelter their weakness in the motherly heart of the mother of our redemption 'shall draw salvation from the Lord.' The heart, into which the tenderest mother-love drew all the agony of the passion and death of our Redeemer, is a tower of strength for the weak. She is our life, our sweetness and our hope; in her we find the beauty of eternal life. To whom shall we go for an assurance of salvation if not to her who, in order to save us, offered both her Only-Begotten and herself to the cruel death of the cross. 'It is not near the cross,' says St Bernard, 'that Mary is found, but on it, nailed to its beams as Jesus is.' She loves us with the same love she has for her Firstborn and the double edged sword that pierced his heart opened wide her heart that it might be the refuge of sinners to the end of time and the gate of heaven for those who hope in her. Her love embraces every child of Adam and there is no power that will snatch a soul from her protecting love. She was made to be the mother of mercy, and her mission on earth and in heaven is not to judge but to show mercy and to open her pierced heart wider and wider to the poor banished children of Eve who fly to her for help. The eternal Father has made her 'full of grace' that her love might bestow it where justice would deny it. As St Bernard says: 'She is impetuous in mercy, she is resistless in mercy. The duration of her mercy is unto the end of the sinner's life. The broadness of her mercy is unto the limits of the earth. The height of her mercy is unto heaven. The depth of her mercy is unto the lowest abyss of sin or sorrow. She is always merciful. She is only merciful. She is our mother of mercy.'"

Mary's mercy is not in contrast with God's: it is a share in his penchant to be merciful and to spare; only hers is expressed in a motherly tonality. "If it is the property of God to be merciful and to spare, surely it is also the very nature of the mother of mercy to pour forth her mercy even where there are no merits. The quality of her mercy is never strained; and the devil, into whose heart a ray of hope can never shine,

190

is the only one excluded from her love. She sees in every soul, even in that of the most wretched, the image of her Son and, if necessary, she would become again the Queen of Martyrs to save the least of her children" (*Mary's Gift*, p. 30-31).

Teaching of the church

With his broad theological vision, Fr. Kilian exulted in Vatican II's teaching on Our Lady. Those who were enthused by his conferences, sermons, retreats on Our Lady will not forget how he often based his own remarks on the teachings of the council. Although firmly rooted in the tradition of the church and of his beloved Carmel, he was delighted by the wholesome teaching on Our Lady which Vatican II provided. He firmly believed that the Holy Spirit was behind the conciliar teaching: "Some are of the opinion that the council downgraded Our Lady. Nothing could be further from the truth. No council of the church ever devoted more time and space to her. It did correct certain exaggerations that had crept in by putting her back in the context of Christ and his church. What emerged was a magnificent image of her. She is the spotless image of all the church desires and hopes to be" (*Mary: Our Inspiration*, in *Carmel in the World* 17 [1978], p. 8).

He meditated long and often, and shared with others the council's richest insights on Mary. Sometimes he quoted them verbatim; at other times he wove the council's thought into his own expressions in an inextricable way. "The Constitution on the Church presents her as the model of all virtues: 'while in the most holy virgin the church has already reached that perfection whereby she exists without spot or wrinkle, the followers of Christ still strive to increase in holiness by conquering sin. And so they turn their eyes to Mary who shines forth to the whole community of the elect as the model of virtues. She is the living mirror of every virtue; the living Gospel of Christ. St Paul calls the glorious Gospel the image of God whose rays reach us through it. Mary reflects those glorious rays and mediates them to us. After

Christ she is the most perfect, human reflection of the holiness of God himself'" (*Ibid.*, p. 8-9).

The council did not wish to base its presentation of Mary on some "fruitless and passing emotion." It "reminds us that true devotion to her 'proceeds from true faith by which we are led to know the excellence of the mother of God and are moved to a filial love towards our mother and to the imitation of her virtues' (*Lumen gentium*, 67)" (*Ibid.*, p. 10-11). Mary is now alive and active for us. "Like her son she lives in heaven to intercede for us and as the council states, 'the Son whom she brought forth is he whom God placed as the firstborn among many brethren, namely, the faithful. She cooperates in their birth and development with a maternal love (*Lumen gentium*, 64).' Like Christ she came into the world to serve, not to be served and she passed along doing good to all" (*Ibid.*, p. 13-14).

A thoroughly catholic Carmelite, Fr. Kilian could not but find grace in the teaching of the popes. Enthusiastically he urged members of the order to celebrate the Marian Year of 1954. Pope Pius XII had asked religious superiors to guide their religious families to a zealous and fervent observance of the "year" honoring Our Lady. Fr. Kilian penned a letter to his brothers in which he called on Carmelites to live up to their "totally Marian" tonality (cf. *The Sword* 17 [1954], p. 113).

Those close to Fr. Kilian will remember with what joyful gratitude he reacted to Pope Paul VI's teaching on Our Lady at the close of the third session of the Vatican Council. The key to authentic Marian devotion, Fr. Kilian kept repeating, was the pope's title: "perfect disciple of her Son." Mary is understood best and honored most when she is seen to be the human person who best exemplified all that her Son did and taught. Her role is wholly in relationship to her Son, from whom, as disciple, she receives all that we admire and love in her. Catholics make no apology for their warm and intense Marian devotion because they are merely admiring the concrete embodiment of Jesus' beatitudes, the summary of Christ's revolutionary value system. "In his address for the closing of the third session of the council, Pope Paul declared her the 'Mother of the Church' and reminded us how in her earthly life she realized the perfect image of the disciple of Christ, reflecting every virtue and incarnating the evangelical virtues proclaimed by Christ. Therefore, in her, the entire church, in its incomparable variety of life and work, attains the most authentic form of the perfect imitation of Christ'" (*Mary: Our Inspiration*, p. 9).

Because of his broad overview of Carmel's traditional Marian devotion, Fr. Kilian never tired of praising the fresh approach of Pope Paul VI's letter, *Marialis cultus*, which could renew the order's Marian charism if taken seriously. Resolutely anchored in the belief that the Holy Spirit guides the church today as in the past, Fr. Kilian accepted contemporary approaches to Marian devotion with enthusiasm and thanksgiving; he could not fail to see the continuity with what Carmel had experienced in the past. His deep knowledge allowed him to critique aberrant tendencies, but never prevented him from affirming the positive contribution that current Marian thinking offered. "The image of Mary was deep in the heart of the church from the beginning. Like some of the sacraments, she was a living reality long before she was the subject of any dogma. Gradually she emerged from the shadows not only as the guardian of true doctrine but as the pattern of Christian living. 'The faithful at a very early age began to look to Mary and to imitate her by making their lives an act of worship of God and their worship a commitment of their lives' (*Marialis cultus*, 21)" (*Mary: Our Inspiration*, p. 7).

Enriched by others

A man deeply imbued with the spirit of Carmel, Fr. Kilian embodied the humble friar. Not only was he dedicated to manual work even of the most menial kind to the end of his days, not only did he accept secondary roles and rejection of favorite projects with detachment, but in his intellectual integrity, he preferred to express his own convictions and experi-

193

ences in the words of others. When he spoke on spiritual matters, and especially on Our Lady, he would hardly express a new thought without citing an author who had verbalized the same experience in effective, incisive fashion. The result was a rich mosaic of texts about the Blessed Mother. These texts were woven together by a keen and brilliant mind.

At times confreres pressed Fr. Kilian to express his opinion in his own terms. He found this difficult: he was too used to finding grace in the expressions of others. The convinced and fervent way in which he cited others proved that he was not indulging in an academic exercise or falling back on others for lack of personal experience, but rather that in his humility, he found it most congenial to borrow from the inexhaustible treasury of Marian writings in the church. One had only to hear how he preached on Our Lady to realize that while the words belonged to others, the experience was his.

Of Carmelite authors, Arnold Bostius is most frequently cited by Fr. Kilian, who probably identified with the cultural depth of the Belgian humanist coupled with the affective tonality of his Marian writings. "As Bostius says: 'The prayer of Mary is founded on justice; the Son can refuse nothing to his mother. She will come to your aid by showing your Judge, who is her Son, her bosom. She will ask for you in the name of her own merits with such insistence that Jesus will show his side and his wounds to the Father and you will not be rejected when so many proofs of love will speak in your favor'" (*Mary's Gift*, p. 24). Again, in the context of the life of prayer, Fr. Kilian cites Bostius' fervid exhortation: "May her loving memory accompany you both in the daytime and in the night, during your actions, your work and your conversation, in the midst of your joys, in your sorrows and in your rest. May she always occupy the first place in your minds" (*Mother of the Contemplative Life*, in *Commentarium pro Tertio Ordine Carmelitano* [1960], n. 4, p. 22).

The fathers of the church often appear in Fr. Kilian's talks, particularly as he grounds Marian devotion on the solid witness of Christianity's best. Sts

Ambrose and Augustine and others are summed up by St John Damascene: "Nothing can celebrate her worthily, neither the language of men nor the intelligence of angels however sublime it may be; for it is in her and through her that the glory of the Lord has been given to our mortal sight" (*Mary: Our Inspiration*, p. 7).

The saints, who themselves had much of God in them, felt a special kinship with her who was "full of grace." Not surprisingly they are able to identify with Mary and recognized how authentic a human person she truly was because she allowed God to have his way with her. One of Fr. Kilian's favorites was—as might be expected—"St Bernard, the golden voice of the Middle Ages: 'with justice are the eyes of all creatures bent upon you, for in you and through you and out of you the loving hand of the Most High has newly created everything he created.' He salutes her: 'She is the peerless and lovely star lifted high above the vast expanse of the world's ocean, her merits a cause of wonderment and her example our enlightenment'" (*Mary: Our Inspiration*, p. 7).

He often returned to St Bernard's poignant description of the mother of mercy, as we saw above. Other saintly apostles of Marian devotion appear in Fr. Kilian's talks and articles. St Louis Grignion de Mortfort whose doctrine had been experienced in Carmel with only slightly different nuances had much to offer. "How true the words of Louis de Montfort: 'be persuaded that the more you look at Mary the more perfectly will you find Jesus Christ'" (*Mary: Our Inspiration*, p. 11). Especially when describing Carmelite devotion as consecration, Fr. Lynch finds much affinity with St Louis. Until the end of his life he repeated one of the saint's favorite themes: far from distracting from Christ, Mary is our surest gateway to him and to his kingdom. "If St Louis Grignion de Montfort were alive today he would repeat with ever greater emphasis his own words: 'God wishes that Mary be at present more known, more loved, more honored than she has ever been. If Our Lord is not known as he ought to be it is because Mary is still unknown. It is she who brought the Savior into the world the first time; a second time, in the modern age, she will give her Son to the world. . ... Being the way by which Jesus Christ came to us the first time, she will also be the way he will come the second time, though not in the same manner'" (*Mary's Gift*, p. 64).

Fr. Lynch comments: "The reformers forgot the lesson of history; namely, that Mary is the recapitulation of the whole body of Christian doctrine, the key to Christian art, the way to life, and that when she is rejected Christ goes with her. The Lord is with her still and refuses to be separated from her. There is no power on earth or under the earth that can snatch him from her arms or deprive her of her place and function in the economy of human redemption. He is, as St Louis Grignion de Monfort says, 'always and everywhere the fruit of Mary, and Mary is everywhere the veritable tree that bears the fruit of life and the true mother who produces it.' If, therefore, we want the light of his faith in our minds, the fire of his love in our hearts, his divine grace in our souls, and his spirit in our social organism, we must find Mary, his mother, and implore her to bear him again for us" (*Mary's Gift*, p. 61).

Often in describing Carmelite devotion, especially the scapular, Fr. Kilian invoked St Alphonsus Liguori's dictum: "It is impossible that a servant of Mary be damned, provided he serves her faithfully and commends himself to her maternal protection" (*Ibid.*, p. 32). But good theologian that he was, Fr. Lynch invariably adds the saint's explanation: "When we declare that it is impossible for a servant of Mary to be lost, we do not mean those who, because of their devotion to Mary, think themselves warranted to sin freely. We state that these reckless people, because of their presumption, deserve to be treated with rigor and not with kindness. We speak here of servants of Mary who, to the fidelity with which they honor and invoke her, join the desire to amend their lives. I hold it morally impossible that these be lost" (*Ibid.*, p. 33).

The multifaceted splendor of beauty, truth and goodness are most authentically mirrored in Mary. Various writers have captured the dimensions of her

196

witness. Fr. Kilian, voracious reader and expert assimilator, neglected no expression of Mary's presence and role in favor of mankind.

"In a recent work, *Myth and Cult of the Virgin Mary*, Marina Warner reaches the following conclusion: ' The Virgin Mary has inspired some of the loftiest architecture, some of the most moving poetry, some of the most beautiful paintings in the world. She has filled men and women with deep joy and fervent trust; she has been an image of the ideal that has entranced and stirred men and women to the noblest emotions of love and pity and awe...'" (*Mary: Our Inspiration*, p. 5).

"Monsignor Ronald Knox, a convert... tells us that his devotion to Mary was a romance he could not express in words. One might quote him for our age. 'As a traveller, shading his eyes as he contemplates some long vista of scenery, searches about for some human figure that will give him the scale of those distant surroundings, so we with dazzled eyes looking Godwards identify one purely human figure close to the throne of God. One ship had rounded the headland, one destiny is achieved, one human perfection exists. As we see God clearer, we see God greater through this masterpiece of his dealings with mankind'" (*Ibid.*, p. 7-8).

"How true to history are the words of the great Ozanam: 'O Mary, you are beautiful and gracious since the mere thought of you has made beauty and grace descend into the works of man.' He had in mind the cathedrals of Europe, but who could measure the living beauty she has inspired in men and women down the centuries?" (*Ibid.*, p. 8).

"Allen Temko, a protestant historian, wrote: 'In the great moment of the Middle Ages Mary lifted up and civilized the entire West, and as long as the Western world responded to her she made it beautiful...'" (p. 8).

"She is the spotless image of all the church desires and hopes to be. As Paul Claudel wrote: 'While Christ's blood flowed on the cross, the heart of the church beat in the single heart of Mary. She was the primal cell of the church born from the side of Christ; and when the church, the bride of Christ, is purified from every stain and wrinkle, she will be what Mary is now'" (p. 8).

"As Schillebeeckx wrote: 'The entire life of the church throughout her history is nothing more or less than a growth, an ascent towards the image of the mother of God'" (*Ibid.*)

"'When Christ,' writes Schillebeeckx, 'in the Sermon on the Mount called the poor blessed he did not have any abstract ideal in mind. He had always experienced the concrete realization of this ideal in the home of Nazareth in the persons of Mary and Joseph. The eight Beatitudes, inspired by the Holy Spirit, are not unattainable Christian ideals; they constitute Christ's canonization of his mother and of all who live according to her example'" (p. 9).

"The beauty of Christ's life is reflected in her in the lovely setting of a tender motherly love. 'One can resist self-love, one can resist force, but who can resist Beauty holding Innocence in her arms?' (Paul Claudel)" (p. 11).

"In his work on Chaucer, G. K. Chesterton quotes a literary critic who was of the opinion that the great poet 'passed through a period of intense devotion more especially towards the Virgin Mary.' Chesterton comments: 'I do not understand why Chaucer must have "passed through" this fit of devotion as if he had Mariolatry like the measles. Even an amateur who has encountered this malady may be allowed to testify that it usually does not visit its victim for a brief period: it is generally chronic and (in some cases, I have known) quite incurable'" (p. 14).

"The true Carmelite will subscribe wholeheartedly to what Thomas Merton writes: 'Without her the knowledge of Christ is only speculation. But in her it becomes experience, because all the humility and poverty without which Christ cannot be known belong to her. Her sanctity is the silence in which alone Christ can be heard and the voice of God becomes an experience in us through her contemplation. The emptiness, interior solitude and peace without which we cannot be filled with God belong to her alone. If we ever manage to empty ourselves of the noise of the world and of our passions, it is because she has come close to us and given us a share in her sanctity and her hiddenness'" (*Mother of Contemplative Life*, p. 12).

Carmelite devotion to Our Lady

Fr. Kilian's portrait of Mary was obviously painted on an enormous canvas. It definitely adopted the approach of his friend, Fr. Xiberta. The maximalist approach, in contemplating Mary, asks a simple question: how can a person not tell *all* the marvels of God's grace in her? Yet, Fr. Kilian's characteristic—and gift—was his ability to build the Marian devotion of his beloved Carmel on the solid foundations of his broad Marian knowledge and affection. His vast erudition was put at the service of his religious family's heritage. Although he was often disappointed by Carmel's shortcomings, he never gave in to self-pity or negative criticism or leaving aside Carmelite subjects for more congenial, generic ones. His love for Carmel was a "constant" till his last breath. Carmel's mother and beauty could bot be separated from the wholesome vision he inculcated. People may have queried and even criticized his acquisition of English castles for Carmel; Fr. Lynch's vision extended beyond walls and mortar to sanctuaries where Carmel might do what it should be best at: making authentic Marian devotion available to God's people.

There have been some who have not been impressed by Fr. Kilian's Marian mystique. The key to understanding his wholehearted endorsement of Carmelite Marian devotion is simple: Mary is not an ideal for Carmel, she is presence. She is not the exemplar of virtue as much as the part of Carmel which has reached the summit of the Mount which is Christ himself. Fr. Kilian's most basic assumption was that Our Lady of Mt. Carmel is the living and loving person who has been part of Carmel's makeup since its beginnings. Any way in which this truth can be stressed and illustrated is good, and Fr. Lynch used

199

it. His manifold interests could be summed up by presenting Our Lady of Mt. Carmel as 'Queen of Prophets,' as the mother of the contemplative life and as the lady of the scapular.

'Queen of Prophets'

Following a venerable tradition, recently updated, Fr. Lynch stressed that Carmel, to be authentic, must be prophetic. Beginning with the ideal founder, the prophet Elijah, Carmel has at its best moments and in its outstanding proponents served zealously and clearly as the mouthpiece of God, particularly at moments when the Lord needed chosen instruments to shake men from their ungodly ways.

Remembering that Mary in her litany is hailed 'Queen of Prophets,' Fr. Kilian sees the connection with the prophets of old: "Like Jeremiah she felt inadequate to the call of God but looked on her lowliness, and the most humble of his creatures became the greatest of his prophets. Hosea is said to be the prophet of God's love. For him God was the husband of Israel, and the covenant relationship was basically one of love. Mary's entire life from her immaculate conception to her coronation in heaven is a revelation in flesh and blood of God's tender love. And all he has done for her bears witness to his loving plan for us. Isaiah is the prophet of the holiness of God. Mary stands next to her Son as the revelation of the fulness of grace and holiness. Her soul was the spotless image of God seeking its source: holy is his Name. It was the profound sense of the holiness of God that made her holy" (*Prophets, their Queen and Carmel*, in *Carmel in the World* 13 [1975], p. 100-101). Mary's *Magnificat* expresses some of the deepest insights of prophets such as Ezechiel and Amos. While exulting in the wideness of God's mercy towards those who repent, there are ominous words of prophecy for the rich who oppress the poor and crush the needy.

Mary the prophetess did not come from the class in power. She "belonged to the remnant of the poor, and the life she lived in Nazareth with Joseph and

200

Jesus was a proclamation for all time of the blessedness of the poor." It was Mary's reaction to the Word of God that most cogently argues for her prophetic charism. "The prophets devoured the word of God and it became a living part of them. It burned like a fire in the heart of Jeremiah and, like every fire, it had to blaze out. The fathers tell us that Mary conceived the Word in her heart before she conceived him in her womb. Her heart was the home of the Word of God before she became his living tabernacle. She was more blessed in how she heard and kept the word than she was in giving birth to the Son of God. Her soul was so perfectly attuned to the word that the fathers compare her to the lyre played upon by the Holy Spirit. The Holy Spirit had all his way with her" (*Ibid.*, p. 101-102).

All her life she pondered the wondrous deeds surrounding her Son. The word shared with her about Jesus she kept in her heart; every time we meet her in the scriptures we find her practicing that same word. "The generations to come would look upon her and find in her the perfect disciple, the most authentic interpretation of the Gospel. She is a living mirror in which we may contemplate Christ. She mediates him to us and reflects him. It was with her in mind that John called the church 'a woman clothed with the sun with the moon under her feet'" (*Ibid.*, p. 102).

Fr. Kilian links Carmel's prophetic call with its Marian dimension. "For the prophet of Carmel the word of God was not just something to reflect upon in silence and solitude but a torch to burn evil out of the hearts of men. And for Mary, humble handmaid, it was a command to rise up and serve; it meant action. The contemplative background of the order compels us to ponder the word of God in our hearts and to proclaim it in season and out of season by word and example. The strong food of the word should build us up into men and women for others, make us light where there is darkness and a leaven in the mass of today" (*Ibid.*, p. 105).

Mary's matchless place in Carmel derives from her reflective attitude even while she was acting as a primary protagonist in the work of the redemption of the world. Pope Paul VI has immortalized this trait of Our Lady in his vibrant *Marialis cultus*. Fr. Kilian had intuited the reflective aspect of Our Lady decades before. He found confirmation of his personal belief in the cultured French author Jean Guitton: "If I were asked what new attribute I should like to see paid to the Blessed Virgin, it would be this: Virgin reflective, Virgin meditating history, Virgin of thought" (cited in *Mother of contemplative life*, p. 19).

Mary's *Magnificat* vibrates with biblical imagery as she expresses the solid points of her religious reflection. "As Our lady stood on the threshhold of her cousin's home and lifted her eyes to heaven to magnify the Lord and rejoice in God her Savior, she teaches all her sons and daughters in Carmel the primary purpose of their vocation, which is to enter with her into unceasing, loving conversation with God by meditating on his law day and night. If there is one thing more than another which she wants us to learn from her example, it is contemplation."

This contemplative spirit is not a spirit of clarity and vision, but of faith. If authentic, it entails growth and deepening. Mary passed on this path. "It is a mistake to think that from the beginning Our Lady knew all God's designs in her regard. The divine plan unfolded itself gradually to her in the solitude and silence of her contemplation. 'In her mind,' writes Guitton, 'as in that of everyone of us, God respected the law of progress which is the law of every creature in time, and the free passage from dim consciousness to exact awareness, the ordinary mode of human cognition'" (*Ibid.*) Fr. Kilian adds: "From her knowledge of the Old Testament she knew the slowness of God's ways and, in the silence and recollection of her soul, she sought to know the divine will."

One of Fr. Lynch's favorite authors, Cardinal Newman, helps him describe the virgin's outstanding faith, a result of her humble reflection on God's dealings with his chosen ones. "Her answer, 'Be it done to me according to your word,' reveals the reflective mind and gives us a glimpse into the spiritual depths of her soul. Here, even before the Word was made flesh within her, she is, as Newman says, 'the pattern of our faith;' Mary is our pattern of faith, both in the reception and in the study of divine truth. She does not think it enough to accept, she dwells upon it; not enough to possess, she uses it; not enough to assent, she develops it; not enough to submit her reason, she reasons upon it; not indeed reasoning first, and believing afterwards, with Zachariah, yet first believing without reasoning, next from love and reverence, reasoning after believing'... Her heart, as Newman says, was 'the Home of the Word,' and her life had been a wholehearted response to it as the Holy Spirit revealed its inner meaning to her. Coming down to dwell within her, the Word found in her all the beauty, grandeur and freshness which he had given to man on the morning of his creation. In her, the new Eve, the winter of man's desolation had passed and the flowers of virtue appeared in all their pristine fragrance. . ... From the moment of the incarnation, she became, as St Thomas Aquinas puts it, 'the golden book of the Lord who brightens the darkness of the world;' a book written by the finger of God's right hand" (*Ibid.*, p. 20).

The French school of spirituality in particular, represented by eminent figures like Cardinal Berulle and Bl Elizabeth of the Trinity, delighted in the beauty of Mary's inner life of reflection, of communion, of silence, of agapeic love. Fr. Lynch borrows the words of Fr. Edward Leen (*In the Likeness of Christ*) to fix his gaze on the virgin as she received God's message from the lips of the aged Simeon: "She practises the same self-effacement and observes the same silence as her child. The words said about Jesus and the actions done concerning him do not betray her into opening her lips and proclaiming aloud to all the wonders to which she holds the secret. She veils herself in modesty and retirement; she says nothing; she allows the incidents to speak for themselves; she watches and adores the action of divine providence with regard to her child, and is content to store up all these things in her mind, in order to meditate on them at leisure and to probe ever more deeply into the unfathomable mystery contained in every incident of the human-divine life that is gradually manifesting itself before the eyes of men. . .. Angels, Elizabeth, shepherds, kings, Simeon, Anna, all in their turn speak, and proclaim aloud the glories of her divine Son whose splendor is reflected in her who gave him birth; she is silent and buries herself in profound meditation on all she sees and hears" (*Ibid.*, p. 21).

But in keeping with the solid tradition of his beloved Carmel, Fr. Kilian did not find in Mary only a "model of the contemplative life." She was something more, precisely because of her role in the work of our redemption. "She is the mother of divine grace and of the life we live in Christ; and it is through her that we are drawn into Christ to live in the bosom of God. It is she who forms Christ in us. And if, as Berulle says, 'we must treat the things and the mystery of Jesus not like things past and dead, but like things living and present and ever eternal from which we have to gather precious eternal fruit,' who, better than she, can make those mysteries lively, sapid and intimate for us? . . . Through the mystic mantle of Carmel which she has thrown about us, our lives are hidden away in Christ through her" (*Ibid.*, p. 22).

Our Lady of the Scapular

Fr. Kilian will be remembered by history as the prior general who generated great enthusiasm and imposing manifestations in honor of the 700th anniversary of the scapular in 1951. Under his guidance the order obtained from Pope Pius XII the only apostolic letter, *Neminem profecto latet*, ever written specifically about the scapular devotion. Not only did he know Pius XII personally, but he was familiar with men like Cardinal Spellman of New York to such an extent that he could ask the latter to write the preface to his book on the scapular, *Your Brown Scapular*

(British Isles edition: *Mary's Gift to Carmel*). While the book betrays the erudition of a doctor of philosophy and theology, it is not a scientific or historical study. Rather Fr. Lynch, in his rhapsodic style, shares some of his favorite spiritual and theological insights on the scapular devotion. The book must be categorized as devotional; however, it is the tribute to the solid bases of Carmel's centuries old popular devotion.

The first chapter seeks out the origins of the scapular, as a part of the religious habit in medieval times. The scapular was the means by which even layfolk could "become Carmelites" and take on Carmel's strong commitment to Mary. "When Carmelites made their profession, they vowed their lives to God and to her, and it was in her honor that the homage of their lives of contemplation was offered to their Lord. Mary was the queen and mistress of the holy mount; Carmel was her land, her vineyard, where they worked in the hope of her guidance and protection" (*Mary's Gift*, p. 4).

But beyond the historically tempered meaning, the scapular has acquired a spiritual significance which the second chapter studies. It must be seen in the context "of the inner life of Carmel" lest it lose "much of its spiritual significance" (p. 7). Divine loving-kindness chose the simple, humble elements of human experience through which to touch men. Not only the sacraments, but the church's sacramentals follow this law of divine condescension. Garments are part of this divine method. Our Lady once wrapped her Firstborn in swaddling clothes and probably provided her Son with the seamless cloak which clad him even to Calvary. Now she uses the scapular in the same way: "It envelops us in the special love of our Blessed Mother. It makes us 'hers' in a very special way (p. 11)... She brought us forth into the life of grace, wrapped us up in the garments of her special love and we became hers forever. We can easily understand the love that led Our Lady to wrap up her Son in the swaddling clothes, but that she should cover the ignominy of our spiritual nakedness is something that only her most merciful love can explain" (p. 12).

The motherly concern of Mary covers the whole of a person's existence; thus traditionally Mary's has been described as a triple promise. Fr. Kilian gives a resumé of the vast scapular literature in chapter three. "The Scapular is the sign of Our Lady's triple promise to assist us in life and in death, and to bring us as soon as possible to the gate of heaven. Since we learned how to pray, we have asked Our Lady to pray for us now and at the hour of our death. And when we came to know the great mysteries of hell and heaven and purgatory, we perhaps added a prayer to be saved from hell and to be brought as soon as possible to enjoy the bliss of heaven. The scapular promise is Our Lady's answer to that prayer, for those who wear her habit worthily shall never suffer the pains of hell; and the special love she exercises towards them will enable them to die well and join her in heaven as soon as her 'suppliant omnipotence' has won the crown for them" (p. 17).

In the fourth chapter Fr. Kilian delves into another "constant" of the scapular devotion, namely, Mary's link with the gift of perseverance. "One of the greatest means of final perseverance we have is devotion to the Blessed Mother. It is the constant teaching of the church that devotion to God's mother is not only a means, but a pledge of eternal salvation. Those who shelter their weakness in the motherly heart of the mother of our redemption 'shall draw salvation from the Lord.' That heart, into which the tenderest mother-love drew all the agony of the passion and death of our Redeemer, is a tower of strength for the weak. ... To whom shall we go for an assurance of salvation if not to her who in order to save us offered both her Only-Begotten and herself to the cruel death of the cross" (p. 30).

In the fifth chapter, Fr. Kilian takes up a subject which recently has again been studied. Since the Holy Father, John Paul II, asked for a consecration of mankind to Mary, theologians and spiritual writers and exegetes have returned to this traditional concept to delve into the meaning of consecration, or entrusting, to the Blessed Virgin. The Carmelite tradition has much to contribute to the current dialogue: from writers like Ven. Michael of St Augustine to Fr. Bartholomew Maria Xiberta, the scapular devotion has been seen as a concrete form of this consecration, something which Pope Pius XII explicitly mentioned in his 1951 letter.

In the penultimate chapter, Fr. Kilian shows how the scapular devotion entails an affiliation to the Carmelite family. He describes the difference between belonging to the third order and the confraternity. Not only does a scapular wearer assume the spirituality of Carmel, but also is given a share in the masses, prayers, sacrifices and good works of the thousands who make up this religious family. "The Little Flower promised to spend her heaven doing good upon earth. She is just one among many Carmelite saints who are spending their heaven praying for the wearers of the scapular" (p. 53).

Finally, from his philosophical background, Fr. Kilian is able to trace how the modern epoch has crowded out Our Lady in favor of innumerable idols and -isms. After showing how the person of Mary once invigorated the whole of society, he goes on to trace the sickness of current society to a rejection of the blessed mother.

Until the end of his days in October, 1985, Fr. Lynch preached in season and out of season that religion was the basic answer to the worst ills that afflict the world. Far from alienating, the faith was the supremely liberating factor because it allowed us to reach authenticity and truth. The Blessed Mother is intimately bound to God's loving plan for all mankind. A return to her is supreme realism. It embodies what is noblest in us. Fr. Lynch's conclusion to his book on the scapular (p. 68) is a fitting way to finish the message of this faithful son of Carmel and great devotee of Mary.

"In Mary there is the beauty of life and her bands are a heartful binding. In her is all grace of the way and of the truth, in her is all hope of life and of virtue for the prodigal world of today. As the executioners retired from Calvary to glory in their victory over her Son, we find her closing the wounds sin had dug in his sacred body and preparing it for the new life of a glorious resurrection. Today she is busy again closing the wounds the same forces of evil have made in the social body, which is the mystical body of that same Son, and preparing it for a new life. The future may seem dark, but she is busy and that new life is already stirring in the womb of the world. As of old, she needs hands to help; so let us offer ourselves as did the holy women and Joseph of Arimathea that all things may be restored in Christ through Mary."

Our Lady of Mount Carmel with Carmelite Saints
Ariel Agemian, mid-20th century
Priory of Our Lady of the Scapular of Mount Carmel
New York City
Photo: Carmelite General Archives

Our Lady of Mount Carmel with Carmelite Saints
Theodore C. Barbarossa, 1965 (dedication)
Chapel of Our Lady of Mount Carmel
National Shrine of the Immaculate Conception
Washington, D.C.
Photo by Riccardo Palazzi, O. Carm.

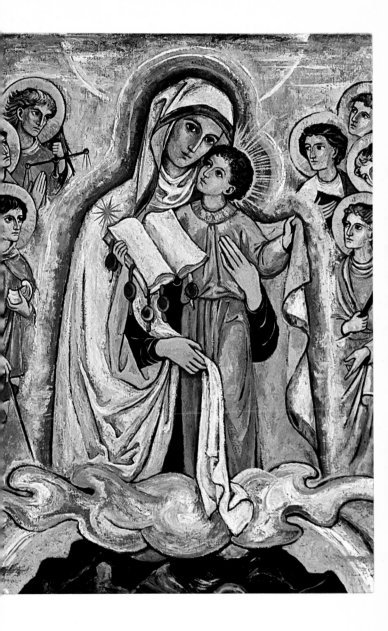

Our Lady of Mount Carmel
Rosvista Bitterlinch Brink, 1954
International Center of St. Albert
Rome
Photo by Riccardo Palazzi, O. Carm.

Our Lady of Mount Carmel
Moira Forsyth, stained glass window, 1957/8
Cloister Chapel, The Friars
Aylesford, Kent
Photo by Riccardo Palazzi, O. Carm.

11

MARY'S PLACE IN CARMEL

Our Lady in the
Constitutions of 1971

For years the Carmelite order was described as *totus Marianus*: completely Marian. The *Constitutions* of the order sanctioned this usage, stressing the centrality of Mary's place in the Carmelite family. Mary, even more than the prophet Elijah, was the inspirer of Carmel; she was indissolubly linked to the spirituality of the order. It was taken for granted that a Carmelite would nurture a filial devotion towards Our Lady, especially under her title of Mt. Carmel, and that he would be a faithful and zealous propagator of this devotion, which was widespread among the faithful especially under the form of the scapular devotion.

The new *Constitutions* of the order (1971) do not contain the phrase *totus Marianus*; this is no denial of the past. In not insisting on phrases such as this, the order wishes to shed any hint of triumphalism, or of exclusivism, or "I-have-something-that-you-don't-have" vis-à-vis other orders. As a matter of fact, other orders such as the Oblates of Mary Immaculate, the Cistercians, the Montfort fathers, to mention only a few, are strongly Marian in their spirit, which also comes through in their apostolate. True love for Mary nurses no secret jealousy that others, too, honor her and preach her.

Thus in post-Vatican II times there is a distinct trend to de-emphasize the small peculiarities of various Marian devotions and to present Mary in a fuller, more biblical framework. In this movement, the trend is to concentrate on the heart of Marian devotion—and thus on the fundamental devotion which must be the basis of all particular Marian devotions. In the past there was a distinct danger that, in stressing the peculiarities of the myriad Marian devotions, the central value of Mary's witness and place in the church would be missed. Thus today there is greater preoccupation with discovering more fully the mother of God as the scriptures present her, than with questions about the contrasting value of various scapulars of Our Lady. There is more study and preaching on Our Lady's part in the whole of the history of salvation than on her many and varied apparitions.

In this process there is a danger of making Mary too distant a figure, more the object of research than a mother who loves her own. However, basically the trend is good because it is based on the deepest point of the mystery of Mary, on the point all Marian devotions have in common. This common treasure should in no way thwart veneration of Mary under her various titles, since Mary's intervention in man's favor is not directed towards them as a mass but as persons, all of whom have a unique worth and thus experience Mary's interest in their lives in unique ways as individuals, and also as members of the various religious families and confraternities within the church. However, these individual interventions of Mary are always from the hands of the same loving mother of all. Her part in our salvation was one, although, like her Son, she knows how to make this salvation personal and singular for everyone.

The factors which all Marian devotions have in common are varied. The new Carmelite *Constitutions*, although alluding to the particular and unique moments of Marian devotion in the Carmelite order, stress above all the basic thrusts which make devotion to Mary such an integral part of Christian faith. For convenience's sake, we would break down this teaching into four points: Mary and Christ, Mary and the church, Mary and Carmel in particular, devotion and devotions to Mary. It will be evident that the order, without sacrificing any of its patrimony—which also enriches the church—wishes to "think with the church" and stress in the very first place the

210

constants of Marian devotion on which all else is based.

Mary leads to Christ

Carmel, like the universal church, in the first place wishes to nip in the bud any suspicion that devotion to Mary derogates from the unique love and commitment that belong to Christ Jesus. Devotion to Mary by its very nature leads further: it is not at the end of the path. It can rest only at the summit of the mount which is Christ himself. If there were exaggerations in the past which neglected this basic fact, the church and the order are bent on deposing them from the very start. The *Constitutions*, then, present devotion to Mary in this context:

"The Blessed Virgin Mary while she lived out her mortal life, best expressed what it means to be a disciple of Christ. She mirrored every virtue. In her way of life she fully reflected those beatitudes which Christ Jesus preached. For this reason the universal church, in developing her own pluriform life and activity, turns to the Virgin Mother of God as to her best model. In her is to be found the perfect way of imitating Christ" (n. 68). These thoughts are taken almost literally from the talk which Pope Paul VI gave at the closing of the third session of Vatican II (1964) when he declared Mary the 'Mother of the Church.'

The basic reason why the church and Carmel do not hesitate to open their hearts to Mary is because she shows more clearly than any other human being what it means in the flesh *to be a follower of Christ*. The saints are Christians who have imitated Christ, taking on his vision of life; Mary's life is the best expression we have of what this commitment to Christ and his message implies. Being a disciple means a committent that considers no suffering too great, that takes on every necessary hardship, that knows how to die to the old man of sin and make room for the new man in the Spirit of Christ, that will go the whole way with Jesus even when it means climbing the slopes of Calvary. Mary, overshadowed

211

by the power of the Most High, was warned by old Simeon that this was to be her lot: "A sword will pierce your own soul too" (Lk 2: 35). How true this was and what true discipleship of Christ meant at its deepest roots Mary experienced only when "near the cross of Jesus stood his mother" (Jn 19: 25).

Like every true disciple Mary had to commit herself wholeheartedly to her Son: this demanded *faith*. This aspect of the faith exhibited by Mary throughout her life was stressed by the Council and is one of the favorite topics of writers today. A disciple is expected to stake his all, to make his fundamental option rest in Christ: who, in this vale of tears, is ever completely secure that the risk he is taking by the commitment of his whole life to Christ is foolproof?. Like all believers Mary was not overwhelmed by the surety of vision: she did not see the divinity of her Son streaming forth from the human in him. Like every mother, she showed her love for her Son by the diapers she changed, by the meals she prepared, by the household she kept in order, by the interest she showed in all her Son said and did. No doubt Mary was spiritually sensitive to the other-worldly side of Jesus, but the fullness of her Son's power and glory she knew only after his resurrection and ascension.

What a refreshingly healthy picture of a true mother Mary presents, for instance, in the episode of the finding of the boy Jesus in Jerusalem when he was twelve. Then, as today, Mary never hoarded her Son away for herself: she shared the joy and treasure of her life with others and in such a spontaneous and natural way that for a whole day, meal times included, Jesus was missing and she was not aware of it. "They, Mary and Joseph, assumed he was with the caravan, and it was only after a day's journey that they went to look for him among their relations and acquaintances" (Lk 2: 44). When finally they did find Jesus, who explained his zeal for his Father's business: "they did not understand what he meant" (Lk 2: 50). Jesus was not constantly whispering in his mother's ear the way in which he was fulfilling his heavenly Father's will. She, too, rooted in the love of her mother's heart, had to believe in her Son.

How she differs from other disciples, and why she is the model for them all, lies in the fact that her faith in Jesus never wavered. Not when he seemingly overlooked her for the sake of getting a point across: "My mother and my brothers are those who hear the Word of God and put it into practice" (Lk 8: 21). Not when his own townsfolk would not accept him (Mt 13: 56). Not when he agonized and died on the cross in her presence. Mary is the perfect disciple of her Son because she lived the essential characteristic of a follower: faithfulness. A disciple throws in his lot with his "master:" but this initial option is but the springboard to a lifetime spent exploring the rich variety contained in that option in every aspect of his life. A disciple is not like the member of a club, whose membership does not imply total commitment. A disciple, by his free choice, agrees to give his life over to the mission of him whom he follows. Mary's "Let what you have said be done to me" (Lk 1: 38) explicitated what she meant in calling herself "the Lord's handmaid." She was staking her all on the mission of Christ. Every other glimpse we have of her in the scriptures shows in what marvellous, faithful ways she lived her *Fiat*.

Mary did this as she *mirrored every virtue*. This is not preacher's rhetoric: every glimpse of Mary in the scriptures shows her resplendent with attitudes that reveal in the flesh the message which her Son is preaching. Mary appears as one whose value system is a splendid reflection of her Son's teaching. Did Christ place the centrality of his message in the dual command of love of God and of neighbor? Then Mary reflects it. And in what magnificent down-to-earth ways! What but love of God made her full of grace, made her sensitive enough to the voice of God through an angel's lips, made her the handmaid of no one but the Lord, made her the Father's daughter, the Son's mother, the Spirit's temple? What but love of neighbor made her go "as quickly as she could to a town in the hill country" to rejoice with and to help her pregnant cousin Elizabeth (Lk 1: 39 ff)? What but love of neighbor made her intercede for the embarrassed newlyweds at the feast of Cana?

Did Jesus preach humility and meekness of heart? Mary's life shines with these attitudes as she assumes her role as the epitome of the *anawim*, the lowly ones of Israel. How she felt part of Jahweh's "little people" when "the time came for her to have her child, and she gave birth to a son, her firstborn. She wrapped him in swaddling clothes and laid him in a manger because there was no room for them in the inn" (Lk 2: 6-7). Like a host of displaced persons, she had to flee before the wrath of local authorities and live for many years in Egyptian exile. The crown of Israel's *anawim*, she remained open constantly to the workings of the Lord; especially when she was caught up with the unexpected, her humble attitude comes through: "His mother stored up all these things in her heart" (Lk 2: 51).

Did Jesus teach his own how to pray? Mary could not but show what this meant. Her *Magnificat* remains a favorite evening prayer of the church through the centuries. As usual, Mary does not take the limelight but after her Son's ascension she is found with the apostles "in continuous prayer" (Acts 1: 14). Whatever Jesus preached Mary epitomized in her way of life. If we could rid the phrase "paragon of virtue" of its negative overtones, it would be a most fitting way to describe Mary.

If this is so, it is to be expected that she should have been the living incarnation of the basic attitudes or virtues announced by Christ in his Sermon on the Mount as the program of his kingdom, *the beatitudes* (cf. Mt 5: 3-10). Reversing so many of the attitudes which animated his contemporaries, as well as men of all times, Jesus wished to give the Spirit that should be the hallmark of the children of his kingdom. He upset many philosophies, many world outlooks, when he pronounced as the truly fortunate, the poor in spirit, the gentle, those in mourning, those who hunger and thirst for what is right, the merciful, the pure in heart, the peacemakers, those who are persecuted in the cause of right. It is to these that the Kingdom of God belongs. Mary's appearances in scripture show us sufficiently how her earthly life reflected this revolutionary, seemingly weak set of values, which in reality, however, are the surest sign of real strength and character.

How gentle and considerate Our Lady, as she whispers to her Son, "they have no wine" (Jn 2: 3); how vividly she shows us how these exalted beatitudes must be translated into the very prosaic and earthy moments of our existence. If the mourner is considered blessed, who could be more so than Mary who held the bruised and battered and dead body of her Son in her arms and has been immortalized as the *pietà*? In Old Testament fashion Mary expressed the words of her Son, "happy those who hunger and thirst for what is right" in her own canticle, the *Magnificat*: "He has routed the proud of heart. He has pulled down princes from their thrones and exalted the lowly. The hungry he has filled with good things..." (Lk 1: 51-53). She was not wrong when she foresaw that all generations would call her blessed (cf. Lk 1: 48): and she was blessed above all because she epitomized the beatitudes proclaimed by her Son.

In her, then, is to be found *the perfect way of imitating Christ*. To put on the mind of Christ there is need to have recourse to the scriptures. But even more important there is need to see that the scriptures have been and are being lived out in the flesh by followers of Christ who show us graphically and convincingly, albeit partially, what it means to imitate Christ. She who comes closest to closing the gap between "partially" and "fully" is Mary. Full of grace, she stumbled over fewer obstacles in being a replica of her Son. Although a creature like ourselves and fully a member of Israel's folk, she escaped from the consequences of Adam's original fall and so had the possibility to harmonize the demands of spirit and flesh in a way that the higher part always predominated.

The whole being of Christ's personality was attached to his Father's will: "Let it be as you, not I, would have it" (Mt 26: 39) is Christ's final option when faced with the horrific vision of the passion. Mary had expressed her reaction to the will of the Father in her regard: "Let what you have said be done to me" (Lk 1: 38). This statement of Mary was not a momentary reaction, it was not her answer to one request that God was making of her. It was a resumé of her life. The scriptures are eloquent in their witness to Mary's submission to God's will, however much it differed from what she believed to be his will for her. Her very motherhood, the birth of Jesus in a strange town, the flight and exile in Egypt, the episode of losing the Christ Child in Jerusalem, Christ's leaving when his public ministry began, the seeming shunting aside of Mary by Jesus during his ministry, her stance beneath the cross: in all Mary shows herself living out her initial *Fiat*. It is not what her vision encompasses, but what God wills that matters. This attitude translated into daily living is the closest imitation of Christ possible. This is Mary's accomplishment.

Mary and the church

The Order's new *Constitutions* could not but reflect the stress which Vatican II put on the rapport between Mary and the church. Whereas in former times Mary was often seen in her unique position and on her own, today her place in the church is highlighted. She is seen as the "image and first flowering of the church" (*Lumen Gentium*, 68; *Constitutions*, 85). She is "the church's model" (*Lumen Gentium*, 53; *Constitutions*, 14) in whom the church joyfully contemplates "that which she herself wholly desires and hopes to be" (*Sacrosanctum Concilium*, 103; *Constitutions*, 14). Thus "the church in developing her own pluriform life and activity, turns to the Virgin Mother of God as her best model" (*Constitutions*, 68).

The Carmelite order cannot but rejoice at the church-directed vision of Mary which is taking ever firmer hold on men's hearts. Because, as we saw above, Mary is such an excellent replica of Christ, she truly embodies in her person all that the church—God's people on pilgrimage—can hope and desire to be. If the members of Christ's body must ever strive to be effective and living members, contributing to the ordered and effective functioning of the whole

216

body, they can find no more stirring model than her who "has arrived." The constant *metanoia*, or change of heart, which must characterize anyone who wishes to be a dynamic member of the people of God, has as its aim the opening up of self to the Other and to others: in all creation there exists no one who accomplished this in such a marvellous fashion as did Mary. If the church strives to be Christ's spouse "without wrinkle or spot," then she can look to no finer model that to her who was preserved from sin from her very conception in her mother's womb.

This is the sense in which Mary is the church's image and first flowering. Because the love of God for men which takes the form of the grace of Christ, overwhelmed her with an unheard-of fullness ("Hail, full of grace, the Lord is with you": Lk 1: 28), she from the first moments of her human existence embodied the holiness which other members of Christ must strive for all their lives. Not that she did not grow in the Spirit progressively through her life: being fully human, she received the grace of God according to the various stages of her development. However, it was always with a fullness which is not repeated again; truly the "Almighty has done great things for me" (Lk 1: 49).

Her faith was dynamic, deepening as she pondered all that God was telling her through the events of her ambient and family and times. Yet, because she kept a priority of values so well, it was in the Lord's ways that she grew. And so she became the model of God's people, who strive all their lives to grow into, relish and become holy in the ways of the Lord. The church must constantly be renewed precisely because the ways of the Lord get confused too frequently with purely human ways. Many times quite innocently, and by slow stages, even the surest way of the Lord is encumbered and sometimes so overgrown with undesireable underbrush that the pilgrims on their way to the Father get confused and even lose their way. Thus the church is constantly in need of renewal. And when she needs a human example of what she needs to "renew to," she need look no further than Mary, who still proclaims to the church daily in her *Magnificat*: "The Almighty has shown the power of his arm... his mercy reaches from age to age for those who fear him" (Lk 1: 50).

Renewal in the church is willed first and foremost by God himself; his power and mercy are constantly at the church's disposal to prune away the un-Christian element, to root in Christian hearts the central witness of Christ. Mary not only reminds the church in words, but by her witness shows how concretely and humanly this can and must be done. Mary in word and deed is constantly telling her sons and daughters in the church that all renewal, all work and prayer, must be firmly rooted in a God-directed thrust. The church is most the church—God's vineyard, the recipient of his fatherly care and kindness, the Body of Christ and the favorite field of the Spirit's action—when it borrows Mary's expression: "My soul proclaims the greatness of the Lord and my spirit exalts in God my Savior" (Lk 1: 46). In clearing away the accretions and useless entanglements which distract her from this attitude, the church looks to Mary as to her who let God have his way with her. And so she conceived and bore the Son who is the head of his body.

In her motherhood, she truly cooperated in the foundation of the church, because, firstly she gave the world Christ, who cannot be adequately distinguished from the church. And under the cross she further accepted the motherhood of all members of the church, represented on that occasion by the apostle John. She becomes, then, mother of the whole Christ—head and members. The ancient Spanish Mozarabic liturgy on Christmas day expressed this truth graphically and beautifully: "Mary gave salvation to the peoples, while the church gives the peoples to their Savior. The one carried life in her womb, while the other carries him in the wellspring of the sacrament. What was once granted in the flesh to Mary is now granted spiritually to the church; she conceives the Word in her unfaltering faith, bears him in a spirit freed from all corruption and contains him in a soul overshadowed by the power of the Most High."

218

In the manifold sweep of her life-giving activity, the church is inspired to look to Mary, in whom is found "her highest example." This does not only obtain through the spirit which animated Mary, but also through the very concrete manifestations of the numberless ways in which the love and the salvation of God can be given flesh in human society. Mary not only accepts the gift of God in becoming the mother of the Messiah, but also forgets her own "privilege" as she hastens to join Elizabeth whose prayers for a child have been answered in her later years; and she stays not only for a couple of days or weeks, but for three months in her concern for her older cousin. Mary not only "treasured all" that happened at the time of Christ's birth and pondered it in her heart (cf. Lk 2: 18), but she spontaneously shared her Newborn with the shepherds and the Magi as they were mysteriously led to his abode. Mary not only willed to observe the laws of her beloved Jewish people, submitting to the purification "laid down by the law of Moses" in Jerusalem (Lk 2: 22), "every year" going up to Jerusalem for the feast of the Passover (Lk 2: 41), but she also joined in the nuptial festivities at Cana. Mary not only stood beneath the cross of the agonizing and dying Christ, but she refused to close herself against a cruel humanity who put goodness to death; she was found in prayer with the disciples and other women. Where could the church look for a higher example?

Our Lady and Carmel

The place of Our Lady in relation to Christ and to the church is the foundation of Carmel's devotion to Mary. No kind of particular devotion may be allowed to supplant the basic truths which are Mary's true glory. In other words, the main thrust of Carmel's devotion to Mary will always surge from hearts imbued with this fundamental vision of Mary, and every manifestation of Carmel's Marian devotion will be measured for authenticity against it.

However, since the person of Mary is of such rich proportions, there will naturally be some aspects which will be stressed by various religious families. These do not mean to exclude other aspects, but mean to highlight various particular graces of Mary. From its inception the Carmelite family was known officially as Brothers of the Blessed Virgin Mary of Mount Carmel (*Const.*, 6). Since their chapel was dedicated to Mary, the original Carmelite hermits considered Mary as their patroness and mother in the strong medieval sense of these realities. The early Carmelites considered themselves brothers of Mary, part of her household: even physically they lived in the land graced by her presence centuries previously. Their life was considered a service of Mary: she was the patroness of their foundation on Carmel. Their life, as a consequence, was a tribute and a commitment to her. Familiarity with her sprang from the fact that early Carmelites saw themselves as part of her family. This led to a way of life, concentrated on the spirit, which sought to emulate and thus magnify that of Mary (cf. *Const.* 11).

Mary as the "Virgin Most Pure" inspired Carmelites in a special way. She who was the "Beauty of Carmel" was seen reflecting the divine beauty precisely in her purity. If God is God because of his purity which allows of no contamination, then Mary, who of all creatures is closest to God, had to mirror this purity. Carmelites see in "her wholehearted purity" (*Const.* 14) the perfect image of all they hope and desire to be. How many times the white cloak of Carmel has been described as a sign of the following of Mary in her unwavering purity.

In today's world the very word "purity" is often taken as a joke. There is much unwarranted, damaging and uninhibited sexual aberration to the extent that this essential Christian attitude seems to have been swallowed up by the various factors that have produced the "sex revolution." Mary most pure was never more needed as an antidote to this trend which, if allowed to prevail, will destroy mankind because it goes so radically against human dignity. Thus, the modern Carmelite is challenged courageously to take his stand and refuse to look back; he has made his choice. In Mary's service, he strives with all the powers at his disposal to witness to the dire need for purity in today's society.

Firstly, *purity of intent*. The Carmelite, in the footsteps of Mary, refuses every compromise with the allurements of a society which gives free rein to every possible pleasure, even the most immoral. A Carmelite has chosen to follow Mary in all her wholesomeness of intent: only a God-directed vision can save the world from disaster. Regardless of how ridiculous the world considers this message, the Carmelite refuses to keep silent. Because of his love for his neighbors and friends, he witnesses in every way possible that God, *the* Pure One, still lives among us.

"Mary was impelled by the faith that God dwells among us and that life finds its beginning and end in God. She indicates that truly human life is not possible without giving God his proper role" (cf. *Const.* 14). No sacrifice will be too great for a Carmelite to follow Mary's lead: to witness to the fact that men can be most authentically men—they can reach the pinnacle of their humanity—only if they allow God to take his proper and essential place in their lives. Mary became *the* woman looked up to by all generations because she embraced with all her heart "the great things that the Mighty One had done for her." She is a living proof that God's will in our regard is not a domineering, tyrannical force that squelches our human possibilities and desires; it is the love of a Father who made us for happiness, made men to fulfill themselves in the deepest roots of their being, and so the will of God which loves men so, aims at nothing else than man's authentic fulfillment. Mary's greatness is rooted in her *Fiat*—in her acceptance of God's will for her. The Carmelite today, even if he must appear a fool, does the same: in the purity of intent he says "yes" to God's design for him and shakes off every temptation to turn back on his choice.

There is also *purity of heart*. How often in today's world even the pious person's heart wavers. There are many tugs on one's love, some of which (and in our days, many of which) would wean one away from the first love offered to God. Often the heart's affection, which begins on a highly spiritual or human level in favor of another, loses its altruistic thrust and becomes concerned with the self-pleasure which the relationship affords. How often today the heart of man suffers violence through the inventive ways of ill-placed love! The momentary thrills of the modern conception of love leave the heart unsatisfied and even frustrated. Only the purity of love according to God's all-pervading design for men can satisfy the hankerings of his heart. What an example Mary leaves us as "her spirit exults in God her Savior" (cf. Lk 1: 46). Whenever she appears in scripture she is in some way opening her heart to the Lord whose greatness she proclaims. Her heart belongs to God and so she can love truly, deeply, even in the prosaic details of daily living. She no sooner opens her heart to the Lord at the annunciation than she is urged by that same thrust of pure love to go to the aid of her elderly cousin. She ponders the mysteries of her Son in her heart, and in so doing opens that same heart to the "no wine" situation at Cana.

The *Constitutions*, then, look to Mary for the Carmelite's commitment to chastity, according to each member's state in life. It is she who inspires Carmelites to face the world and enrich it by *internal purity* (cf. *Const.* 42). It is this internal purity, which is but the substratum of a purity which embraces the whole man even in his outward comportment, which the Carmelite, in imitation of Mary, believes can save and enrich the world. A heart which is pure and which expresses itself in consequent action acts in a Godlike fashion: it never uses persons for one's own pleasure, it is intent on allowing each loved one to preserve intact the inner sanctuary in the depths of his being. A pure heart is convinced that, far from being constrained, it is capable of sharing its love with others in a far more altruistic and wholesome way. A pure heart is the heart which realizes that total love of God in no way implies having nothing else besides, but rather being able to offer self to others in a spirit that looks for no personal advantage, but is as disinterested and gratuitous as is God's love.

One of the surest means of fostering this purity is a familiarity with the blessed virgin, which must be sought for increasingly each day (cf. *Const.* 42). An outlook on life which is pure is no "do-it-alone" affair; it follows on an intimacy with Mary since she, the handmaid of the Lord, is the mother of all, and in her mother's love wishes that her sons love one another not in word but in deed.

The Carmelite vision of Mary takes special note of another of her characteristics: *her all-pervading readiness*, which led her to be open to the Lord constantly (*Const.* 14). This openness to the Lord's slightest wish led her to occupy a unique place in the history of salvation. Carmelites take as their mission the continuation of the work of Mary. They are to "witness to the living presence of Mary in the history of salvation and to cooperate with the Incarnation of Christ in the world of today" (*Const.* 15). Mary's readiness is above all expressed by her "Let what you have said be done to me" and this availability is what the Carmelite seeks to perpetuate in today's world. Mary continually acquiesced to her unique role in the Incarnation; the Carmelite takes as part of his very vocation the continuation of the work of the Incarnate Word today. He is a son of Mary in the deepest sense when he commits himself to the incarnation of the life and work of Christ in the world of his strivings. Many times this assiduity will lead to uncharted paths and to unexpected events, but the true son of Mary is ready at every moment to repeat—and to repeat with enthusiasm and joy—his own *Fiat*.

The readiness of a Carmelite means to be at the beck and call of the Lord: not when he is good and ready, but whenever the Lord intimates, and so often he calls at awkward moments. In disposing himself for the call of the Lord, he takes as a personal message from Mary her words to the servants at Cana: "Do whatever he tells you" (Jn 2: 15). Mary's Son recalls the way in which Mary herself lived this out; he remembers that Mary's readiness led her eventually to stand beneath the cross, and only then would she be overwhelmed by the grace of her Son's resurrection and glorification. Readiness for the Carmelite, then, refuses to be deluded; as in Mary's case, it will have to be exercised with a great deal of faith, hope and charity : and so the *Constitutions* (n. 14) call

223

Mary "the source of inspiration in the order of faith, hope and charity." Though these virtues unite us immediately to God, they do so through the darkness of faith, the insecurity of hope and the constant wavering of charity. This readiness will often not lead to a brave, courageous, unflinching witness, applauded by grateful spectators. It will more often than not imply a dogged faithfulness even in the face of lack of success, of imputation of unworthy motives, of lack of cooperation and enthusiasm, of lack of appreciation for the effort expended. Mary's life, and her subsequent place in Christian hearts, is a powerful incentive to retain this spirit of readiness without counting the cost.

Devotion and devotions

In a strong statement, the *Constitutions* (n. 69) bring out the Carmelite's responsibility vis-à-vis Marian devotion. "Veneration of the Blessed Virgin Mary and the spread of this veneration are part of the very vocation of the order in the church." There can be no ambiguity: the Carmelite order, following a hallowed tradition and seconding the expectations of the church, openly professes that an essential part of its mission is to propagate devotion to Our Lady. The basic calling of the order within the church, the charism of the order, must, include this devotion to Mary.

This first of all on a personal and community level. To propagate something, it is not enough to read up on the subject and preach it. It must be a lived reality. Preached devotion to Mary must spring from a heart committed to her. This is what the *Constitutions* say: Veneration of Our Lady touches the very essence of the order. This is in line with the view of Carmelite writers like Ven. Michael of St Augustine, who believed that each order had a specific attitude of Christ to perpetuate and stress. Franciscans would continue to stress Christ's poverty and joy. Carmelites would perpetuate in the church the love Jesus had for his mother. For if Jesus was a perfect Son, he had to have a tremendous reservoir of love

224

for his mother. This aspect of his person is precisely what older Carmelite writers saw to be Carmel's charism. Whatever be the expression of this basic commitment, the fact remains that a true Carmelite cannot remain blasé about Marian devotion; it is not a question of choice. Veneration of Mary pertains to his very being as a Carmelite.

This obtains not only on an individual basis, but also extends to the whole order. The church rightly expects of Carmel a robust Marian devotion. Communities and provinces are to be in the forefront of those who witness to what a true, updated devotion to Mary implies. This brings up the final point: the distinction between devotion and devotions. *The* important element is devotion: to have a heart committed to the person and mission of Mary, to appreciate her place in the history of man's salvation, to make her presence and interest in men of today the final result of her being "Mother of the Church." This inner conviction cannot be supplied for by any amount of devotions, which are external manifestations of devotion itself. If there is a valid criticism of some Marian devotions today, then it is due to the fact that the devotions forgot that their soul is devotion. And devotion implies commitment, imitation.

However, it would be an extreme error to rule out devotions for fear that aberrations will result. Man is no angel; he has constant need of an outward expression of his inner self. His body and its senses are the expressions of his soul with its faculties. And devotions mean to link the two elements into a harmonious whole.

Vatican II expressed concern that devotion begin with the liturgy. Not only should extant devotions be updated so that they are imbued with a liturgical spirit; but also the place of Mary in the paschal mystery of Christ her Son, which is perpetuated for us in the Eucharistic celebration, should be duly stressed. If Mary cooperated in the work of redemption standing beneath his cross, it would be most strange if she did not have a part to play in the perpetuation of this redemptive reality which takes place primarily at the celebration of Mass.

225

15

The *Constitutions* urge, further, that a catholic view be taken of other devotions. There should be high esteem for those practices and devotions which the church's teaching authority has recommended through the years. Among these the scapular and the rosary are mentioned explicitly, citing the Council document (*Lumen Gentium* 67). But fresh efforts to express Marian devotion are also contemplated. Without doubt there will be different approaches according to the characteristics and needs and mentality of the various peoples within the church. What would express Marian devotion in Malta might not find resonance in Dutch hearts; what Latin American ingenuity would demand to manifest devotion to Mary might not suit the Australian. The present vision of the church and of the order has this advantage: that the essentials are stressed. These then are left to be translated according to the characteristics of the various peoples. It is seen today that unity does not demand uniformity except in essentials.

This grace of the present moment in the church's history should not be allowed to lie fallow. It should not allow the insinuation of the temptation to leave Marian devotion to other, more romantic times and peoples. Mary is too important for the church's life to allow her to be neglected. She is too much part of Carmel to allow for her quiet demise, leaving Marian devotion for a medieval mentality. Mary is too central to *the* mystery of our faith, the Incarnation, to be shunted aside. As the history of the church has amply shown, the view that is had of Mary greatly influences the view of her Son, Our Lord. A minimalistic, downgrading vision of Mary leads to misunderstandings, and worse, about Christ. As the church through Vatican II has spoken about Mary in a way that no other magisterial pronouncement has, so Carmel cannot but rejoice that an essential of its calling in the church is given fresh impetus. With renewed zeal, Carmel is grateful for this moment of grace, because it is convinced that where there is Mary there is hope and salvation, because there infallibly is Christ, the summit of Carmel.

12

IN MARY'S HOME

*The Blessed Virgin Mary in the Constitutions
of the Carmelite Sisters of Bologna*

The 1982 Constitutions of the Carmelite Sisters of Bologna (Suore Carmelitane delle Grazie) are a humble but effective proof of the enrichment which recent years have brought to the order's Marian dimension. When compared with previous Constitutions (e.g. 1881, 1950, 1971), the most recent ones are noteworthy for their theological solidity in affirming the integral role that Mary has in the Carmelite charism. A comparative study of the various editions would give the lie to those who lament the disappearence or impoverishment of the Marian aspect of Carmel's charism; in many ways Carmelite "marianism" was never expressed better than in these most recent Constitutions.

On several points the sisters' Constitutions are more explicit about Carmel's approach to Mary than the Constitutions of the friars. For example, they affirm what Carmelites of the past have held so dear, that Carmel's characteristic mission is to continue in the church the effort "to express towards Mary the filial love of Jesus for his mother and to take her into our home" (n. 49, p. 41).

Various orders and congregations in the church seek to live out the Christian life in all its breadth, but because of human limitations and for the sake of effective witness, they highlight one characteristic of Jesus' life more than another. Thus the Franciscans, while seeking to mirror the whole spectrum of values lived out by Christ, are known for their poverty, simplicity and joy. Dominicans seek to deepen the Chris-

tian meaning of truth by means of their contemplation and to share such convictions with others. The
characteristic of Carmelites is to continue the attitude
of filial love and veneration which Jesus, the perfect
Son, has for his mother.

Jesus was the perfect man in all things; as son of
Mary he showed himself the perfect Son. Throughout the centuries, Carmel is expected to perpetuate
this dimension of the rich personality of Jesus.

The Constitutions summarize under four titles
the sonship to be lived by a Carmelite: "with cult of
veneration and of love, of prayer and of imitation"
(*Ibid.*) These permit Carmel to develop the Marian
presence in a fruitful, deep and plurifaceted way.

It is significant that the Constitutions stress this
honor paid the Blessed Mother precisely under her
title "of Mount Carmel" and "following the traditions
of the order" (*Ibid.*) Far from distancing us from
Christ Jesus, Carmelite devotion for Our Lady is firmly rooted in Christ-centeredness in the sense that our
veneration, our love, our prayer, our imitation of
Mary, wish to enflesh and continue what transpired
in the heart of Jesus with regard to his mother. In
the words of St Therese of Lisieux, the Carmelite
takes no account of her own activity, of her own talents, but humbly begs the Lord Jesus to lend her his
own love, his own holiness, his own prayer. The Carmelite is happiest when she can, according to her limited possibilities, perpetuate this attitude of Jesus towards his mother.

Mary, essential to Carmel

The Constitutions stress that this attitude is essential to the Carmelite charism. The first words,
which preceed the Prologue and are printed in capital letters, announce this glad proclamation: AVE
MARIA! Thus they practice the exhortation of Ven.
Michael of St Augustine, to preface with the name of
Mary everything that is done, is said, or is written.
Far from being a pietistic usage suited to other times,
it reminds the Carmelite in everything that happens

that the order owes its foundations to Mary. Although the Constitutions do not make this explicit statement, still they do state vigorously and categorically: the order "was founded in service and in honor of the Blessed Virgin Mary" (n. 47, p. 40). In other words, in order to be faithful to the original inspiration of the order, service and honor towards Our Lady enter into the fundamental makeup of the order. Were they denied, Carmel would not be united to its roots, which in the end would lead to its death.

With rapid but incisive thrust, the Constitutions give a precious interpretation of this primaeval choice. First, "this commits us to live intimately united with Our Lady." If the foundational reason for the order includes Mary, then she enters into the very life and vitality of the order. In the divine realm, by the will of God himself, his gifts do not remain on a psychological level, only the object of our minds, and in this way presented to our meditation. Eternal reality is new life, our sharing in the life of God himself, now by faith and in the afterlife by the intimacy of the divine presence. This is applied to her who was "full of grace," that is, filled with this divine life. We are bound to Mary with filial bonds in such a way that, to be authentic, we cannot prescind from an intimate bond with her. Communion with Our Lady means a life of common interests, of sharing one's goods, among which first place is held by her motherly affection.

Second, Carmelites are committed "to offer her a special cult of filial devotion and to spread it among their brothers." With great joy Carmelites join contemporary efforts, sponsored by qualified experts, to imbue our Marian cult with the liturgical spirit. In fact, during the first centuries of Carmel's existence, "the special cult of filial devotion" was liturgical celebration more than anything else; it was rendered to the blessed virgin in many forms, e.g., by the antiphon *Salve Regina* proclaimed after every hour of the Office and after every Mass. In the recent past it was to be found in the Little Office of Our Lady according to the Carmelite Rite, which was prayed by many of our sisters, including those of Bologna. To guarantee a healthy devotion towards Our Lady, rooted in the other truths of our faith, there is no surer source than the liturgy. Pope Paul VI explained this in his magisterial *Marialis cultus*, one of the most beautiful church documents on Our Lady. He shows that today's liturgy presents a most authentic image of Mary derived from biblical data and the more authentic intuitions of the fathers. Naturally, liturgical cult towards Our Lady is not only external, but it means to confer, deepen and bring to life the reality which it symbolizes. Liturgical worship is sterile only if it neglects the symbiosis between the interior life and the life of worship, between the individual's spiritual life and that of the community. How incisive for Carmelites should be the connection between the pauses of silence in the liturgy and the silence of Our Lady (cf. Servites, *Do Whatever He Tells You*, Rome, 1983). The Carmelite also tries to spread this cult among his brethren. The Marian characteristic, love for Mary, should be apparent in every form of Carmelite apostolate.

Third, "we are dealing with realities that are part of our vocation in the church." In other words, our devotion for Our Lady is not just something reserved for us, but it redounds to the well-being of the whole church. There is no need to prove from history how in the past the life of the church throughout the world was decidedly marked by Carmelite devotion towards Our Lady.

In our own day, this Carmelite Marian presence has dwindled noticeably, but more because of confusion in the ranks of the Carmelite family than to rejection on the part of the faithful. A Carmelite is not obliged to prove that his devotion for Our Lady redounds to the good of the church; there are testimonies from all over the world in this sense. It is a shame that our own generation has not known how to adapt to the needs of our times with the same enthusiasm and the same creativity as our forefathers in Carmel, who never finished sharing their treasure, Our Lady and her scapular, with their brethren.

Fourth, these realities "characterize our religious family, the individual sisters, community life and the apostolate." Put into other terms this is the traditional motto: *Carmel is totally Marian*, namely every

230

aspect of Carmelite life should be pervaded by a Marian tonality. It should not only permeate the devotion of individual religious but it should also be reflected in each individual community life-style and in the various fields of the apostolate. The wholesome presence of a Carmelite community should breathe and make breathe the beneficent and tender presence of so noble a mother.

A fine paragraph explains the presence and importance of Our Lady in Carmelite life. Without claiming that Mary is a model exclusively for religious as distinct from other Christians, Carmelites acknowledge through their life the clear, inspiring example of Mary who incarnates in herself values both of a contemplative and of an apostolic life. "The Blessed Virgin Mary is the perfect model of uniting prayer with the apostolic life. For while she lived a life just like everyone else here on earth, full of concerns about family and work, she remained united to her Son, cooperating in the work of the Savior in an eminently particular way" (n. 48, p. 43).

Carmelites, often troubled by the tensions between contemplation and action, and only with difficulty finding solutions to so many concrete situations of commitment in the church, breathe with more calm and hope when they are able to recognize in Mary that harmony of values which in other realities they so often find in conflict. Mary knew how to dedicate herself totally to home and family, to work shared by every housewife, but at the same time to remain intimately united to her Son Jesus. The important fact is that both elements elicit Mary's cooperation in the work of Jesus as he saves mankind.

Herald of every Carmelite, Mary is the concrete guarantee that Carmelite life, both with divine intimacy and with apostolic commitments, can and should be redemptive. St Therese in her Carmelite authenticity exults: it does not matter what is done—great or small, important or banal—what counts is love which animates the Carmelite, whose vocation it is to be love in the heart of the Church. Mary was so dear to Therese because she lived this element more authentically than anyone else.

The Prologue to the Constitutions underscores other aspects of this same reality: "We tend towards perfection of evangelical charity, supported by the example of the Blessed Virgin Mary, mother and beauty of Carmel. Like her we open ourselves to the grace of the Lord in prayer and in self-giving to others. With her we listen to, harbor and meditate the Word of God. In her we live out our humble commitment of love and service of the church and of the brethren" (p. 14). It is useful to note here a characteristic of the Carmelite charism, incarnated so effectively in Mary; she, the beauty of Carmel, shows us how to live in humble, silent service.

Mount Carmel itself was the symbol of beauty, a place graced with greenery in contrast with the arid dryness of the plains and deserts of Israel. Mary is beauty in a world darkened by so many shadows and deviations. She mirrors the glory and beauty which God shared with creation at the beginning.

The beauty of Mary is an essential part of the life of contemplation to which the Lord calls Carmel. Contemplation means to be amazed, to be left breathless by the greatness, the goodness and beauty of God who lovingly reveals himself to men. We discover Mary to be filled with God, resplendent with his splendor, with his glory (cf. *Do Whatever He Tells You*.)

With realism the Constitutions speak of "our humble commitment." The Carmelite order never has been distinguished for famous schools, for systematic and sustained series of publications, nor for missionary work which pervades all other forms of life. Assimilated into the movements of apostolic fraternity (the mendicants), Carmelites dedicated their efforts above all to the poorer classes, providing a contribution that is modest but faithful and vibrant of involvement in the ups and downs of the people. In this area, what better model is there than Mary, who is magnified by all generations not by reason of her extraordinary works, but because of her "littleness" which allowed the omnipotent God to do great things in and through her.

Mary, who gave "both name and origin to the Congregation," continues to be its prime inspiration, especially in three sectors. Firstly, "with her the Congregation seeks to live in the spirit and traditions of Carmel, the Gospel of the beatitudes." Mary is the concrete realization of the Magna Carta of the message of Christ, the beatitudes. As outstanding member of the *anawim*, Mary incarnates in herself the values which Jesus designates as the vital core of his message, and which are the only means for attaining authentic happiness.

This Gospel "makes of us creatures fully disposed for the action of the Holy Spirit." Far from atrophying the followers of Christ, the beatitudes make them pliable under the constant interventions of God. One's proper projects, fixed ideas, all give way to the Good News. Mary submitted to the annunciation of the Archangel Gabriel, overturning her whole vision of the future. Following her, the Carmelite allows himself to be led by the action of the Spirit of Jesus, who is always the source of freshness, of surprise, of the perennial youthfulness of the church and of Carmel. From the beginning—from the annunciation as she was overshadowed by the Holy Spirit—to the end—in the cenacle awaiting the new coming of the same Spirit—Mary in the scriptures is linked with and open to an invasion of the Spirit. Thus she becomes a model for those who give free access to the Spirit in their lives.

Thirdly, in this way Carmelites become "transmitters of the joy of Jesus in the world." The venerable Carmelite Rite chanted even on Good Friday: "Your cross, O Lord, brought joy to the whole world." Through his paschal mystery, Jesus made it possible for men to smile even when faced with tense and mortifying situations. The more that we appreciate the true treasure which God gave us in Jesus and in Mary, the more wayfaring man can be pervaded with joy, a foretaste of eternal beatitude. Mary carried in her womb the joy of all the peoples, she prepared him for his mission, she accompanied him, collaborating even under his cross.

Carmelites can never forget the crucial part played by Mary, and thus with fervent love they invoke her: "Cause of our Joy." What need we have for joy in a world torn asunder by divisions, injustices, the threat of nuclear holocaust! The only joy that is not passing derives from Jesus and comes to us from the hands of Mary.

Model of religious

Certainly Jesus and Mary are models for every state in life; but as religious life is the intensification of the baptismal life of every Christian, and the highlighting of the evangelical values of obedience, chastity and poverty, it is not surprising that religious look to Mary in a special way to understand the path their consecrated life is to follow. "We lead a life which aims to follow the life which Christ and his mother chose for themselves, in complete chastity, in poverty and in obedience, taking the holy Gospel as the supreme norm" (n. 20, p. 15).

How many times recent popes have reiterated: religious life is necessary for the church, not so much to perform various acts of charity, which certainly are valid realizations of the perennial concern of the church for human needs, but even more for the quality of life which allows religious to mirror in an incisive and vital way, the very heart of the church. Ideally, the religious family is the church in miniature, concentrated in its most authentic manifestations. Our Lady is part of this very dimension: "Our self-giving to God and to Mary, accepted by the church ... unites us in a special way to the church and to its mystery" (n. 5, p. 16).

In the three vows, religious life specifies the Christian values which a consecrated person wishes to incarnate in the church with urgent incisiveness. The new Constitutions for the first time explicitly link the vows to Mary, model of chastity, poverty and obedience.

Chastity: among the means, both natural and supernatural, which make it possible to live chastity

234

with fidelity and enthusiasm, is numbered: "recourse to the immaculate virgin, to whom we are consecrated in a special way and in whom we should trust as in a mother and sister" (n. 13, p. 21). Here is a description of the familiar way in which a Carmelite entrusts self to Our Lady of Mt. Carmel, as brothers and sisters of so noble an older sister.

Poverty: "We shall be grateful to the Lord whenever he allows us to lack something. We shall be happy to help the sisters and to deprive ourselves even of some things that are indispensable. We know that when we are truly poor, we deeply share in the happiness reserved for the poor in spirit and about which Mary our mother chanted in her *Magnificat*" (n. 23, p. 26). Mary, the modest servant of the Lord, is at the head of the *anawim*, those who have no voice in things that matter, who are rich only in their hope against all hope in the promises of God and in the faithfulness of God to his word. This interior richness means that a person can even rejoice to be deprived of material things. Spiritual riches are more than enough to provide authentic happiness.

Obedience: "Daughters of the Virgin Mary, in our obedience we look to her who precisely by means of her obedience cooperated in an eminently particular way in the work of the Redeemer, becoming our mother in the order of grace. We rely on her in the hour of trial and in faith, so that our generous 'yes' to the will of God collaborates in the salvation of the world" (n. 30, p. 29). The allusion is to the mystery of the annunciation, always dear to Carmelites. Mary became our mother when she became mother of Christ the Redeemer, which means from the moment of her consent to the Archangel Gabriel. Carmelites continue the same mission of Mary in the church; they too are bringers of peace, of reconciliation, of mercy, of holiness into the world by means of their unconditional, generous and zealous "yes."

The life of prayer puts into an ever more "Carmelite" context the way to live "in allegiance to Christ Jesus" inspired by the example of Our Lady. Carmel may never forget the scriptural example of Our Lady who was immersed in the Word of God, intent not only on hearing it, preserving it, but also on putting it into practice. "Prayer ... has a central place in Carmel which is called to follow in the footsteps of Mary, to listen to, to preserve and to meditate the word of the Lord with one's heart ..." (n. 31, p. 31). The contemplative attitude of Mary, the humble listener to every word pronounced by God, does make an impression on and does inspire Carmel, a fortress of contemplation (cf. Constitutions, 1287).

Life of devotion

The life of devotion which fosters and flows from prayer is also marked by the presence of Our Lady. Her image, which in Carmelite tradition has affinity with the traditional Eastern icon—namely, it is not only an image appealing to one's memory, but rather a sacramental which makes present in some way the realities which it depicts—should adorn all the places destined for use by Carmelites so that they can make explicit this presence of Mary. "In an eminent place in our churches and chapels, in community rooms such as the chapter and the refectory, at the entrance and in the rooms, there should always be a devout image of the Blessed Virgin Mary of Mount Carmel, who inspires our communion with God and our self-giving to our brethren" (n. 50, p. 41).

The scapular devotion is linked to the meaning of the religious habit. Recalling the use of the habit, with exceptions reserved to the discretion of the superior general, the Constitutions acknowledge that we are not angels, and that even something as intimate as religious consecration cannot remain purely interior, but following the rules of a healthy anthropology, affirm the importance and even the necessity of visible signs in order to express invisible realities. "As a sign of consecration and of the common vocation in the family of Our Lady of Mt. Carmel, we wear the habit of Carmel according to the description and the norms of the Directory" (n. 18, p. 18).

The scapular, symbol of the habit and of a way of life in the Carmelite spirit, permits us to concretize the rich symbolism of clothing. The scapular is a reminder of the need to put on the virtues of Mary, which Carmel takes as a constitutive element of its charism. "Devotion to the scapular, a sign of our consecration to Mary, expresses our belonging to her and our will to be faithful in her imitation and in union with her. As mother of grace, she leads us to intimacy with the Father in the Son through the Holy Spirit" (n. 51, p. 41-42). The deep roots of Catholic spirituality—always immersed in the life of the Blessed Trinity—are stressed by this sentence. The scapular is not in competition with the practise of the sacramental and devotional life of the church. Ideally, it is part of it, and leads to a more robust ecclesial life.

The new Constitutions go further; on this point too they are more explicit and inspiring than the 1971 Constitutions of the friars. The scapular is described in its characteristic aspects: in outline form is given of an entire theology and spirituality of the scapular devotion.

"As far as we are able, following the teaching of the magisterium of the church and of the order, we shall spead the devotion of the scapular, presenting it as the clothing of Mary which unites a person to Carmel, and as a reminder of the virtues of the blessed virgin, of the interior life, of mortification, of the need for good example in humility and charity" (n. 51, p. 42). The allusion to the letter of Pope Pius XII on the scapular, *Neminem profecto latet*, is apparent; obviously it has a magisterial validity. These Carmelites propose not to reserve this part of the treasury of the church to themselves, but to spread it according to the possibilities and to the indications of the competent authorities. Simple in form, simple in its meaning, the scapular is eminently suited to Carmelite spirituality, rooted as it is in humility, in submission to the loving approaches of God, and in belonging to the family of Mary.

To honor Our Lady, the Carmelite sisters will find the necessary time each day to pray the rosary either in community or privately (n. 52, p. 42). As far as possible they will look after a lay Third Order group or a Carmelite Confraternity in each house of the Institute (n. 53, p. 42).

Other devotions recommended to the sisters often have a link with the blessed mother. Like St Teresa of Jesus, so the sisters "delle Grazie" foster "a special devotion towards St Joseph, spouse of the Blessed Virgin Mary" precisely because he was so intimately linked with Our Lady (n. 53, p. 42-43). Even devotion for the Prophet Elijah is projected in harmony with the unique place that Our Lady enjoys in Carmelite hearts. "We shall extend special devotion to the Prophet Elijah, in whose life—as also, and in an eminent way, in that of Mary—we see a reflection of our vocation... In him, as in Mary, we can recognize that a fully human life can only be had insofar as we allow God to be God in our whole existence..." (n. 55, p. 43). This description derives from the Constitutions of the friars, in which Elijah and Mary are underscored as symbolic exemplars of life in Carmel; this is not just something added to the Christian life, but in reality is a concrete and committed realization of that very life which permeates Carmelites from the deepest roots of their beings.

When speaking of evangelical penance, the Constitutions return to the admirable example of Mary who crowned a life of suffering by standing under the cross of her abandoned Son, giving his whole life because of the love he bore for all men. Rightly, the most radical mortification is recognized as linked with the sufferings, with the failures, and with the opposition that mark every human existence. In this field too the spirit of Mary, faithful disciple of her Son, is of greatest importance. Although the Constitutions wisely provide some of the traditional penitential practices (v.g. abstinence on July 15 in honor of Our Lady of Mt. Carmel, n. 61, p. 45), they go more deeply. They recall Mary under the cross, showing us how to become coredeemers: "In the practice of mortification, animated by church sentiments, we always seek to keep before us Jesus and his ministry of salvation completed on Calvary, keeping ourselves constantly united to the Lord, as was Our Lady, even under the cross" (n. 62, p. 46).

In Part II on Formation there are few allusions to Our Lady. However, if the contents of formation should include what was established in Part I, this already ensures a full and healthy assimilation of the Marian dimension of Carmel. In dealing with the specific character of the order, the Constitutions require that "the educative process proper to each person" preserve and transmit "the Marian and Elijan spirit" (n. 97, p. 60). These teachings are solemnly concretized in the formula of religious profession, in which the role of Mary in Carmel is invoked twice: "... in allegiance to Christ Jesus, imitating the example of the virgin mother of God ... with the grace of the Holy Spirit and the help of the blessed virgin Mary" (n. 146, p. 80-81). Although secondary, the provision made about a new name in the order is significant: "The sisters retain their baptismal name, with the addition of Mary and some devout title, but only as a private devotion" (n. 145, p. 79).

In Part III, on Government, references to Our Lady are even more rare. Wisely, the mistress of novices is advised to deal with each novice according to her individual character, and that she help her to be "penetrated with a solid and truly filial devotion towards the blessed virgin and the scapular" (n. 255, p. 128).

In conclusion, the Constitutions suggest that Our Lady remain as guide and protector throughout life, that the way of life described be lived with authenticity and faithfulness. Our Lady will see to it that the longed for harbor is reached through helping the sisters to put the prescriptions into daily practise (p. 135-136). "From the novitiate all will have a copy of the Constitutions, on which we shall form ourselves to the glory of the Holy Trinity, trusting in the aid of our faithful God and of the faithful virgin Mary. With her motherly help we shall seek to fill with charity our faithfulness to every norm and prescription, knowing that love is the fullness of the law and that at the end of our lives we shall be judged on love."

13

THE SCAPULAR

Reappraising a Marian devotion

More than once the scapular has been called Our
Lady's habit or Mary's 'sacrament.' For centuries it
has been one of the prime Marian devotions in the
church. Not many decades ago a First Communion
class would be expected to return to church during
the afternoon of "their" day to be enrolled in Our
Lady's Carmelite scapular. In Latin countries mothers often would bring their infants to be enrolled in
Mary's scapular immediately following baptism: the
infant who had been baptized into Christ and now
belonged to him, also belonged to Mary. Both truths
called for outward signs to complete their message.

The scapular devotion has fallen on hard times,
as have other devotions. The cry has been raised: the
two pieces of cloth which are but a miniscule frag-
ment of the habit of Our Lady's Carmelite order are
too often used as a talisman, as a superstitious practice. Amulet, good luck charm: accusers have reduced the scapular to nothing more. Only too often
these wagging fingers have been too simplistic: even
in the "old" pre-Vatican II church, the ordinary Catholic appreciated the value of these devotions far better than he is given credit for. Not untypical is the
episode of the fourteen year old Carmelite seminarian
returning home to his down-to-earth Catholic mother
for the summer holidays, bringing her a scapular as
every Carmelite should. He explained to her that Our
Lady had promised to save whoever wore her "little
habit." The mother, with the wisdom of centuries of
Christian belief in her heart, replied, "By all means,

son, I will wear the scapular, but I doubt that I will be saved if I do not try to live a good Christian life."

Catholics as a whole have never been duped: in their wholesome, simple faith they have never been content with mere externals. "The habit does not make the monk" is a saying that indicated a healthy vision of spiritual realities. The habit—the external sign—was taken for granted; it was useful, perhaps even necessary, but it was never the core value. It was an outward sign that bespoke something far more essential. Man is a social being and needs to communicate his values and insights to others; he might consider the use of an external sign necessary to his sharing and communicating with others. But presupposed is the fact that there is something else— within the spiritual spectrum of values—which is of greater import.

What is this deeper, more important dimension of the scapular devotion? What spiritual message does the outward sign of the scapular wish to convey? If the scapular is one of the best known of Marian devotions, what are its most important spiritual dimensions? In other words, how should we view the scapular in an updated way which follows the mind of the church in our time, and yet incorporates all the worthwhile dimensions from the past?

Scapular devotion is consecration

Too often the heart of devotion has been identified with various acts of piety, perhaps certain prayers or rites to be practiced. The scapular devotion in this vision would be reduced to a certain formulary of prayers to Our Lady, or perhaps to an effort to imitate some virtue of Our Lady such as the altruism which she showed on her visit to her aged cousin Elizabeth or in her intervention at the marriage feast of Cana. It would be wrong to minimize these forms of devotion: when they rise from sincere and faith filled hearts they can be the stuff of holiness. However they do not capture the central point of true devotion. They are outgrowths of what should be prime.

242

This same factor obtains when we attempt to answer the question: what makes a Christian. We would answer: certain practices like Sunday mass, periodic penance, morning and evening prayers, the attempt to assimilate the virtues of Christ into our own lives. All these factors are valid and contribute to form a true follower of Christ; but the heart of the matter is deeper still. To be a Christian means above all to live a life that is no longer just a natural life, such as we receive from our earthly parents. A Christian does more even than "put on Christ" like he puts on a garment; regardless how befitting a garment is, it always remains something other than the person who wears it. Certainly, to be a Christian means to make every effort to put on the mind of Christ—to share his world outlook, and above all, to lead an altruistic life as he did. But beyond this level, and more basic, is the fact that we now live the life of Christ Jesus in a real sense, over and above our natural lives.

St Paul himself sees that it is something more than "to put on Christ;" he goes on to use some very realistic images. He calls us all members, parts of one body whose head is Christ. We, Christ and ourselves, live the very same life, as do all members of one body. He even uses the marriage union to express how we belong to Christ: as a married couple become one in body and soul, so the Christian is united to Christ in a like way. St John uses the image of the vine and branches: the same life vivifies both. What these biblical images mean to stress is the basic belonging to Christ Jesus: "you are no longer your own," St Paul cries out. Radically a Christian is the property of Christ; in baptism he is sealed with a "character," an indelible sign something like the marking on slaves and soldiers in ancient days, which marks a Christian as belonging to Christ forever. This is the basic truth of being a Christian. This radical belonging to Christ is often called a consecration or a definitive commitment.

Consecration basically means to reserve a person or an object for a given purpose. A consecrated person is one who is taken from among others and dedicated to a given type of life or work. This act of consecration, in effect, means that a person is made different from others: he is reserved for a special mission; taken from the ordinary and common way of life, he is separated and designated to work for the good of others in a unique way. A Christian is different from other men, not just by a juridical title—because he is *called* a Christian, a follower of Christ—but because from the depths of his being he is now possessed by Christ. Not even serious sin can break off this radical belonging to the Lord; a Christian may turn his back on God and throw all his gifts back in his face; but because he is marked by his baptism, the church may never give up on a member of Christ. Until his dying breath he has the right to be ministered to and cared for by the church because he is a member of Christ's body, a sick, ailing and even dead member, but nevertheless, a member.

Basically the scapular devotion is a consecration. Pope Pius XII in his letter commemorating the Centenary of the scapular devotion could not have put it more clearly: "May the scapular be to them a sign of their consecration to the most sacred heart of the Immaculate Virgin, which [consecration] in recent times we have so strongly recommended" (*Neminem profecto latet*).

Just as baptism plunges a person into the life of Christ in a way that makes the Christian radically different; so investiture in the scapular most fundamentally is a commitment to the life of Mary, which she shares with her sons and daughters. She herself collaborated with the Holy Spirit in a unique way to give life to her firstborn Son Christ Jesus. We call her the mother of God because she was not just an inert instrument, but contributed everything that every human mother contributes to the formation of a human being: and she contributed more, because there was no human father to complement her contribution.

Mary is mother of all Christians because she is the mother of Christ. She gave birth to him whose life we share; she shared her humanity with him; his human nature was taken entirely from her and so we who live in Christ are also dependent on Mary, on whom our head depends. A mother's role is irrever-

244

sible; once a mother, no distance, no absence, no legal fiction can break the unique bond that obtains between mother and child. This is why Marian devotion in the church has never been considered something that can be dispensed with.

God in his goodness wished to depend on a woman's contribution when he took on our human flesh. He could have done it differently; he did not wish to do so. Thus there is an irrevocable bond between Christ and Mary; once a son always a son. In the case of Christ his relationship with Mary is extended to us. We are given to live "in Christ" (the favorite expression of St Paul), and so are of the same nature. He took this dual nature from God and from Mary. Christians, too, brothers of Christ, owe their origins to God and to Mary; to God in a supremely unique way, to Mary in a secondary, but nonetheless real way.

Mothers who, after they bring their children to the baptismal font to attach them irrevocably to Christ and then bring them to Mary's altar to consecrate their children to the mother of us all, are performing not just a "pretty, traditional" act but are being deeply theological. When mothers want to enroll their little ones in the scapular soon after baptism, they are openly professing what their motherly hearts know by experience: a mother is a mother always. A mother is responsible for the child, but never more so than in the helplessness of infancy and of childhood. If Mary is 'Mother of the Church,' i.e. mother of us all, then this cannot exclude her little ones, the children who need the guiding hand, loving protection and unalloyed affection of a mother. If Mary is the mother of the whole Christ, then she is mother of all Christians. The scapular devotion is a recognization of this basic fact of Christian existence.

Christians belong to Mary in a different way than they belong to Christ, but "different" does not mean unreal. They are consecrated to her and whether they acknowledge this consecration of not, they benefit from the motherly charity of Mary all the days of their lives. The scapular devotion, then, is fundamentally a constant reminder and stimulus to reawaken and deepen this sense of belonging to Mary. The sight of the scapular and its veneration has no deeper purpose than to remind Christians that just as they have been engrafted into Christ in baptism, and so are his, so they have put on the life that Jesus received from Mary, and so belong to her as her sons and daughters. In itself the scapular is only an outward sign, but what it points to is the depths of Marian devotion: when Jesus told John beneath the cross "Behold, your mother," he was not just telling the beloved disciple to care for his mother in his own absence, because in this case he never would have added the significant words to Mary: "Woman, behold your son." Mary was to have a special, motherly relationship to John. As the church has seen and taught, John was merely the representative of the church beneath the cross. Christ offered John (and us) his own mother; he made his own mother our mother.

This mutual gift, sealed at the most solemn "hour" of Christ's life, which was his physical death, is not a pious nicety of the faith. It is not a truth that may be accepted or rejected at will. Catholic faith is crystal clear: Mary is the mother of Christ, and as such, of the whole Christ. Thus Pope Paul VI's favorite title of Mary as "Mother of the Church" is as Catholic as the fact of the divine maternity or of the presence of Christ in the Eucharist. The Catholic church may never retreat from those glorious acquisitions with which God has graced her in regard to Our Lady: her motherhood, her virginity, her immaculate conception, her assumption. These are precious pearls, gifts of God to us; he is able to raise man to such heights despite his misery and limitations. Admittedly, the scapular as a form of devotion could conceivably disappear from the life of the church; as a matter of fact, for many centuries Marian devotion was not fostered under this form. But the church could never go back on its profound consecration to and dependence on Mary simply because by God's plan she is essential to his way of showing his saving love for us.

Among the early fathers of the church the dependence of the church on Mary was so deeply appreciated that in their discourses they often described Mary in order to bring out the nature of the church, and vice versa. They saw, perhaps more clearly than we today, that the two are actually on the same level: both are virgins, preserving the integrity of the faith without admixture of error or exaggeration; both are mothers, begetting many sons and daughters for the kingdom of God. St Augustine puts it concisely (*Sermon*, 192, 2): "She [the church] generates the peoples, but they are members of him whose body and spouse she is at the same time. In this, the church preserves an analogy with that virgin who among many is the mother of unity." A disciple of St Augustine, St Caesarius of Arles, went on to explain: "The Spirit overshadowed Mary, and his blessing does the same to the church at the baptismal font. Mary conceived her Son without sin, and the church destroys all sin in those whom she regenerates. By Mary there was born he who was at the beginning; by the church is reborn he who perished at the beginning. Mary brought forth for many peoples, the church brings forth these peoples. The one gave us her Son, remaining a virgin; through this Son, who is her virgin Bridegroom, the other continually brings forth children" (*Homily* III).

The scapular devotion mirrors holiness

A second characteristic of the scapular devotion follows from the basic consecration to Mary. Only too often in recent times have we heard it said: "Get rid of those medieval accretions to the faith such as medals, scapulars, novenas, pilgrimages, processions ... Let's get back to the essentials. The important thing is to have interior devotion to Mary. All these other things are distractions, palliatives that often are a cover-up for lack of sincere, interior devotion." This attitude has upset many people whose devotion to Our Lady took these various forms. In their humility, these good people examine their consciences and admit that at times the external may obtrude on the internal, which is fundamental. But to deny the need for externals in the faith is entirely un-Christian and inhuman. This attitude is a newfangled dualism, or angelism, that would make man all interior, spiritual. It actually is a remnant of Jansenism, which could never admit any good in the material or fleshy side of things.

A man is only half a man if the affection he stores in his heart does not become transparent in a smile, in a hug, in an embrace, in a handshake. A person can have all the compassion imaginable in his heart, but if he does not extend his hand spontaneously to somoene in need, no one will know it, and we can legitimately begin to doubt whether he really does have compassion, because all virtue is action, dynamism, and not the static definition that is memorized in class. In the church this same principle applies: God in his condescension treats man as he is; the tremendous lover of mankind extends his fatherly love not just through some interior sentiment nor purely by blind faith.

We have *signs* of faith, the sacraments, by which God introduces us and preserves us in his life and love. This sacramental way is just a prolongation of the Incarnation. God did not save us by an act of his will. He could have, but he loved us too much for that. Authentic love calls for a certain equality: God would become a man in all the concreteness that we find in Christ Jesus. He became man so completely that some people even missed the point that at the roots of his being he was God. This is God's way of doing things: he never disdains his creation, but enhances it to be an instrument of his eternal lovingkindness for man. He uses the most simple elements of nature to direct his love to men and does so in order to make his access to them in the human way.

The church takes its cue from the way in which God works; it uses the outward, the external, to bring God's life and love to men. Devotion to Mary takes the same form. The scapular devotion is one concrete way in which this is exemplified. How? Fundamentally, the scapular devotion weds the internal and the external aspects of devotion. As a symbolic garment the scapular is a sign of a person's putting

248

on of Mary, of belonging to her, of rejoicing in her motherly charity.

True devotion cannot remain hidden. It is something supremely attractive; it attracts people's attention. Spontaneously, naturally, without apparent effort, a person who is aware of his Christian commitment and who strives to live it daily—willing to take on any sacrifice in order to be possessed by the Lord—this person irradiates the spirit that pervades his whole being. Define it—impossible; deny it— equally impossible. It is that reality that impresses when we meet a genuinely holy person. There is something about him that exudes goodness, kindness, Christlikeness.

With a variety that is worthy of a richly simple God, each holy person incarnates a spark of the blaze of divine perfection. Men are struck by it; they encounter something fresh, outside their ordinary, everyday experience. Holy people enrich others with treasures which cannot be priced because they are the treasures at the deepest part of man's spirit, which, however, cannot be hidden. In an authentically human way, they reveal themselves in outward deportment and appearance. This experience has been noted by those who have had the fortune of visiting a fervent cloistered convent of nuns. There is something in the attitude, in the bearing of the nuns, which reflects their interior richness. And there is nothing more uplifting in the world. The same holds true of an encounter with a person who is deeply in love with God: what an impression on the whole world Pope John XXIII made. In our own Carmelite family, how the simplicity of the learned Fr. Bartholomew M. Xiberta and of Bl. Titus Brandsma fascinated and attracted those who knew these good men. Their holiness was, yes, above all an interior stance, a consecration, a commitment, which could not help but make itself evident in their everyday lives.

The scapular devotion shares in this characteristic: it is not only consecration to Mary. It is also a spontaneous, natural revelation of this interior reality. A true Christian stands out among his peers, not self-consciously nor self-righteously, but as an embodiment in the flesh of Christ's Gospel. Similarly, an authentic scapular wearer cannot help but show exteriorly what it means to be the son of so great and so tender a heavenly mother. This witness is not necessarily manifested through specific acts of piety, prayer or sacrifice; rather it is an attitude that pervades his whole life. When a scapular wearer becomes aware of how much Mary his mother means to him, when he comes to realize that she is a mother always interested even in things as banal as more wine at a marriage feast; when he recognizes her kind heart in the assistance she brought to her aged cousin Elizabeth, then he cannot but reflect these higher values in his own life. What happens is that he is weaned away from the meaningless trivialities, in which he thought he would find his personal satisfaction, and is now overwhelmed by the things above—in the case of the scapular devotion, by the presence of a heavenly mother who never abandons her sons and daughters.

In other words, an authentic scapular devotion intensifies the basic Christian commitment to put on Christ. It is an attempt to appreciate Mary's role in our belief. When this role is recognized and its inestimable worth appreciated, then certain basic Christian constants are lived more fully. If Mary was "the perfect disciple of her Son," then appreciation of her role can only bring to light untapped dimensions of Christian living. A scapular wearer sees in Mary as in a mirror the most perfect human image of Christ Jesus, and his reaction is to reflect in his own way and according to his possibilities this same image. If Christ became like us in all things but sin, he was also formed and influenced in many ways by his mother. In Christ we detect traits and ways of acting that Mary first showed him, not by verbal communication, but by the daily life she committed herself to with Jesus and Joseph in Nazareth. Thus a true disciple of Christ owes an inestimable debt to Mary, and the scapular wearer considers no duty more pressing than that of putting on Mary and her attitudes, precisely because she, better than any creature, showed the true depths of Christ her Son.

The scapular devotion, then, denotes a decision about one's scale of values. In putting first things first, it gives primacy to the spiritual values which Mary reflected so well. The scapular devotion means to gaze on our heavenly mother, which makes us prefer God's will to every other reality: "Let it be done to me according to your word." It makes us receive God's Word and ponder it constantly in our hearts, as did Mary. It makes us active in charity towards those in need. It makes us gather together in prayer and praise with the disciples of the Lord. It makes us stand beneath the cross of Christ, bearing in our hearts and even in our bodies that share of his cross that we are meant to carry. Above all and through all, it makes us strongly Christ-grounded, since every appearance of Mary in the scriptures is in reference to Christ her Son. The scapular devotion, then, because it rivets our attention on Mary and makes us more aware of our sonship and dependence on her, makes us more joyfully and more zealously eager to reflect her Son not in any one act or practice, but in the very roots of our being, body and soul, inwardly and outwardly.

The scapular devotion is hardly a crutch for poor benighted Christians who do not enjoy the wisdom of the "enlightened." It is a devotion of the strong-hearted and of the generous. It is a radical devotion that demands the leaving aside of many good things in order "to choose the better part," namely the part of Jesus and Mary. The scapular devotion is a constant reminder that many times, especially in our hedonistic, pleasure-seeking society, we too have to carry a heavy cross in going against the current. To be faithful to Christian principles, to which Mary witnessed, there is often need for pure heroism. To remain constant in one's Marian orientation and priorities—especially in the daily living out of these values—calls for a faithfulness best exemplified in Mary herself. She did not give up on humankind even after men had put her beloved Son to atrocious death on the cross. We find Mary with the early Christian community, sustaining its prayer. She is the soul of the first followers of her Son, never content to retire into a hurt attitude after having written off the wicked world which assassinated goodness itself.

Devotion to Mary through the scapular, which is worn constantly, means to stress this element of faithfulness. Scapular wearers are meant to be reflections of a basic optimism in the world. They can never compromise with evil (and progress in technology and science has done anything but rid the world of evil), but neither can they ever cease offering a hand, a word, a heart full of pardon and peace as did Mary and Jesus. To reflect this attitude day in, day out, without becoming discouraged when one's words go unheeded, when one's hand remains unclasped by another's, when one's heart receives no satisfaction of mutual affection and esteem, is to live the scapular devotion integrally. The scapular is meant to be worn constantly: the wearer is meant to be unwearying in his efforts to make Mary's motherhood appreciated and her Son's kingdom come. The scapular wearer, following the very best in Carmelite tradition, will never reach the heights of this devotion more surely than when he can rejoice in suffering—in derision, in misunderstanding, in indifference, in rejection, in solitude, in lack of appreciation, in lack of affection—because then his heart is most like the heart of Christ Jesus and his mother, who did nothing but seek to do good. For their trouble one was nailed to the gibbet of the cross; Mary's heart was pierced with the sword of sorrow as she stood beneath that cross. The scapular wearer knows he must reflect the faith in men that Jesus and Mary reflected on Calvary: when things seem blackest, and the powers of darkness seem to triumph, at that very moment, life—and life in abundance—was being earned for the whole world. The scapular wearer is convinced that like Mary he can hope to reflect his consecration to her most faithfully when he strives to witness, whether he is listned to or turned off, loved or despised or even ignored, to the concrete values which Mary showed under the cross and which she shares with those who are graced with her scapular.

252

The scapular as a "piety"

The third and final characteristic of the scapular devotion is the dimension which in the past has received the most attention, namely, the practice of acts of piety and imitation of the virtues of Our Lady. As mentioned above, these are integral and even necessary elements of devotion. Devotion stored up in the heart is essential but incomplete, because it is not completely human. If a person is so overwhelmed by the goodness of God in giving us so great a mother, whose protection and tender kindness are symbolized in the scapular, he cannot keep silent. If he is truly holy, he must share this grace with others. The more he values Mary in his life, the more he will wish to "share the wealth." He will want to pray with others that they will open their hearts to so great a gift. He will join in acts of piety to praise and thank God for so many benefits from Christ's mother and ours, not just towards himself but towards others as well. He shall want to beg her that his wavering and even rebellious heart remain constant. Above all, he will realize that there is no more efficacious praise and thanksgiving than imitation. He will want to assimilate the attitudes, virtues, values of Mary into his own life.

The scapular devotion embraces Mary in her entirety, but it does place particular stress on some of her virtues: universal charity, humility, purity, simplicity (cf. Pope Pius XII, *Neminem profecto*). Without exhausting possibilities, we will here briefly consider these four virtues as the basis of a deep spiritual life, proferred to those devoted to the scapular of Our Lady of Mt. Carmel.

Universal charity

First, Mary's universal charity. Early church writers exulted in a fact of our faith that is not overly striking to us: that Jesus is for everyone. After millenia during which the chosen race was the beneficiary of God's favor, the explosion of God's favor-for-all was a strong point of St Paul's preaching to the gentiles who also benefitted from God's loving-kindness. Jesus died for everyone without exception; his salvation was proffered to every human under the sun, not excluding the apostle who betrayed him, or those who drove the nails into his hands and feet. If these gifts of God in Christ Jesus are not reserved for any one category, but are universal, could exception be made for the gift that God gave us of Mary?

Mary too is for everyone. "Mother of the Church" she is called, and whoever reaches God does so because he belongs somehow—even most tenuously and remotely—to the church. Mary's motherly charity extends to all men. It extends to them, as befits a mother's love during life, in death and after death. This is the universal charity to which the scapular wearer is challenged. If he wants to practice the scapular devotion worthily, his charity must tend towards the same universality as Mary's.

Concretely, this means that the scapular wearer constantly strives to overcome the cramping restrictions of a self-centered existence; he rejects an outlook that would make himself the center of his interest. Universal charity implies that the scapular wearer, like Mary, knows how to think of others even before thinking of himself. The scapular is available to everyone who loves Our Lady; it is meant to be worn constantly and as such becomes the symbol of Christian charity, which is not an occasional virtue, nor a frequent attitude, but the very basis of Christian living. It is meant to permeate Christian lives and reach out to everyman, especially to God's little ones—the needy, the solitary, the unwanted, the unattractive, the shunted aside, the unimportant, the silent. Universal charity as practiced by scapular wearers must reach out to those who have never experienced what Christ's love is. If Christ proclaimed "by this shall all men know that you are my disciples, if you love one another ... that you love those who hate you, that you pray for those who persecute you," the scapular wearer can do no less than follow the example of Mary, refuge of sinners, solace of the afflicted.

Mary, sinless because she mirrored her Son, has such great compassion for sinners precisely because she realizes how sin enslaves, how it makes man less a man and restricts him in his joy and freedom and openness. A scapular wearer likewise has a heart of pity for the wanderer; he never gives up on people. He finds nothing more natural than praying for those who are most inimical to the church. The scapular wearer knows how to do the harder thing: take the initiative, and after praying for the scoffer, treat him as if he were his friend. These are the heights of holiness (e.g. the example of the Little Flower), which are not reached overnight, but which are the ideal to which the scapular devotion points, urges and assists, because Mary to whom this devotion is directed is the haven of erring souls.

Charity to be universal must take the initiative. True charity, like true love, exaggerates: it does not wait for people to beg for help; it has a delicacy all its own that will save the needy the embarrassment of asking for help. It is a mother's heart which senses her children's needs even before they explicitate them. The scapular wearer strives all his days to put on this mentality, to be so aware of when others are suffering, of when others are isolated in piteous solitude, of when others feel unwanted and unloved, that even without being notified he already senses it with Christian charity that knows no limits; he does all he can to bring light where there is darkness, hope where there is despair, charity where there is selfishness, reconciliation where there is resentment and rancor. To be able to do this without obtruding, without condescending, without seeming to make the other person an "object of charity" is a gift for which the scapular wearer prays every day and asks Mary to share with him.

Humility

The scapular devotion is a devotion of humility, not of the strident, sorrowful kind which brings so much attention to self because of constant protestation of one's own unworthiness; but the humility which is radiant and grateful and praisefull because it acknowledges what great things God does for us despite our miserliness, selfishness and self-centeredness. The scapular itself is an undistinguished sacramental: two pieces of cloth worn over the shoulders, often but not necessarily adorned with an image of Our Lady of Mt. Carmel. The color is brown, that of the earth—the *humus*, from which we derive the word "humility." It is an earthy thing, for ordinary folk who wish to live the Christian life in their everyday lives with a freshness that makes it truly extraordinary. The scapular wearer takes his cue from the very ordinariness of the scapular itself: it is readily available because of its simple form. It is almost as if it were free—and this is what true humility is: a recognition that the best things we enjoy in life are free, because they come from the hands of a heavenly Father who counts the number of hairs on our head and who knows when a single sparrow falls from the sky.

The virtue of humility is characteristic of the scapular wearer because it was so characteristic of Mary. She who declared herself "the handmaid of the Lord," i.e. the slavegirl of God, yet did not hesitate to declare "all generations shall call me blessed." Why? Not because she had some talents within herself to elicit all this praise, but because "He who is mighty has done great things for me." The humble person, the scapular wearer, strives to imbibe this spirit of acknowledging the marvels God is working for him. He is so overwhelmed by God's loving-kindness that he forgets to think, self-consciously, of his own exploits. A humble person is an optimistic person because his hope is placed not in his own projects and plans, activities and ideals, but on God's marvels in him. A humble person would be ashamed to call attention to himself by protestations of guilt, of ineptitude, of failure: these are only too evident and need no commendation. What he is amazed at is the marvellous way in which the Lord can work even through the dullest of instruments to see to the accomplishment of his will.

The scapular wearer, because he strives to be humble like Mary, is a dynamic person. So often

256

humility is taken as passive virtue, not suitable to our frantically active times. There is nothing further from the truth. It is passive only to the degree in which the humble person allows the Lord to work through him; he is constantly at work to remove the obstacles to the Holy Spirit's action in his life and he seconds every initiative that the limitless goodness of the Lord proposes to him. It was the humble virgin Mary who hastened to the hill country to be with her cousin Elizabeth in her days of pregnancy. It was the humble Mary who pleaded for the newly married couple when they had no more wine. It was the humble virgin who would not interrupt her Son's preaching, but who stood outside during his mission. Humility is supremely active, because God is nothing but act, with no passivity in him at all. And when a person allows himself to be overtaken by God—and this is the humility of the saints, which the scapular devotion inculcates—there is no Christian more dynamic and alive and and life-giving than he.

Purity

The scapular devotion also includes the virtue of purity, a purity that reaches the heights of the beatitudes. Christ Jesus promised that the "pure of heart" would see God. Purity goes beyond a preoccupation to avoid sexual sins; more fundamentally it has to do with something more challenging—a single-minded vision which sees all things in the divine milieu. Purity means lack of contamination; it means freedom from what detracts from beauty and wholesomeness; positively it means integrity, consistency, faithfulness to what a person should be. The pure of heart are those who do not let their hearts deviate from their supreme good and goal. They are adamant on one thing only: to let the Lord have his way with them at all costs. Their hearts have been captivated by the tremendous lover of mankind and they cannot do otherwise than follow his will for them.

The scapular devotion follows the Carmelite vision of Mary as ever virgin, she who was so captivated by God's plans for her life, which upset all her personal projects and became completely human by opening herself to the approaches of God in her life. Her attachment to the Word of God was eminently pure, despite the sorrow and suffering which her sharing in her Son's destiny involved. Her heart never wavered: she *stood* by the cross. Images of Our Lady fainting or swooning in the arms of St John beneath the cross betray the Gospel image of this valiant woman who all her life had accepted the fact her Son was to redeem mankind under the shadow of a cross. Simeon had forewarned her. What a travesty of Mary's true spirit it is to deny her this winning purity of heart under the cross. There her virginal heart, which had been given to no other than her Son, surely was not clouded over or contaminated for the first time. Her whole life of purity had been a preparation for this "hour," which had already been anticipated with Mary's presence at Cana. She was not found wanting.

The scapular wearer emulates this purity of heart. He belongs to Christ and to Mary. Whatever state of life he follows, he seeks to keep his heart and body uncontaminated. The scapular wearer is single-minded; he has no ulterior motives; he is not seeking status or recognition nor even a reputation for holiness. All he prays for is that he remain pure in his intent to let Christ and Mary reign supreme in his life, that his life might reflect the single purpose that motivated their lives, so that he too might be ready even to die for his first love. Everything in the world is his because his heart belongs to the Lord and to the world's mistress.

Simplicity

Finally the scapular devotion engenders the virtue of simplicity. This attitude is characteristic of the modern generation who has had a surfeit of surrogates which have been meant to make them happy and free but which have failed. There is a general trend to return to the simple things of life which tend to be taken for granted by those who are seeking to get ahead in life. The simple person is anything but

258

a dull, boring or monotonous person. He is a person fully alive because he takes life as it is lived minute by minute and strives to appreciate it all—even—and especially in its most banal and routine manifestations. For a simple person a "Hello" or "Good morning" or "So long" are not conventional phrases, but communications of interior wealth to another.

The simple person is one who has found the unity in his life, who sees life full of meaning at every moment, even though most of these moments are anything but exciting and world-shaking. A simple person has found his peace within himself, and so he irradiates a calm and a serenity that are inexplicable, except that he has opened himself up to someone greater than himself and so can really live.

The *anawim*, the faithful remnant of Israel, were a simple people, those who hoped against hope that God would be faithful to his promises. Even when all seemed to militate against the Word of the Lord, they blindly clung to their belief. Mary was the prototype of these "little people" who knew no other way than that of blind trust in God. Mary was a simple person, whose life held its mysteries: but rather than stymieing her, they challenged her to grasp ever more deeply God's loving-kindness. When she pondered the mysteries of her Son's life in her heart, she simply grew in her capacity to magnify the Lord and to allow her spirit to exalt in God her Savior.

The scapular devotion is nothing if it is not simple: wearing the symbol of Mary's garment and seeking to live up to the expectations of so great a mother. There are no fixed prayer formulas, no set penitential practices (though both these are laudable and should be adapted to each scapular wearer's needs and state in life). The constant wearing of the scapular is an ever present reminder that life is to be lived gratefully and intensely every moment—not with puckered brows and clenched fist that denote too much reliance on human effort, but with joyous freedom of those who belong to God and need nothing else. Their hands are turned to him constantly, knowing that he fills the simple with good things, and that Mary as mother is with them always—always available, always watchful, always anxious to help, especially in moments of stress and difficulty and weakness.

* * *

From what we have seen, the scapular devotion takes its place in the mainstream of Catholic life. In our own time a whole generation of Carmelites have been impressed by the childlike devotion to Our Lady of the Scapular of the order's greatest theologian, Fr. Bartholomew M. Xiberta, who sat with Karl Rahner and Henri Lubac at the debating table of Vatiacn II. The learned theologian wrote in his typically precise terms, but with a heart brimming over with unique . love for Mary, his eyes often in tears when he remembered her goodness towards her Carmelite brethren. A favorite way of counting the days of the year was for him counting how many more days until the celebration of July 16. He described his vision of devotion to Our Lady of the Scapular thus:

"A true devotion to Mary, one that is felt in all its fullness, does not limit itself to a few acts of devotion practised at certain definite times, but is a constant, permanent orientation of the deepest affections of the Christian soul. A true devotion to Mary involves much more than the performance of one of the many Marian practices that have been added to the observance of the commandments; it embraces the whole person, and becomes as much a characteristic of that person as that of being a Christian.

"The person who is truly devoted to Mary assumes towards her the attitude a child takes towards its mother by giving her one's whole being. This feature of devotion to Mary is expressed in one word, 'consecration,' that is, a total and exclusive gift by which what is consecrated remains the whole property of the one to whom it is consecrated, and not for a limited time, but forever."

14

CARMEL IS ALL MARY'S

Popular devotion in honor of
Our Lady of Mount Carmel

The thirteenth century Western hermits on Mt. Carmel, who dedicated the chapel in the middle of their cells to the Blessed Virgin Mary, gave the Carmelite Order an inspirational impact which has only grown stonger with the years. The patroness—"to whose praise and glory the order itself was especially instituted in parts beyond the sea" (1282 letter of Prior General Peter of Millau to King Edward I of England)—of the Carmelites' first chapel has been so much of an indispensable presence in the order that there is no aspect of Carmel's life which does not have a Marian tonality. Future centuries would proudly—and with commitment—declare: "Carmel is wholly Marian;" everything in Carmel bears a Marian imprint.

Blessed Titus Brandsma expressed this perennial conviction: "Both superiors and members should help to promote the double spirit of the order with the cooperation and the help of the order's patroness, Mary, under whose patronage they should place every work and in whose honor they should sanctify all their labors. The order is totally Marian not only in name but also in its works, for if it were not Marian it would not be Carmelite." This Marian dimension is not above all a question of exterior display on the July 16 feast, but "the intensity of our interior life is what will give Our Blessed Mother the glory that she deserves" (Bartholomew Maria Xiberta, O. Carm., *Fragmentos doctrinales*, p. 175).

While Carmel's faithful sons and daughters have striven to perpetuate the Marian tonality of their interior life, spontaneously this interior devotion has expressed itself in innumerable ways. Carmel has consistently avoided the minimalistic approach to Mary, nor has it ever espoused the theory that all authentic Marian devotion must be exclusively within. From Marian works of art to popular prints of Our Lady of Mt. Carmel, from majestic Marian sanctuaries to simple altar pieces, from statues of Our Lady which have won national prizes for art (e.g., at Aylesford), to mass-produced statues of Carmel's patroness: the order's presence throughout the Catholic world has been characterized by outward symbols of Mary's indispensable role in Carmel.

Even in areas where Carmelites are basically committed to the promotion of justice and peace among the downtrodden and exploited peoples, it is significant that "the little people of God" are the first to ask for some outward representation of Mary's perennial interest and charity. How many requests there are for scapulars, for holy pictures, from the humble and little ones of this world, whose grammar may be tainted, but whose interest in Christ's and Mary's love for them cannot be shaken by any earthly force. The world's oppressed know experientially the limitations and abuses of all social systems; in their rigorous simplicity they know that even when their rights and dignity are better safeguarded, the only definitive state of happiness is embodied in Christ Jesus and secondarily in the blessed mother who has the motherly role of guiding and caring for them until they are safely home.

Although Carmelites can be found in any number of apostolic commitments, still over the years a "constant" witness of Carmel has been in sanctuaries and churches dedicated to Our Lady. When Carmelites took refuge in Europe, they dedicated their first churches to Our Lady, particularly in the mystery of the annunciation (e.g., the 13th century churches in Trapani, Catania, Marsala in Sicily, Genoa, Milan and even Avignon). Even when Carmelites were assigned already existing and dedicated churches such as San

Martino ai Monti in Rome in 1299, devotion to Our
Lady became a hallmark of their pastoral service.

Confraternities of the scapular

A typical manifestation of the effectiveness of the
Marian dimension was the establishment of various
Marian confraternities in churches served by Carmelites. At times these were not scapular confraternities
but rather lay associations whose function was to
honor Our Lady and to offer their members a sturdy
Marian oriented spirituality. In some places they
were named *Laudesi* (praisers), as they were characterized by the public praise and honor paid to Our
Lady in her joys and sorrows, or other mysteries. In
1267 the confraternity in Toulouse, France, had five
thousand members. Florence (1280) and Cambridge
(c. 1300) have historically documented confraternities
of this type. Carmelites were obviously "natural"
sponsors of these popular lay movements of Marian
spirituality. The Siena group explicitly acknowledges
its submission "to the custody of the brothers of
Blessed Mary of Carmel and to their advice" (cf. J.
Smet, *The Carmelites* I, p. 25; C. Catena, *Le Carmelitane*, p. 57).

At their origins these confraternities were valuable expressions of the good which Marian devotion in
the church can attain: by the celebration of the sacraments, by processions, by preaching, by penitential
practices, by a sustained prayer life, by imitation of
the virtues of Our Lady, these confraternities were a
popular manifestation of the mystery of Christ and of
his mother Mary. Often these spiritual practices
were complemented by charitable works of mercy in
favor of the poor, the sick, prisoners, pilgrims and
the deceased. From a robust devotion towards Mary,
who showed her motherly charity towards all, especially towards those most in need, her devotees understood that they must provide the same type of loving, humble service to the needy. Although with the
passage of time, these confraternities often lost their
original vision of true devotion both in spirituality
and in service and became too concerned with the

salvation of the individual through "guaranteed" practices of piety, still at their roots they were valid and valuable movements of lay participation in the life of the church.

The scapular confraternity grew out of this movement. Layfolk wished to have closer ties to the order and asked to join the confraternity of Carmel, with the possibility of wearing the habit or at least a part of the habit, as the typically medieval sign of belonging to the order of Our Lady. In all likelihood this is the origin of the scapular devotion; lay persons asked to be invested in the "small" habit or scapular, in order to be linked to the spirituality of Carmel, to its perennial devotion to Our Lady, to become part of the liturgical and paraliturgical service offered to God at the hands of and in the spirit of the Blessed Mother (cf. Valentino Macca, *Maria tra pietà, devozione e culto,* in *Religiosità populare,* p. 234-236).

The root meaning of the scapular confraternity, then, is a characteristic movement through which layfolk wished to be associated with the spirituality of Carmel. Wisely integrating internal renewal with external observances, the confraternity aimed to give Gospel witness to the values of Catholicism. Particularly when attacked by protestant accusations of infidelity to the Gospel, the church found a potent embodiment of her values in the scapular confraternity. This is how one contemporary writer describes the scapular confraternity's role:

"In our days Spain is outstanding; there is not a house in that land in which the habit of Carmel is not worn in order to obtain the infinite Carmelite indulgences. Both daughters of King Philip of Spain and all his courtiers wore Our Lady of Mt. Carmel's habit or 'patience' and the long, wide one at that, as worn by the friars of the order. It was given to them personally by the Most Reverend General John Baptist Rossi of Ravenna. Does not all of Spain and Portugal seem to be one great Carmelite convent? ... In Italy, especially in the kingdom of Naples and in Lombardy, there is an infinite number of confraternity members who meet frequently with great devotion. At Piacenza more than ten thousand members are in-

scribed in the register of the confraternity; men, women, laymen and religious of other orders, secular
priests and nuns of diverse orders. Upper and Lower
Germany have an infinite number of confraternity
members, but because of the doomed heretics many
fell away. France had the most members of the
whole order, but today it is oppressed by sac-
ramentary enemies" (Joseph Falcone, cited by J.
Smet, *Carmelites II*, p. 25).

Until the twentieth century, the scapular devotion
remained one of the hallmarks of Catholicism. In
some places mothers had their infants enrolled in the
scapular at baptism, or whole classes of first commu-
nicants were asked to return to church on the afternoon of their First Communion Day in order to be
enrolled in the scapular. Recently, from Zaire, the
story of Isidore Bakanja has witnessed to the strength
of the scapular devotion as a sign of one's Catholic
faith. In 1913, Isidore, a young native worker and a
convert to Catholicism, was introduced to the rosary
and scapular devotions by the Belgian missionaries
who were his spiritual guides. A hostile, non-believ-
ing foreman from Belgium resented Isidore's spontaneous show of his faith. After other episodes of
hatred for the hired hand, the foreman at a certain
point demanded that Isidore throw away the scapular
he had hanging around his neck. When Isidore
politely refused, he was beaten to such a degree that
he died some time later. He had been inscribed in
the Carmelite scapular confraternity by the missionaries: a modern martyr, for whom the scapular had
become a symbol of his new found faith, for which
he was willing to suffer even death.

The La Bruna *shrine in Naples*

Devotion to Our Lady was so much part of the
Carmelite mystique that sanctuaries and churches en-
trusted to the pastoral care of Carmelites were dedicated to Our Lady, or else became the venue of a popular, fervent devotion adapted to the culture and tem-
perament of the various peoples. Some of these
sanctuaries have survived to our own day.

265

Probably none has been better known within the order than Our Lady *La Bruna* of Carmine Maggiore in Naples. Like so many other ancient images of Our Lady in the Carmelite tradition, so this one, painted on wood, reputedly was brought to Europe from Mt. Carmel when the friars were chased out by the Saracens. Although there is no official image of Our Lady of Mt. Carmel, *La Bruna* comes closest and is probably the most widespread. Ven Michael of St Augustine, as provincial of the reformed Belgian province, ordered a copy of the picture for each house. Many in the order followed his example. In some Carmelite houses every room had a copy of *La Bruna*, e.g. until a few years ago, in the International College of St Albert in Rome. In some places this image evoked the devotion of the Seven Joys of Our Lady, celebrated on Wednesdays in particular.

The Neapolitan Madonna, with blue mantle and brownish tunic, is pictured holding the Child Jesus, pressing his cheek to hers. The image, enshrined above the main altar with an ambience behind the altar in which the faithful are able to come close to the Madonna, is a masterful combination of stateliness and humanness. Rare is the Neapolitan who has not heard of this Madonna, or rather, the 'Mamma of Carmine.' To the Neapolitan soul the proper way to celebrate the patronal feast of July 16 is with a fireworks display around a brightly illuminated facade of Carmine. But much deeper is the experience of Mary's motherly touch in the people's lives. Mary for the Neapolitan is not a mere pretty picture but a living icon, a living presence who is part of one's family, or better, who invites her friends to be part of her family.

Wednesdays in particular are dedicated to popular dislays of devotion to Mary. The Basilica is filled with faithful who come from various zones of the city and its suburbs to keep their weekly visit with the 'Mamma' of their families who has consistently proven herself in ways that her devotees consider wondrous and even miraculous. Casual visitors are struck by the fact that many of those present are men. One of Our Lady's clients gave this rationale for his weekly visit: from my mother's knees I learned to look to our 'Carmine Mamma' in all the ups and downs of life. My joys and sorrows, my needs and fears, I poured out before her whom I have come to love as a mother. How could I miss my weekly visit to so good and concerned a mother? I was a member of the *carabinieri* (select police force) all my life. Now in retirement, I try to share my debt of gratitude to the Madonna with my children and grandchildren.

The little people of God make up the vast majority of visitors to the Madonna di Carmine. Unsophisticated trust in the motherly charity of Mary draws them week after week. They come to Our Lady to learn how to be better disciples of Christ Jesus. One woman put it so: "Father, please pray with me to *la Mamma* of Carmine. At home I have my aging mother whom I am taking care of. She would die if I would put her in an old age home. But how difficult it's becoming! She is getting more and more senile and capricious. Sometimes I just don't seem to be able to cope any more. I've come to ask Our Lady to teach me how to be patient and loving towards my mother until the end. After all, my mother put up with me and my stupidities in the past. Pray with me that Our Lady always stand by me."

At other times people come to Our Lady to ask for favors and for her protection. One mother explained why she was at Carmine: "So far my teenage children are great. But Father, you know what it's like out there. Our 'Mamma' of Carmine cannot refuse me when I ask her to keep my children good, can she?" A worried husband gave this reason for his presence: "I've just come out of the hospital myself. Now my wife has just been admitted and it seems she'll have to undergo a serious operation. I've come to beg our 'Mamma' to spare my wife. She's been a wonderful companion and spouse. The Blessed Mother has always understood my poor prayers. I think she'll hear me out this time too!"

Another Marian shrine which is as vibrant today as it was at its opening in the thirteenth century is Trapani at the Western tip of Sicily. Dedicated to the annunciation, this Gothic basilica, transformed into a baroque temple in the 1600's, has become the diocesan Marian shrine. Although also known for devotion to native son St Albert of Sicily, Carmelite, the shrine above all is a Marian sanctuary. Its jewel is a lifesize, marble statue of Our Lady, probably from the 1200 or 1300's, whose beauty has been universally acclaimed and often imitated. The blessed virgin is holding the Child Jesus; the two are looking at each other smilingly. The virgin's serene smile has captured the wholesome interior world of Mary.

The people of Trapani pay their Madonna their reverence and gratitude year round, but particularly in the months of July and August when the Carmine and Assumption feasts are celebrated with special devotion and warmth. The best available preachers are invited in order to make the feasts into grace filled moments of evangelization and catechesis. Throughout the year the sanctuary is frequented by thousands of faithful, and in particular there is a daily visit by many youngsters on their way to the adjacent school. Often young engaged couples are seen praying before Our Lady's shrine; small wonder that many of them ask for permission to celebrate their marriage before their heavenly mother. The sacramental life of the sanctuary has been one of its strong points over the years, as the Carmelites provide yet another example of how our sacramental encounter with the Lord Jesus is effected in the house and at the intercession of Mary. She who brought forth the Savior of the world continues the same mission in the perennial celebrations of the sacraments, of the Eucharist and of Reconciliation in particular.

Carmelite devotion towards the Mother of God has taken many forms particularly in those places with venerable traditions that often go back for centuries and literally to time immemorial. Several towns like Mesagne (Puglia) and Ispica (Sicily) honor Our Lady of Mt. Carmel as their principal patroness with the attendant celebrations of July 16. The custom of inviting special preachers for the solemnity has been used effectively to introduce the faithful to a more wholesome appreciation of the role of the blessed mother in Christian life. Following the inspiration of Vatican II and the numerous helps which have been provided since, preachers go beyond the privileges of Mary to her solidarity with God's people on the pilgrimage of faith to the Father. From excessive stress on the miraculous, Mary's role in the plan of salvation—as described particularly in the scriptures, in the liturgy and in conciliar documents—has become much clearer.

While Mary does not deal with people *en masse,* but as individuals, she does so like every mother in the context of the Christian family. An overly individualistic approach to Mary is slowly giving way to the full import of Pope Paul VI's title "Mother of the Church." Rather than casting Mary's beauty and incisiveness in splendid isolation, contemporary preaching stresses her role as the perfect disciple of her Son Jesus, in complete subordination to him and to his mission.

The updated teaching on Mary's place in Carmelite hearts has for the most part been judiciously harmonized with the obvious need for external manifestations and celebrations. When the friars have not been able to organize the feast, often confraternities or the Third Order have taken on the external celebration of July 16.

This feast began as the solemn yearly commemoration of the benefits enjoyed by confraternity members, so it is a return to the roots when confraternities in places like Palermo and Catania, Sicily, insure a worthy and even exuberant honor paid to Our Lady of Mt. Carmel for her unremitting goodness towards members of her family.

Even when modern traffic problems have caused church and civil authorities to question the feasibility of an outdoor procession in a frequented zone such as that around Our Lady of Traspontina on the main street leading to St Peter's Basilica in Rome, the local people have not been impressed. They have demanded their procession which traditionally finishes in St Peter's Square. The popular and deeply seated dimensions of this devotion are evident by the fact that some of the most ardent supporters are those who politically are on the left side of the spectrum!

Rome and Malta honor Our Lady of Mt. Carmel

Significant is the fact that the four parishes which the Carmelites service in Rome all have a sturdy Marian orientation. The image of Our Lady of Mt. Carmel in the Basilica of San Martino ai Monti is the most revered icon in the church. It is fittingly encased in the Blessed Sacrament chapel, where most of the liturgical life of the parish is celebrated in the course of the week. In Traspontina, not only is there a venerable Byzantine Madonna over the main altar, sheltered under an artistic baldacchino, but there is also a life-sized statue of a seated Lady of Mt. Carmel at a side altar. People not only from the parish venerate Our Lady dressed in the brown and white of Carmel, but many devotees, including government ministers, come from considerable distances to show their esteem and trust in the Carmelite virgin and mother. The constant floral and candle tributes are symbols of grateful and trusting hearts in her who has proven herself a faithful and loving mother. The many people, men and women of all social ranks, who kneel before Our Lady to dialogue with her, are the best manifestation of Christians' abiding faith in the living presence and intervention of Our Lady. The saints and Our Lady are not just pious, useful memories; they are alive—more than we, because they now live the life that knows no end and so are able to offer us benefits that are beyond momentary contentment.

The two new Carmelite parishes in Rome are both dedicated to Our Lady. The first, in the populous Torrespaccata section, teeming with a populace from many parts of Italy, especially the south, is dedicated to Our Lady Queen of the World. It was the first church dedicated under this new title after Pope Pius XII's letter on this Marian mystery. The other new parish, in the modern EUR section, is dedicated explicitly to Our Lady of Mt. Carmel.

The island of Malta, which has given many illustrious Carmelites to the order, has been a fortress of devotion towards Our Lady of Mt. Carmel since the province's foundation in the 1400's. The first foundation was dedicated to the annunciation (and is currently being restored with its hermit's caves and chapel in the ancient Carmelite tradition). The Basilica of Valletta, recently restored, honors a most precious image of Our Lady of Mt. Carmel (by an unknown artist, c. 1600). The scapular vision depicted on it made history in our day when, for the centenary celebrations of the scapular vision, the Maltese obtained permission from the British authorities to issue a three value series of postage stamps reproducing the Madonna of Carmine, but without the portrait of the Queen of England which, until then, had been *de rigeur* on all stamps of Commonwealth countries. The people's daily devotion to Our Lady of Mt. Carmel is climaxed on July 16 not only by processions throughout the island but also by other symbols of the people's commitment to Carmel's mother and beauty. Specially composed music in polyphony for solemn vespers, celebrated in an overflowing church, is a typical expression of the Maltese devotion for Mary of Mt. Carmel, who has been an integral part of Maltese history through the centuries.

Aylesford, Carmel restored in England

In 1949 the Carmelite Order was blessed when, under Prior General Kilian Lynch, the ancient friary of Aylesford in England was reacquired. One of the original English foundations in 1242, The Friars had been expropriated at the time of the reformation. Not only was the friary linked to a tradition that made it the venue of the scapular vision to St Simon Stock, but its medieval church had been dedicated to the assumption of Our Lady. Although the church had completely disappeared, the restoration of Aylesford, ably inspired by Fr. Malachy Lynch, aimed at the building of an outdoor shrine in honor of the

271

same assumption. Combining the talents of top ranked artists with the needs of a popular Marian shrine, Aylesford has provided the church in England with one of its most frequented Marian sanctuaries. The open air shrine church features a prizewinning statue in gold gilt wood representing the Assumption of Our Lady, but throughout the shrine there are numerous affirmations of the presence of Mary and of other Catholic pieties. Visitors have often spontaneously expressed this reaction: "In this place the living presence of Mary becomes a deeply felt experience." With its offshoot community at Allington Castle, two miles down the Medway River, Aylesford has become a model for the order of the possibilities of a Marian shrine in service of the upbuilding of the people of God in a secularized world.

Traditional pieties such as the rosary and the scapular are still basic fare. The Rosary Way behind the church, featuring ceramic representations of the fifteen mysteries of the rosary by renowned artist Adam Kossowski, is part of the pilgrims' devotion. The particular intentions of the shrine for which special prayers are offered are: a return to the fold of those who have wandered off; a renewal of faith and religion; conversion to the true faith of Jesus Christ. On Sundays and greater feasts, a venerable statue of the Blessed Virgin giving the scapular to St Simon Stick is carried in procession, often made up of thousands of participating pilgrims. These afternoon devotions are climaxed by a sermon, often on Our Lady, and by benediction of the Blessed Sacrament in the outdoor shrine. Afterwards people are invited to be enrolled in the scapular. A brief explanation of the scapular is followed by the ceremony of enrollment. A newsletter edited by the Prior of Aylesford keeps people abreast of the activities and of the life at The Friars, as well as of their commitment to the Aylesford apostolate.

Taking to heart the recommendation of Pope Paul VI in *Marialis cultus* (n. 24), Fr. Hugh Ckarke has attempted "to promote a genuine creative activity" with regard to the rosary. Noting that there are many other mysteries of Christ's life and of Mary's presence which could be the object of our medita-

272

tions during the praying of the beads, he has proposed in pamphlet form other mysteries: apostolic, merciful, eucharistic. While giving the apposite scriptural passages in each case, he has singled out five apostolic mysteries as: 1) the Baptism of Jesus; 2) the Wedding Feast at Cana; 3) the True Family of Jesus; 4) the Sermon on the Mount; 5) Mary Chooses the Better Part. The Merciful mysteries he lists as: 1) the Name of Jesus; 2) Jesus and Sinners; 3) the Pharisee and the Publican; 4) the Good Shepherd; 5) the Good Thief. And finally the Eucharistic mysteries he proposes as: 1) the Feeding of the Five Thousand; 2) the Promise of the Eucharist; 3) the Institution of the Eucharist; 4) the Death of Jesus; 5) the Glorification of Jesus.

Besides being a pilgrimage center, Aylesford over the years has taken on many other dimensions. The retreat center is a fulltime operation and nationally advertized. Carmelites preach many of the retreats, while others are conducted by guest speakers or retreat masters. The retreatants are able to be inserted into the daily schedule of religious exericises which characterize the shrine. They also are able to make use of the sizeable community of friars for the sacrament of reconciliation and for counseling and spiritual direction.

The ecumenical aspect of Aylesford has broadened over the years. About a third of the visitors are not Catholics. Some, especially of the Anglican communion, make frequent use of The Friars for retreats and study days. A humble but very effective ecumenical gesture has developed into the annual Anglican pilgrimage to this Marian shrine, usually led by some distinguished leader of the Anglican church. The common love and devotion for the mother of God is a unifying factor which grows with the years.

In England, where Mediterranean exuberance is not the rule, it is again the little people of God who frequent Aylesford, proud that their country has been entitled "the dowry of Mary" and confident that Mary will be as benevolent to the modern generation as she has been to their forefathers. The mother of two youngsters, nine and eleven years old, comes on pilgrimage from Northern Ireland: "Father, my one prayer to the Blessed Mother and the reason I came here is to beg that these children of mine keep their faith unsullied all the days of their life." A worker from a nearby Ford factory takes a week of his holidays to ask for a private retreat, "so that I can give better witness to my Christian faith on the Ford assembly line." The vocation director of a boys' school brings a group of youngsters for a weekend retreat to discern with them the meaning of a priestly and religious vocation. The father of two young teenagers brings his children to Our Lady's Shrine begging for Mary's aid in bringing up the children, left to him by his wife who had deserted her family for another man. An elderly widow is begging Our Lady to help her in her plight to find a new flat, as she is being evicted from her present one.

The simple devotion taught by Fr. Malachy Lynch—venerating one's scapular each morning while praying, "Mary, use me today"—has affected the lives of thousands. Aylesford itself is a sign of the spontaneous, unexpected ways in which the blessed mother can make use of us if we commit ourselves to her. Much of Aylesford's apostolate has developed spontaneously without precise planning.

While making himself available to a crowd of up to 5,000 people gathered for a Sunday afternoon service, a friar may find himself confronted by a young, engaged couple from London. "Why are wearing a brown habit of a different color from that other friar?" is a first innocuous question. The second is the real one: "How can you know that Christianity and not Buddhism or Islam is the religion revealed by God to mankind?" A tract on revelation must be condensed into a 5-8 minute respite before the buses leave. The next day the girl comes cycling from London and praying the rosary the whole way, in order to thank Our Lady that because of yesterday's visit her fiancé is going to take instructions and they will be married in the Catholic church.

The priest explaining the scapular devotion to a group of 25-30 people on a Sunday afternoon notices that one woman is standing to the side, taking everything in, but obviously embarassed to come forward. When the others have left she approaches the priest and explains: "Father, I am one of those lost sheep of which the Gospel speaks. I've been away from the church and from religious practice for forty years. Today, I stopped here by chance. I've heard the message of Aylesford. I hear Our Lady's call and concern and the fact that she has been watching over me all this time, even while I paid no attention to her and her Son. Please enrol me in the scapular so that I never forget this moment of grace and return to the flock."

Carmelite devotion in Ireland

Across the Irish Sea in Dublin the Carmelites' Whitefriars Street church enshrines the treasured statue of Our Lady of Dublin. A "black Madonna" carved out of dark oak in the German school of Dürer, the statue probably belonged to the Cistercian Abbey of St. Mary, but during penal times was used as a trough. Rescued from a secondhand shop by well-known Dr. John Spratt, O. Carm., it was finally given a suitable niche in 1837 when the Carmelites were permitted to return to their Whitefriars Street Church. Subsequently the statue was suitably mounted and crowned in a chapel to the left of the main entrance of the church. It remains a memorial to the often turbulent conditions of the faith in Ireland. The statue of Our Lady of Dublin is a plastic reminder that the mother of God has accompanied her devoted people through their troubles.

The Carmelite brown scapular has served as the pledge and reminder of Mary's motherly concern and solidarity through many a trial and persecution. In fact, in penal times it was recognized as the sign of a faithful Catholic in Ireland. The Irish tradition of being buried in a Carmelite habit, of which the scapular is but a symbol, is epitomized by the final wishes of President de Valera, whose devotion to Our Lady of Mt. Carmel was proverbial. Even protestants attest to the fact that the scapular devotion was widespread in the troubled times (cf. Peter O'Dwyer,

Mary's Keepsake, p. 12-22). A popular poem from probably the 17th century embodies the meaning of the scapular for the Irish people:

In scapular of brown ye walk who hear
The message I would speak, lest pain
And fear and friendless woe be near
Thy final hour on deathbed lain.
In Mary trust, thy heart keep true
or, false, thy heart shall learn to rue.
And Wednesday's meat thou shalt not share
Nor reck the anguish of thy care.
Thy pride of self sustain the least
Her humble child, before the priest.
Five feasts of Mary will thou keep
To win her loved one's peaceful sleep.
Confess at least thy sin-soiled state
And thou will see her dear Son's fête.

The Carmelite presence at Ireland's national shrine to Mary at Knock, carried on in the person of ex-missionary Stephen Josten, O. Carm., is the continuation of a long history of Carmel's contribution to Marian devotion in that country.

Our Lady of Mt. Carmel at Fatima

Another initiative of Fr. Kilian Lynch's years as prior general was the establishment of a Carmelite community in Fatima, Portugal. Assured by one of Fatima's visionaries, Sr. Lucy, that the scapular devotion was an integral part of Fatima's message, Fr. Lynch initiated the building of Casa Beato Nuno. Originally the site was destined for an international center of lay Carmelites. While never discarding this finality, the Casa is at present a pilgrims' hostel administered by the Carmelites of both first and third orders. Not only is an atmosphere congenial to pilgrimage inculcated, but spiritual care of the lay help is so assiduous that one of the youngsters who worked at the reception desk for several years entered the friars' novitiate, and a girl who was part of the staff entered the novitiate of the Third Order Regular Sisters of Orihuela.

While offering their services at the sanctuary and in neighboring parishes the friars aim to make the Fatima stay of pilgrims a genuine spiritual experience. The reverence and simple devotion of the Portuguese people for Our Lady, who honored their land with her presence in 1917, is a lasting impression made on a foreign pilgrim. The abundance of youngsters and of whole family units at the shrine is a grace filled symbol of the incisiveness of Mary's touch on human lives and hearts in Portugal.

The monthly procession of Our Lady's statue the length and breadth of the immense square before the basilica leaves living vignettes of a faith that is imperishable—because simple and humble. The mother and father clutching their two sleeping youngsters to themselves, but intent on covering the whole route of the procession with the others; the humble people whom God loves standing for hours under the blazing sun during the celebration of the Eucharist; the last persons in the procession are two nuns in their 80's, one leaning on the other, hobbling along with the help of canes but with the glistening eyes of children who will not be deprived of a good thing; the gnarled hands of a peasant whose clothes show he is used to sleeping outdoors with his flock, but whose baritone voice can be heard devoutly singing the praises of Mary, verse after verse after verse; the little children, led by their mothers, enthusiastically practising how they will kneel when the statue of Our Lady passes by; a young couple praying quietly, reverently before Our Lady's statue, begging Mary's blessing on their blossoming love; lines and lines of people waiting to receive the saving word of reconciliation through the sacrament of penance; the silent tears of a grandmother and her teenage granddaughter as the statue of Our Lady of Fatima hovers over them for a moment during the procession; the thousands of handkerchiefs waving their adieu to their blessed mother as the statue is being returned to its regular niche and the all-night vigil officially comes to an end. And these are but external symbols; what of the internal work of grace which is so powerfully at work at Fatima?

The Carmelite connection with Fatima goes back to the origins of the order in Portugal. Our Lady was always a prominent element in Carmel's presence. When the national hero, Bl Nuno Alvarez, wished to enter an order dedicated to Our Lady at the end of his days, he was most impressed with the Marian spirit of Carmel, which he entered as a lay brother. He finished his life as such, acting as porter in the Lisbon friary, dying in 1431. Actually after his victories over the armies of Castille, which insured Portugal's independance, he built a monumental Marian temple in Lisbon as a thanksgiving to Mary whom he had invoked all this life and to whom he had confided his armies before battle. He assigned this church and its adjacent friary to the Carmelites precisely because of their well-known Marian traditions.

Carmel in Portugal kept the memory of Our Lady and her help in time of need alive by means of the scapular devotion. The latter was on a par with the rosary as the ordinary fare of Catholics. Even when the friars were prohibited in the country by anti-clerical laws, the scapular confraternities kept on flourishing and nourishing a solid, tender devotion towards Our Lady of Mt. Carmel.

Sr. Lucy, seer of Fatima, has stated that when she was a youngster in 1917, both rosary and scapular were very much part of the scene in Fatima and its environs. In fact the last time that Our Lady appeared, on October 13, she appeared surrounted by dazzling light and changed aspect several times. First she appeared with St Joseph and the Child Jesus, often identified with the joyful mysteries of the rosary. Then she seemed to be Our Lady of Sorrows, identified with the sorrowful mysteries of the rosary. Finally, she appeared as Our Lady of Mt. Carmel, with reference to the glorious mysteries, easily related to the scapular devotion's connection with Our Lady's protection at the hour of death and with its challenge to live a Mary-like life so as to gain the eternal happiness destined for all authentic followers of Christ Jesus (cf. Kilian Lynch, *Our Lady of Fatima and the Brown Scapular*).

Spain's contribution

An historian of Marian devotion in Spain could not fail to note the contribution of Carmel. In the Golden Era of Spain's world-wide influence, the Carmelite presence was extremely strong, as evidenced by the firm roots this devotion took among Latin American peoples evangelized from Spain. This popular devotion has survived particularly in centers of Marian devotion as in Jerez de la Frontera (Andalusia) and El Henar (Castille). In Zaragoza (Aragon), the Carmelite church housed the popular and ancient statue the *Madonna de la Candelaria*. The six-foot painting on wood was cared for by the confraternity in its own chapel. Our Lady is depicted seated on her throne and with sceptre; the Infant Jesus is supported by her other hand. He is looking away from Mary at the instruments of the passion being offered to him by an angel (cf. Smet, *Carmelites* III, p. 488). In Catalonia the Marian devotion of the order can be traced in such ardent apostles of Mary as Fr. Bartholomew Maria Xiberta and the teaching of Ven. Liberata Ferrarons, Carmelite tertiary.

The Slavic countries

In Slavic countries, Carmel's love for Mary found congenial terrain. In Poland even today if a parish priest is looking for a preacher for a Marian celebration, he will think of approaching a Carmelite, as a man of Mary. The present Holy Father often came to the Carmelite church in Krakow which prizes an ancient image of Our Lady of the Sands, miraculously preserved through centuries of destruction and anti-Catholic persecution. The naturally Marian soul of Poland spontaneously makes of this shrine a much frequented and beloved center of devotion. The pope obviously remembered his diocese when he told the capitulars of the General Chapter of 1983: "There is in your order, and powerfully so, a deep Christological and Marian tradition: to follow Christ by imitating Mary. I hope you keep these treasures; be loyal to them, deepen and update them, because they are indestructible treasures that the world and humanity greatly need" (cf. *Carmel in the World* 34 [1984] p. 86).

The statue of the sorrowful Mother venerated at the Order's Church in Obory since 1605 has attracted much devotion. People to this day talk about miracles worked at Mary's intercession. Another widely beloved Madonna is honored in the Carmelite church at Wola Gulowska. Marian devotion is also intense in Pilzno and Gdansk, where Solidarity members like Lech Walęsa are frequent worshippers.

In neighboring Czechoslovakia, Our Lady of Mt. Carmel is venerated particularly in the parish church built specifically for Carmelites in the village Kostelni Vydrí. In 1984 the last Carmelite pastor of this Church, Fr. Melchior Karásek, died. He had just finished hearing confessions on the solemnity of Pentecost and collapsed as he was leaving the church. He was clutching his rosary which he had been praying when the final summons came. Although the church, filled with Carmelite mementos, is now served by a non-Carmelite, the latter has stated that he would maintain the devotion to Our Lady of Mt. Carmel, particularly by sponsoring the pilgrimage which has survived very difficult days and still attracts two to three thousand people on July 16 or on the following Sunday when the solemnity is celebrated.

* * *

Carmelites from various parts of the world may be upset by the fact that in this cursory review of popular devotion to Our Lady of Mt. Carmel, their country or region has not been mentioned. This fact in itself confirms our basic premise. It is right that Carmelites protest when this overriding element of their spirituality is not acknowledged.

Recently an International Marian Commission has been convoked to study the future of devotion to Our Lady of Mt. Carmel, and in particular of the scapular devotion. A first communiqué of this study group, addressed to all Carmelites as well as confraternity members and those associated in other ways, has been distributed. Hopefully, in the next few years, there will be various local, national and regional Marian congresses sponsored by interested Carmelites. Ideally, there will be an International Congress on this dimension of Carmel's charism in two or three years' time. The final goal is a well-documented study of the meaning of devotion to Our Lady of Mt. Carmel and of the scapular in our time as we approach the 21st century.

CARMEL AT PRAYER

**Prayers in honor of
Our Lady of Mount Carmel**

POPE PIUS XII ON PRAYER
TO OUR LADY OF MOUNT CARMEL

July 19, 1946

The Virgin of Carmel, Patroness of seafarers who every day hand their lives over to the instability of wind and waves! From our position as steersman of Peter's barque, when we experience the rage of the storm and before our eyes we see the sea fiercely tossed, threatening to destroy our ship, we raise our gaze, serene and confident, to the Virgin of Carmel— Look to the Star, call upon Mary—and we beg her not to abandon us. And even if hell does not cease its assaults and its violence and the daring and furor of the forces of evil constantly increase, while we count on her mighty protection we never have doubt about the final victory.

AYLESFORD
PILGRIMS' PRAYER

O Holy and Immaculate Virgin, Ornament and Splendor of Carmel, look with an eye of special kindness on those who wear your blessed habit.

Strengthen my weakness with your power; lighten the darkness of my mind with your wisdom; increase in me faith, hope and charity, that I may pay to you, day by day, my debt of humble homage.

May your scapular keep your eyes of mercy upon me always and give me your special protection in my daily struggle to be faithful. May it help me to be humble, charitable and patient, and may it keep me always mindful of your joyful presence and never failing love.

Be always near, O Mother of Carmel, to offer my life and works to Jesus through your pure hands. Help me to pray well, and to be always aware of the presence of God.

Enfold all lost and wandering souls in the mantle of your protection. Be with me and all sinners in life and in death, that with the saints of Carmel I may bless and glorify you for ever in the kingdom of your Son. Amen.

PRAYER
TO OUR LADY OF MOUNT CARMEL

O most beautiful Flower of Carmel,
Fruitful vine, Splendor of Heaven,
Blessed Mother of the Son of God,
Immaculate Virgin,
Assist me in this my time of need.
O Star of the Sea
help me and show me that you are
    my Mother.

O Holy Mary, Mother of God,
Queen of Heaven and Earth,
I humbly beseech you from the bottom
    of my heart
To assist me in this my urgent need.
O show me that you are my Mother.
God, our Father, never leaves unaided
Those fur whom you pray.

O Mary, conceived without sin,
Pray for us who have recourse
    to you (*three times*).

Sweet Mother, I place this cause
In your hands (*three times*).

THE SEVEN JOYS
OF OUR LADY

I

Blessed are you, Father, source of all life and love,
   who filled Mary with grace and joy
at the annunciation of your Son's taking on flesh
   from the beloved daughter of Sion.
As Mary rejoiced that she was called to be associated
   in the work of bringing mankind back to the
   home of the Father,
so may we too be filled with glad enthusiasm as we
   allow ourselves to become instruments of your
   life and love in favor of the world.

II

Blessed are you, Father, who loved us so much as to
   send your Son to us in the form of a child, the
   most beautiful of the sons of men,
at the birth of our Savior you overwhelmed the Virgin Mary with the joy of motherhood by which
   she was able to call Son him whom until then
   you alone called by this name.
As Mary collaborated joyfully in bringing the Word
   made Flesh into our world,
so may we too be an 'additional humanity' for Jesus,
   that we may continue his saving mission to our
   fellow man.

288

III

Blessed are you, Father, who willed to manifest your salvation to all the nations,

and who, at the epiphany of the Lord, flooded Mary's spirit with gladness as she presented her Child for the veneration of the wise men, our forebearers in faith.

In order to make complete the festivities of the marriage feast at Cana, Mary trustingly turned to her Son who brings joy to the whole world.

As Mary became the cause of our joy by pointing out her Son, mankind's Redeemer,

so may we be the heralds of joy and peace in our weary world by witnessing to the presence of Jesus and of his Spirit among us.

IV

Blessed are you, Father, who raised Jesus to new life and by his resurrection inundated the spirit of Mary with gladness.

As Mary exulted in the victory of her Son over sin and death, and in our newfound dignity as members of your household,

so may we proclaim and witness to the heart of the Gospel message.

V

Blessed are you, Father, who welcomed your Son to your right hand as Lord of heaven and earth,

and by his ascension made Mary's heart exult at her Son's full glorification.

As Mary celebrated the recapitulation of all creation in Jesus her Son,

so may we be untiring and joyous in our efforts to extend Christ's lordship to all men and to all creation.

VI

Blessed are you, Father, who sent another Paraclete
to lead your sons and daughters into all truth,
and who, in the mystery of pentecost, once more
overshadowed Mary by the gift of the Spirit,
making her the glorious Queen of Apostles.
As Mary was attentive to every initiative of the Holy
Spirit,
so may we be transformed by the Spirit of Jesus and
by his merciful love.

VII

Blessed are you, Father, who filled heaven with jubilee
at the assumption of the Blessed Virgin Mary, granting her, body and soul, a full share in Christ's
glorification.
As Mary became the delight of angels and saints, and
brought to the heavenly family the tender
warmth of motherly love,
so may we live in imitation of her, in order to be
found worthy one day to share in her eternal
exultation.

SCAPULAR PRAYER
TO THE MOTHER OF THE INCARNATION

O Blessed Virgin,
I consider the small habit which you were so good as
    to give me
as a likeness of the great and precious vestment
which you provided for the Word of God of your very
    substance.

In this symbol I recognize the unique benefit
which all of mankind received from you,
and through you from the Word of God,
covering the nakedness or sin of our first fathers.

You brought us back and enriched us with graces
    which Christ's sacred humanity merited for us.
This benefit is supreme and the source of all other
    graces which God sends to men through your
    goodness,
And by means of which they continue in their natural
    and moral existence during this present life.

I wish this livery to rouse my spirit
to as actual a remembrance as possible of this bene-
    fit,
and my whole being to a constant homage
towards the excellence of the mystery of the Incarna-
    tion.

I wish this small habit to act as a means
by which I can preserve and renew in my soul that
    baptismal grace
with which all Christians are clothed in Christ Jesus.

As the apostle tells us,
I constantly remove the clothing of the old man

and clothe myself anew with all justice, truth and
holiness.

I also wish this small habit to help me
to render homage to you in your quality as Mother of
God.

This latter is the most wondrous and eminent thing
apart from God.

Therefore, I infinitely cherish this livery
which mystically represents the effect of your motherhood.

It roots me all the days of my life
in the very special sentiments of piety and reverence
towards this imposing dignity.

Mathias of St John, O. Carm.

PRAYER TO OUR LADY OF MOUNT CARMEL
EXEMPLAR OF ALL VIRTUES

O Blessed Virgin,
it is with the grace of God that I wish to act.

According to the thought of one of your great servants, St Ambrose,
Your life should serve as a model and rule for all
kinds of persons.

Foliowing his advice, I desire
that your witness and the actions of your life
be always like a mirror before my eyes.
Constantly gazing at your way to perfection
I shall try to assimilate it into my own activities.

I am greatly indebted to you
for having admitted me to the ranks of those who by
means of the scapular
make special profession of honoring and serving
you.

But I realize that I cannot pretend
to acquit myself more worthily of this obligation
than by becoming attentive in imitating your virtues.

St Augustine, one of your great servants, warns us
that the nature of true devotion is to imitate the person being honored.

I acknowledge that the disorder and lack of concern
of my spirit,
together with the weakness of my nature,
will be more apt to alienate me from my goal
than to allow me to approach it.

O kindly Mother,
obtain for me from God the necessary attention, strength and faithfulness
to reach this goal.

This is what you desire most of those who wear your holy habit,
to which you have attached all the blessings and favors
that you promise to those who will wear it devoutly.

Mathias of St John, O. Carm.

FAITHFUL VIRGIN
PRAY FOR US

You are the faithful Handmaid, the faithful Virgin, well accepted and beloved. You know how to run your household: you take all on yourself; you are able to manage well. Pray for us, commit yourself to our needs, as today we place in your hands our firm resolution of amendment.

We ask you to be our intercessor for two things, because there are two houses of God: one on earth and one in heaven. On earth is the church, in heaven paradise. All faithful Virgin, never allow us to be separated from the church, nor in death allow us to be excluded from paradise.

We profess the faith in which we were born, and in which we intend to live and desire to die. May our hearts be torn from us a thousand times before our faith be torn from our hearts. All the blood that courses through our veins, we are ready to shed in the profession of the catholic faith.

Not only are you the faithful Virgin, but you are the Mother of the faith, so that we call you Mother of the Revelation of the Faith. By your intercession set our minds firmly on the truths of our faith, that we may always be obedient to them. Obtain for us the grace to die in the arms of the mother who welcomed us at our birth: our one, holy, catholic, apostolic, Roman church.

But this does not suffice. From the house of faith we wish to pass over into the house of love, to that blessed kingdom in which charity is never ended. I know that we pretend too much: we who are deficient servants aspire to the wages of faithful servants. We need your protection: obtain for us the grace to be faithful servants in order to merit the reward promised them.

Allow us one more word. The promise of an upright person becomes an obligation. We have your promise: I will love those who love me. You are the faithful Virgin. We love you very much. We have nothing else at heart, nothing else fixed in our minds. There is noting we desire so much: we would be faithful in serving you. Nothing do we wish more than your commands. Our lives, such as they are, we wish to spend in your holy service. We die of desire to see you.

We love you, most loveable Virgin. All of us love you. In your gracious faithfulness answer us with your precious love. With that we have all that is good. Amen.

Andrea Mastelloni, O. Carm.

CAUSE OF OUR JOY
PRAY FOR US

Most loving and gracious Mother, obtain for us true happiness. In order to welcome into our hearts that joy which alone can fill them, dispose us to receive that delight of which our hearts are not capable.

You are the teacher of exultation. Draw us to follow your example. You teach us true joy. You said: My spirit rejoices in God my Savior, teaching us that we shall not truly rejoice nor exult except in God. Be for us the cause of authentic and constant joy so that through you we may hear that most welcome invitation: Enter into the joy of your Lord.

You, Joy of heaven, to whom St Cyril of Alexandria addressed himself: The heavens exult through you;

You, Joy of the world, whom St Germanus congratulates: The common joy of the world; and of whom the church sings: Joy of the world, new star in the heavens;

You, Joy of the angels, to whom the same St Cyril says: The heavens exult through you, the angels are glad;

You, Joy of all mankind, when you gave birth to the Son of God, you spread joy over all. There come to my lips the words of Pope St Leo: Because our Lord, the destroyer of sin and death, found no one free of guilt, he came to free everyone. And he adds: Let the saint exult because he draws near to his reward; let the sinner be glad because he is invited to receive pardon.

Cause of our Joy, pray for us. Obtain for us this one grace, the grace that supplies for all our desires, for all that we need, the grace of graces: that God be with us in this life and we be with God in the next.

Holy Mother, you who are the mother of Jesus are also the mother of his members. You give birth to them continuously; you give them access to the lasting joy of eternal happiness. Be so good as to bring us to birth to the life of eternal jubilee. Amen.

Andrea Mastelloni, O. Carm.

TO THE MOTHER OF GOD

Holy Virgin, esteemed Queen of heaven and earth, Mother and Patroness of Carmel,

I offer you this book as an expression of my desire to honor you and as a public testimony to the complete dedication I have made to you of my heart and my life from the moment I came to know you.

Even before my birth, my parents vowed me to the service of your Majesty; on coming of age I fulfilled their vow by entering your holy Order; and since then I have always considered you my sovereign Princess.

Without the slightest hesitation I have considered myself entirely yours, realizing that, as one of your faithful and dedicated servants, I must work day and night for your glory, and that I can accomplish nothing without referring it to you in a special way.

I have acquitted myself of this task very poorly.

On this occasion, however, though I have so often failed you, I offer you the fruit of my studies.

Receive it, incomparable Virgin, on your own terms, for I present it to you, submissive to your dominion and ever devoted to the service of your Majesty.

Take this book into your care that your brightness may dispel whatever shadow I have cast on it, and that it may enlighten those who read it and may guide them happily in the ways of religious perfection.

Etienne de St Francis Xavier, O. Carm.

DEDICATION

Most pure Virgin, holy Mary, Mother of God, special glory, ornament and patroness of Carmel! It is I, one of your children, who confidently present you in this short work, consecrated to arouse veneration of you, the fruit of my vigils, the firstfruits of my pen. This homage, this public witness of my gratitude is due you for many reasons. After God, I owe everything to you. I have been under your protection from the moment I began to exist; my birth was the fruit of your powerful intercession. Every day of my life has been marked by some sign of your motherly goodness.

Happy would I be if I had but known how to profit from such and so much powerful help! Happy would I be if my feeble efforts could make up for my unfaithfulness in your service. My heart, sensitive to whatever touches your glory, will not cease to publish your mercies. Under your auspices I was introduced into the land of Carmel, added to your holy family, instructed in the wonders you worked in favor of our fathers. For the welfare of the church I hasten, holy Virgin, to celebrate—for your glory and for the edification of your children—the prerogatives of your confraternity, the wonders of the holy scapular, this precious gift, this unique privilege, with which you have deigned to adorn the Order of Carmel. I hasten to proffer the exquisite fruits of virtue which abound in this blessed land of Carmel where the milk and honey of authentic and solid devotion flow on all sides.

My hopes shall be fulfilled if this small work, dedicated to the instruction of the faithful who attach themselves to your service, can in some way contribute to enlighten their devotion, to increase and perfect their veneration. Amen.

Venerable Martinien Pannetier, O. Carm.

FLOWER OF CARMEL

Flower of Carmel,
Tall vine blossom laden;
Splendor of heaven,
Child-bearing yet maiden,
    None equals thee.

Mother so tender,
Whom no man didst know;
On Carmel's children
Thy favors bestow,
    Star of the Sea.

Strong stem of Jesse
Who bore one bright flower,
Be ever near us
And guard us each hour
    who serve thee here.

Purest of lilies,
That flowers among thorns,
Bring help to the true heart
That in weakness turns
    and trusts in thee.

Strongest of armor,
We trust in thy might;
Under thy mantle,
Hard press'd in the fight,
    we call to thee.

Our way uncertain,
Surrounded by foes,
Unfailing counsel
You give to those
    who turn to thee.

O gentle Mother
Who in Carmel reigns,
Share with your servants
That gladness you gained
    and now enjoy.

Hail, Gate of Heaven,
With glory now crowned,
Bring us to safety
Where thy Son is found,
    true joy to see.

PRAYER
TO OUR LADY OF MOUNT CARMEL

Peerless Virgin, most pure flower of Carmel, your motherly intercession before the throne of God and your love for us give us complete trust that through you our prayers will be heard by Jesus your Son and our Redeemer. Because you, Mother mild, know our spiritual difficulties and the many trials of our human existence, we hope to be refreshed by you, above all by means of the holy scapular which in your hands reveals itself as an authentic mirror of humility and of chastity, a compendium of modesty and of simplicity, an eloquent remembrance of Christian living, because it consecrates us to you, the patroness, mother and sister of all members of the family of Carmel.

Splendor of heaven, grant to our spirits, wounded by sin but redeemed by the innocent blood of Jesus, the abundance of your favors.

May the light of your comfort and of your motherly tenderness descend on the needs of the church and of the world, on our personal needs, on the needs of those who suffer, on the souls in purgatory, and on the aridity of each and every person.

Star of the sea, assist us in all the ups and downs of life until you see us safe with you for all the eternal ages. Amen.

PRAYER OF THANKSGIVING
TO OUR LADY OF MOUNT CARMEL

Blessed Virgin of Mount Carmel, incomparable mother of all your children, blessed are you because our afflictions were not hidden from you and we are able joyfully to proclaim your mercy.

We wish to render you our humble thanks for the benefits we have received from you, and we are delighted to try to express this to you. But far beyond what words are able to do, you can read the gratitude in the depths of our hearts.

We beg that your watchful intercession assist us during the rest of our lives, so that we persevere in faithfulness to the Lord and in our love for you, so that we can be united with you in eternal thanksgiving to Jesus, who lives and reigns for all the eternal ages. Amen.

THE CARMELITE FAMILY'S
ACT OF COMMITMENT TO OUR LADY

Flower of Carmel, Vine in Bloom, Splendor of Heaven, you alone are Virgin and Mother.

We greet you, gracious mother, with these words which generations of Carmelites have addressed to you. Never were they disappointed.

We know that your Immaculate Heart, overflowing with motherly love, does not change. We are certain that under the protection of so great a mother we will never wander from the way that leads to the summit of Mount Carmel, which is Christ the Lord.

The whole Carmelite family is gathered, linked not by material bonds but by the proofs of your love toward us. These bonds cause us to reply spontaneously with love, with gratitude, with confidence.

We cannot hoard this treasure for ourselves. We wish to share it with all those who were committed to your motherly care under the cross of your Son. You became the mother of every disciple of Jesus through your suffering on Calvary; you are thus always at the side of those who suffer and are in anguish. For this reason, most tender of mothers, you are so loved in the entire catholic world under the title of Our Lady of Mount Carmel.

Pope Pius XII often recommended the devotion of Carmel to the faithful as a symbol of the consecration of the whole world to your Immaculate Heart. We, seconding the wish of Pope John Paul II, renew this consecration enthusiastically.

Mother and Beauty of Carmel, the refreshing dew of the entire catholic world, as members of the one Body of your Son, in our act of commitment to you we wish to include the world of the second millennium, a world rich in promise but beset by so many evils: our world, this world which we must love.

The church has recently encouraged us with the words of the present Holy Father: "Continue to follow Jesus in imitation of Mary. The church needs always to be the church more fully in its component parts, and among these you are important, basic components, because you come directly from the Gospel." Imitating you, allowing ourselves to be transformed into you, our mother, we can become what the church rightfully expects of us.

We gather under your mantle of motherly love. Protected and led by you, the perfect disciple of your Son, we wish to be nothing other than an 'additional humanity' for Jesus. Stammering, we consecrate ourselves as a perpetuation of what Jesus did out of love for us: "For them," he told us, "I consecrate myself, so that they too are consecrated in truth." Our one hope is to be inserted into this consecration which issues from the pure grace of our Redeemer. Buffeted daily by evil from within and from without, we affirm our trust in the power of this consecration. It is Christ's, and so it can triumph over all the ills: all hatred, all wars, all sins which afflict our contemporary world, so advanced and at the same time so weak.

We recognize our insignificance; but gazing at you, the humble handmaid of the Lord, we understand that he works redemption through the little and the weak, through things that are despised. We commit ourselves even to the most humble tasks, to our annoying daily routine, with faithfulness and enthusiasm, hoping to bring love and light and reconciliation where these are lacking.

The Carmelite family will never be able to thank God adequately for the gift of yourself, who were the inspirational force at the very foundation of Carmel. In your stainless virginity, so dear to our fathers, we see how intimately and integrally you are united to the redemptive consecration of your Son.

306

You wrapped your Firstborn in swaddling clothes; you never cease to care for Jesus' brothers and sisters. In our family you have clothed us with the scapular, symbol of your presence, but also of your virtues which we mean to assimilate and so to put on Jesus more radically. We commit ourselves to you, not so much for your favors—which we know will not be lacking—but in order to pledge ourselves the more to the faithful service of your Son Jesus.

Your motherly heart is the refuge of our commitment. How our world would shine with the splendor of your beauty and of your heart full of love. Yet it is marked with too many evils that sully our consciences and our spirits, so that at times we fear for the future.

Procure for us a generous spirit that will lead us to feed the hungry.

Calm our hearts so that peace, the root for the elimination of all war, reign in them.

Grant us more trust in the power of God's love than in the need for arms.

Instill in us a love for life in all its forms.

Beg for us the gift of reconciliation, as the greatest happiness of a mother who sees her children live in peace, harmony and charity.

Share with us your marvelous humility, which refuses to take advantage of the other and which leads us to serve without conditions.

Make us ever more deeply aware of our prophetic charism, so that we love the Lord's commands even to the shedding of our blood, as did our fathers.

Fill our hearts with an unreserved faithfulness to God's truth, which today is so often menaced and transgressed.

Flood our consciences with a lively sense of right and wrong.

Give us an awareness of being temples of the Spirit of your Son, as you were, and the strength to live accordingly.

307

Mother of the whole Carmelite family, we know we are far removed from these ideals. But as a mother, you are used to love more tenderly the needy and weak child. We trust in your goodness, that you will help us overcome our weakness with your power, make us strong in faith, hope and charity. With your purity help us to overcome our temptations, in order to show that the pure of heart are truly blessed. By the power of the Holy Spirit, with which you were filled, obtain for us the grace to conquer sin, both personal and social.

The merciful love of our Redeemer is the most potent love in the world. Mary, you were the creature most permeated with this merciful love. This is why we trust in you to preserve our consciences, wholesome and transformed.

Lead us on our pilgrimage of faith until we reach merciful love in person, Jesus Christ. Even after our death, help us complete our purification so that we might speedily reach our goal and our true home, where we shall be reunited in your family together with all our loved ones, with you, and in the all-fulfilling love of Father, Son and Holy Spirit for all the eternal ages.

Most gracious Mother, purity itself, protect those devoted to you, O Star of the Sea.

Finito di stampare
nel mese di giugno 1988
dalla
Scuola Tipografica S. PIO X
Via degli Etruschi, 7
Tel. 490919
00185 Roma